MACWORLD HOME OFFICE COMPANION

MACWORLD
HOME OFFICE COMPANION

by Kathi Vian and Howard Bornstein

IDG BOOKS WORLDWIDE, INC.
AN INTERNATIONAL DATA GROUP COMPANY

Foster City, CA ■ Chicago, IL ■ Indianapolis, IN ■ Braintree, MA ■ Southlake, TX

Macworld Home Office Companion
Published by
IDG Books Worldwide, Inc.
An International Data Group Company
919 E. Hillsdale Blvd.
Foster City, CA 94404

Library of Congress Catalog Card No.: 95-81939
ISBN: 1-56884-792-0
Printed in the United States of America
10 9 8 7 6 5 4 3 2 1
1A/RV/QV/2W/FC

Distributed in the United States by IDG Books Worldwide, Inc.

Distributed by Macmillan Canada for Canada; by Computer and Technical Books for the Caribbean
Basin; by Contemporantea de Ediciones for Venezuela; by Distribuidora Cuspide for Argentina; by
CITFC for Brazil; by Ediciones ZETA S.C.R. Ltda. for Peru; by Editorial Limusa SA for Mexico; by
Transworld Publishers Limited in the United Kingdom and Europe; by Al-Maiman Publishers &
Distributors for Saudi Arabia; by Simron Pty. Ltd. for South Africa; by IDG Communications (IIK) Ltd.
for Hong Kong; by Toppan Company Ltd. for Japan; by Addison Wesley Publishing Company for
Korea; by Longman Singapore Publisher Ltd. for Singapore, Malaysia, Thailand, and Indonesia;
by Unalis Corporation for Taiwan; by WS Computer Publishing Company, Inc. for the Philippines;
by WoodsLane Enterprises Ltd. for New Zealand.

For general information on IDG Books in the U.S., including information on discounts and premiums, contact IDG Books at 800-434-3422 or 415-655-3000.

For information on where to purchase IDG Books outside the U.S., contact IDG Books International
at 415-655-3021 or fax 415-655-3295.

For information on translations, contact Marc Jeffrey Mikulich, Director, Foreign and Subsidiary
Rights, at IDG Books Worldwide, 415-655-3018 or fax 415-655-3295.

For sales inquiries and special prices for bulk quantities, write to the address above or call IDG
Books Worldwide at 415-655-3000.

For information on using IDG Books in the classroom, or for ordering examination copies, contact
the Education Office at 800-434-2086 or fax 817-251-8174.

Welcome to the world of IDG Books Worldwide.

IDG Books Worldwide, Inc., is a subsidiary of International Data Group, the world's largest publisher of computer-related information and the leading global provider of information services on information technology. IDG was founded more than 25 years ago and now employs more than 7,700 people worldwide. IDG publishes more than 250 computer publications in 67 countries (see listing below). More than 70 million people read one or more IDG publications each month.

Launched in 1990, IDG Books Worldwide is today the #1 publisher of best-selling computer books in the United States. We are proud to have received 8 awards from the Computer Press Association in recognition of editorial excellence and three from Computer Currents' First Annual Readers' Choice Awards, and our best-selling ...For Dummies® series has more than 19 million copies in print with translations in 28 languages. IDG Books Worldwide, through a joint venture with IDG's Hi-Tech Beijing, became the first U.S. publisher to publish a computer book in the People's Republic of China. In record time, IDG Books Worldwide has become the first choice for millions of readers around the world who want to learn how to better manage their businesses.

Our mission is simple: Every one of our books is designed to bring extra value and skill-building instructions to the reader. Our books are written by experts who understand and care about our readers. The knowledge base of our editorial staff comes from years of experience in publishing, education, and journalism — experience which we use to produce books for the '90s. In short, we care about books, so we attract the best people. We devote special attention to details such as audience, interior design, use of icons, and illustrations. And because we use an efficient process of authoring, editing, and desktop publishing our books electronically, we can spend more time ensuring superior content and spend less time on the technicalities of making books.

You can count on our commitment to deliver high-quality books at competitive prices on topics you want to read about. At IDG Books Worldwide, we continue in the IDG tradition of delivering quality for more than 25 years. You'll find no better book on a subject than one from IDG Books Worldwide.

John J. Kilcullen

John Kilcullen
President and CEO
IDG Books Worldwide, Inc.

For Ken Burke and Chris Schacker
Who helped us keep our home office busy for years

PREFACE

This book is about your home office—and how to use your Macintosh to get the most out of it.

If you own your own business, this book will help you set up your Mac to manage your days as well as your accounts, and to promote your products as well as your well-being.

If you work at home while working for someone else, it will help you acquire the skills to get ahead, from better data management to better contact management.

If you're just starting to think about working on your own, it will explain all the steps from getting set up to getting connected to getting down to work in your home office.

About the book

Each chapter has something for everyone. Chapters begin with an overview of concepts you need to know—from the mysteries of the System folder to the principles of information management to strategies for presenting your ideas in text, graphics, or even video.

Then come the home office solutions. No home office is the same, and no single solution will work for everyone. But you might decide you're a little like Andy Fine, who spends a lot of his day on the phone, networking, bringing people together—and looking after a four-year-old. Maybe you manage events, like Ellen Gant or conduct research on behalf of others like Susie Hu. Or you might be more like the Delacruzes, a husband and wife team who run a deadline-oriented service business with the help of two part-time assistants. Or maybe you're like Sam Post with his mail order business.

The solutions show you how each of these people has set up his or her space, hardware, software, and system. They show how they've solved their unique communication problems and the strategies they've developed for organizing their work, marketing their products and services, presenting information, and managing their money. Andy, Ellen, Suzie, and the rest are fictional characters. We made them up to make our points. They may not be exactly like the real private investigator or the real wedding consultant you know, but they should give you an idea of the kinds of choices you have to make—and how to make them.

After the solutions, we give you the nuts and bolts. If you're just getting started, follow the steps under "Jump Start." Often the hardest step is figuring out where the starting line is. We've tried to do that for you—and to coach you to get off to a quick start.

If you've been on your own for a while, you may have reached a plateau. You think you could use your Mac more effectively. You know there are tools out there that could help you do what you do better if you just had the time to sort through them. You want to grow. You want your business to grow. Look at the section in each chapter called "Upsizing." There you'll find tips on how to expand everything from your Mac's memory to your client list. You'll find out how to gain new skills in everything from online research to online sales.

Then go for a little extra power with our "Power Plays." In each chapter, we try to show you special tricks, tools, or strategies. These are hands-on projects, with step-by-step instructions for getting them right.

And just to keep you at the cutting edge, we tell you what we think is "On the Horizon"—and sometimes not too far away.

How this book is organized

We've organized everything into four parts.

In Part One we start out with four chapters on the basics of setting up your own office:

CHAPTER ONE Your Home Office Space gives you tips on how to choose the best spaces in your home for work, as well as sample floorplans, legal requirements, and options for expansion. *Power Play*: How to use your Mac software to draw floorplans of your own office space and try out different office designs.

CHAPTER TWO The Tools of Your Trade is a guide to the basic equipment you'll need to make your office work for you. We tell you what to look for in a Mac and its peripheral equipment, and include guidelines for calculating your system requirements, finding a source, setting it up, and expanding your system once it's up and running. *Power Play*: how to use a Mac spreadsheet program to help you decide whether to buy or lease new equipment.

CHAPTER THREE The Right Applications surveys the types of software products you'll need to run your home office, with tips on how to make the best choices, get updates, and fix bugs, as well as tips for expanding your skills with templates, plug-ins, classes, and user groups. *Power Play*: How to set up project worksets to get you working faster—with all the tools and documents you need at hand.

CHAPTER FOUR System Smarts is a guided tour of the System folder, with everything you need to know about managing extensions, control panels, and fonts, as well as backup strategies, security, and utilities for top system efficiency. *Power Play*: How to use a copy utility to schedule quick, automatic backups of files you can't afford to lose.

In Part Two we help you get connected to the world beyond your office with two chapters on telephony and networking:

CHAPTER FIVE Tangle-Free Telephony untangles the sometimes confusing world of phone-based communication with a close look at telephone answering options, fax choices, data transmission requirements, and even video conferencing options. We help you figure out how many phone lines you need and how to use them—and all the services that will make those lines more valuable to your business. *Power Play*: How to turn a Mac into an automatic phone answering service with mailboxes that your customers can navigate through to find information about your products or services.

CHAPTER SIX Weighing In on the Web gets you Internet savvy in just a few pages and then walks you through the steps from getting your modem to getting your e-mail. It also highlights some of the many plug-ins that expand the possibilities for work on the Web—including URL managers, audio and video options, and ways to plug applets and animations into your Web pages. *Power Play*: How to set up your own page and launch it on the World Wide Web.

In Part Three we get down to business with four chapters on basic business tasks:

CHAPTER SEVEN Management by Mac is all about organization—from your phone book and calendar to complex databases of products and customers. We zoom in on personal information managers, with tips for choosing one that's right for you. And we provide guidelines for setting up your contact file, calendar, and alarms to remind you of things you can't afford to forget. *Power Play*: How to use a phone book CD and a PIM to build a custom database of potential customers anywhere in the country.

CHAPTER EIGHT The Marketing Plan maps the marketing landscape, including direct marketing, word of mouth, public relations, advertising, and using distributors. It gives you the basics of setting up your marketing plan as well as tips creating a strong corporate ID and making your market grow. *Power Play*: How to create and use effective press releases for free publicity.

CHAPTER NINE The New Information Game is a tutorial in using Mac tools to present yourself and your information in the most effective ways. It helps you choose media and tools, and explores the ways in which you can use stylesheets, templates, digitizers, clip art, stock media, special effects, and audio and video to enhance your presentation. *Power Play*: How to build your corporate style into your tools for a convenient, consistent corporate identity.

CHAPTER TEN Fast-Track Finances introduces the basic legal, professional, and practical requirements for your business bookkeeping, and then outlines how to set up your Mac-based books, create budgets, and use spreadsheets to analyze your financial health. *Power Play*: How to create a business plan to guide your own business decisions and attract investors or to just get a business loan.

Part Four closes the book with two chapters about how to handle problems with your Macintosh when you don't have a corporate technical support group to back you up:

CHAPTER ELEVEN Troubleshooting gives simple, succinct instructions on what to do when disks don't show up on your desktop, when your computer crashes, when applications can't be found, when you can't empty the trash, when your Mac is slow as molasses, when your printer doesn't work, and when your Mac isn't communicating with the world at large.

CHAPTER TWELVE File Recovery takes a close-up look at what can go wrong with files—and the tools you can use to recover from those problems. It also gives you step-by-step instructions for using those tools for some of the most common file recovery problems.

Finally, Resources shows you where to find all the products and services we mention throughout the book.

Conventions used in this book

If you're the sort of person who likes to scan a page for quick information, here are some cues to look for:

 The Internet is a business hot spot these days, so we use this icon to highlight all the places throughout the book where we talk about the Internet and how it fits into your business plans. We also use it to mark all the Web and

Internet addresses in the book—for everything from the IRS small-business accounting guidelines to search engines you can use to find just about any address you need.

Wherever you see the Mac Smart icon, you'll find power tips for how to use your Mac more effectively—lots of arcane tricks that the manuals don't always tell you about.

Want a close-up look at some of the best products for your Mac home office? Look for the Product Focus icon.

It's a jungle out there, but look for this Street Smart icon to help you make street-savvy choices about equipment, products, and services for your home business.

The Solution icons mark the pages where we offer a look at possible solutions to different home office needs—with the help of our five fictional home businesses.

Andy Fine   Suzie Hu   Dave & Darcy De la Cruz   Sam Post   Ellen Gant

Also check the margins throughout the book for cross-references to related information and for brief tips on all sorts of topics.

About our recommendations

We are not *Consumer Reports*. We don't do scientifically controlled taste comparisons and computer crash tests. What we do is earn a living from our home—we have for at least 15 years—using our Macintosh computers for all they're worth. We also happen to write about the Macintosh for our living, so we've had the opportunity to try out lots of products and put them to the test in our day-to-day work. We want to share our opinions with you.

About lifestyles

Home offices are about business. But they're also about lifestyle. You can make a lot of money working on your own, but you're probably not in this just for money.

Maybe you hate commuting. Maybe you like figuring out what's next instead of having someone else tell you. Maybe you want to watch your kids grow up or eat breakfast at noon and dinner at midnight. Maybe you'd rather spend your money on musical instruments than career clothes. Or maybe you like career clothes, but not career politics. It doesn't matter what your personal preferences are. What matters is that you find a way to make them work for you. After all, that's why you're working at home.

A lot of home office manuals tell you to get organized. We tell you to get organized, too, but what we mean is get to know yourself and the tools that will help you be yourself. We want you to save time on things that have nothing to do with who you are so you can spend time doing the things that bring you health and happiness. We hope this book helps.

May you prosper.

ACKNOWLEDGMENTS

This book covers so much territory that no single person—or married couple —could possibly write it alone. Many friends, family members, and colleagues gave us insights and facts. We would especially like to thank Alan Brightman at the Worldwide Disabilities Solutions Group at Apple Computer; Bob Bornstein who gave us the model for Andy Fine in this book; Sally Bornstein who helped us understand Sam Post; Annie Ross, who pointed us to resources for setting up healthy offices (and vans); Talei Jean and Tenea Trujillo, who lent us their photographs; Les Paver, our accountant; John Anderson, who knows lots about computers and telephony; and Corey Vian, who helped us with both architectural and networking details. We're grateful for their help and, of course, assume responsibility for all mistakes we made in interpreting the information they gave us.

At IDG Books Worldwide, we'd like to thank Nancy Dunn for suggesting this book and guiding us through the initial vision. Many thanks, too, to Kenyon Brown for all the hand-holding throughout the process and to Suki Gear (forever Suki Dear in our minds) for help with the product inquiries.

Perhaps most important to thank are all the smart, creative, and friendly people who produce all the smart, creative, and friendly Macintosh products we describe in this book—as well as the folks who made those products available to us. Without them, working at home wouldn't be nearly as much fun.

Contents at a Glance

Contents

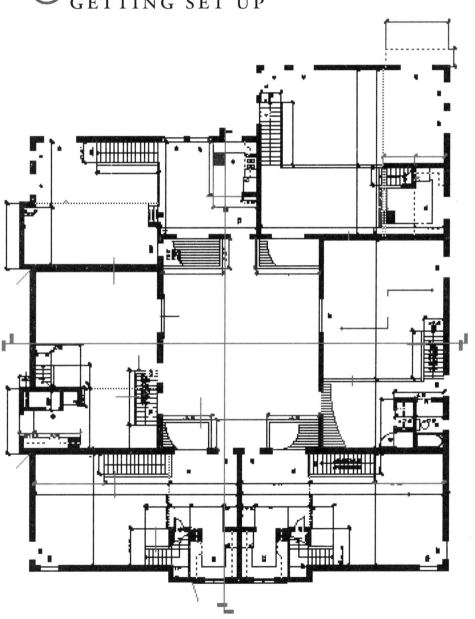

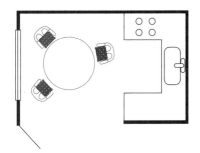

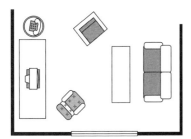

CHAPTER ONE

YOUR HOME OFFICE SPACE
How to find it and furnish it

I f you took all your odd closets, junk-filled drawers, useless nooks, and crammed crannies—if you emptied them all and mushed them all together in one spot—you'd probably have a perfectly respectable space for an office in your home.

This, in fact, is the basic strategy for setting up a home office. You may not be able to mush a lot of little spaces into one big space, unless you have a big budget and a creative architect, but you can and should become a master at stealing space.

How much space?

The first question, of course, is how much space do you actually need? You obviously need space for your Macintosh. And a place for you to sit in front of your Macintosh. A large closet would do. Particularly if you like cozy spaces and have never been a big fan of daylight.

This is not a joke. Some people are happy as clams when they can reach out and touch a wall in any direction. We have a friend who set up his home office in a food storage cellar under his house, a space about six feet by six feet by six feet, with stone walls all around and a kind of overhead, lift-up, double doorway like the ones in the storm cellars in the *Wizard of Oz*. He worked all day at his regular job and came home and worked most of the night in his cellar office. Daylight was irrelevant. He loved this space. Of course, he once lived for a year in a structure the size of an outhouse. He's a particular type. If you're that type, you'll have a pretty easy time finding office space, no matter where you live.

If you're not, you have some decisions to make. Basically, you have four choices: Steal space that you've been using for something else and turn it into an office. Steal some time in a space that you've been using for something else and turn it into a multipurpose space. Add on to your home. Or move.

Spare space

Stealing space that you've been using for something else is often the best solution. Good candidates are spare bedrooms, dining rooms, breakfast nooks, attics, basements, and garages. Spaces with doors you can close work best if you have trouble concentrating, if you need to meet clients in private, or if you have children or animals that could make a mess of your work in less than a minute, given the opportunity. Spaces with real walls and floors and electrical outlets and heat are easier to convert to an office than spaces without those amenities—you sort of just move in. If you're considering an attic, basement, or garage that hasn't already been refinished, you have some work ahead of you. How much depends on how much time and money you want to spend.

If you have in-home clients, some of these spaces may work better than others. A small bedroom tucked at the back of the house may be the perfect place for you to cuddle up with your Mac, but how will you feel about giving your clients a tour of the two for-real bedrooms and a bath on the way down the hall? Kitchens, too, can be public-relations disasters. Look for spots that appear professional.

THE COST OF CONVERSION

What will it take to turn that dark, spider-infested attic into a space where you'd love to spend your days? Or your oil-stained garage into a Macintosh workshop?

The cost depends mostly on the labor charges in your area. In urban areas where there's a lot of demand for contractors, you'll spend more than in a sleepy town. For big cities on the coasts, figure $100 per square foot of space—if the job includes heating and plumbing. If you're converting spaces that don't have heating and plumbing needs, you can probably do it for $80 per square foot. The costs are about the same whether you're doing structural remodeling or new construction. For more accurate estimates, check with a contractor in your area.

Multipurpose space

Multipurpose spaces can work—sometimes as well as spare spaces. Family rooms, living rooms, and dining rooms may all lend themselves to time-sharing. Here are some ways to decide whether yours qualify:

- Are other family members gone for most or all of the day?
- Does a home-like atmosphere—either cozy or gracious—make your clients smile softly and write big checks?
- Are your social life and work life one big tangled knot that you have no desire to unravel?
- Do you think that it's a little silly to dedicate the largest room in your house to four hours of formal entertaining per month while you toil all day, every day in a broom closet?

If you answered *yes* to more than one of these questions, you may want to start moving your office supplies into your china cabinet, or your printer into your entertainment center.

Some tricks can make multipurpose spaces work better. Screens, book-cases, plants, and sculptures of large animals can divide your workspace from play spaces. An area rug can define your work zone. Unless you have nerves of steel, these devices won't help if someone is trying to play at the same time you're trying to work. But they create a psychological separation that you may find useful if you're still worrying about your Excel spreadsheet while you're watching "The X-Files"—or vice versa.

Furniture that folds your work up into a neat little box when you're done is also useful. So is portable furniture. A lot of office furniture now comes on wheels: computer desks, file cubes, printer carts. You just wheel your office into a closet at the end of the work day. However, if your work has a tendency to spread out and devour things like some of those "X-Files" creatures, fold-up desks and rollaway printers may not be as suitable as the slick furniture ads suggest.

A final word of advice (from all the home office experts): Don't try to time-share your bedroom. For most humans, it's just not healthy to spend all day and all night in the same place. Some possible exceptions are writers who need to eat, drink, and dream their novels in order to feel intimate with them, or people who spend a large portion of their working day out and about, but use their home-office Mac to get them started in the morning and organized at the end of the day.

Oh, one other minor detail. Multipurpose spaces aren't tax-deductible.

See Chapter 10, "Fast-Track Finances," for more information about taxes and your home office.

Surface space

When the Macintosh first hit the streets, it was smallish. Meant to be transportable (though more often called transluggable), the computer actually took up less desk space than the keyboard and mouse. Then it got biggish. Now it's smallish again, particularly if you happen to have a PowerBook as your main machine. If you don't, figure a minimum surface space of about two feet by three feet.

Plus space for your printer, your external hard disk, your modem, your telephone and answering machine, a fax machine, and a cup of coffee.

Plus paper space—which is really the killer in a home office. Despite all claims, no one we know has a paperless office. First, you have half a trillion manuals to teach you how to use all the software that's going to save you paperwork. Second, you can't do much of anything on your computer without printing something. Third, a lot of the somethings you have to print are drafts of things you're going to print about fifty times before you're satisfied. And you have to put all that paper somewhere.

This is a lot of surface space, probably comparable to what you'd find in a well-laid out kitchen. So if you see one of those cute little computer desks in some furniture catalog, think twice. Think first about whether you need to look at manuals, reports, specifications, photographs, schematics, or blueprints as you work on your Mac. Then think about how much you'll enjoy balancing those manuals, and so forth, on chairs placed strategically around your cute little desk, or what great exercise you'll get craning your neck to see them on an adjacent tabletop.

Storage space

When you're not using your manuals and reference materials and multimillion drafts, you need to store them. You also need to store printer paper, floppy disks, CD-ROMs, mailing materials, incoming correspondence, financial records, professional magazines, paper catalogs, software catalogs, office supply catalogs, and—yes—pencils, pens, and paper clips. If you actually produce nonpaper products, you may need to store your manufacturing materials and your inventory as well.

All this stuff tends to be messy. If you have floor space and budget, get a large, handsome wall storage system. Get the kind with deep shelves, drawers, and cupboards that close. Or get an architect to design you some built-ins. Or get a do-it-yourself book and do it yourself. Just be sure you can hide everything behind doors.

If you don't have floor space and/or budget, you'll have to steal storage space.

Do you have a coat closet? Get a coat rack for the coats and then build shelves in the closet to store your office supplies.

Do you have a linen closet? Store your lovely linens on open shelves in your bathroom and put your ragged supplies in the linen closet. (Don't do this if the linen closet is in the bathroom—damp office supplies don't work well.)

You may have one or two kitchen cupboards or drawers that you can dedicate to office storage—which is handy if your office is in your dining room or breakfast nook. A lot of the stuff people keep in their kitchen cupboards can actually be displayed in the open. You can hang pots and pans from a rack, use a wall-hung spice rack, keep onions and potatoes in attractive baskets on the countertop, store your silverware in terracotta pots to free up the silverware drawer.

When you buy furniture, think storage. A coffee table can be a trunk where you keep old drafts until you're sure you don't need them anymore. So can under-the-bed drawers. Or an antique chest in the entry hall.

There's another part of this story, though. It's the quarterly clean-out. Put it on your Mac calendar with an alarm. Make an event out of it. Buy pizza and listen to old Beatles tunes while you go through all of your storage bays and toss as much as you can. Or buy sushi and listen to Mozart while you do it. (Researchers have found that students who study to Mozart do better on tests than those who study to rock music. The same might be true for office organizing. Researchers haven't compared the intellectual benefits of pizza and sushi.)

There are lots of ways to set alarms. See Chapters 4 and 7 for some of them.

Healthy space

Speaking of pizza and sushi, your choice of workspace and furnishings (and snacks) can affect your health—and that of the planet. On one hand, by working at home and avoiding the daily commute, you're reducing air pollution, the drain on natural resources, and the general level of tension in the human race. On the other, you may be introducing some unpleasantness—of the chemical, electrical, and emotional type—into the home environment.

The main things that people seem to worry about in the home office are lighting, body-friendly furniture, electromagnetic radiation, and chemical toxins, primarily from printer toner. The good news is that at home, you're more or less in control. You don't have to subject yourself to fluorescent light all day long unless you like the slightly green cast it gives your skin. You can put your printer in the garage with your washer and dryer if you're sensitive to chemicals. You can use ergonomically designed chairs and desks and choose from a range of methods for shielding yourself from electromagnetic radiation—there's even a beanie-style antiradiation cap!

For information about body-friendly furnishings, see Step 2 under "Jump Start" in this chapter.

You may not be as naturally inclined to take care of Mother Nature in your home office—or you may not know how. A lot of corporations these days actually would get better marks for environmental protection than home office folks. Many products in the office, home or otherwise, are recyclable. Printer paper, magazines, toner cartridges—all can find new life if you can find your way to the proper recycling center. Your city or county government can usually give you directions. They may also be able to answer questions about the disposal of any potentially toxic materials that you work with.

If your work materials are too toxic, however, they may not let you do your work in your home, which brings us to the next topic.

Legal space

For information about business licenses and permits, see Step 1 under "Jump Start" in this chapter.

You may not be allowed to work at home. All towns and cities have zoning regulations. The purpose of these regulations is to keep residential areas separate from industrial and commercial areas—because people have an idea that residential areas are basically bucolic while commercial areas are anything from noisy to poisonous.

The truth is that, on some days, you could die from the gas fumes of leaf blowers on a residential street. You may have to postpone business calls while the band next door tunes up for two hours. And the express delivery truck may not be able to park in front of your house because the teens next door have turned your street into a drive-in, after-school party.

But the regulations remain, nevertheless. And violations of them are punishable by fines—daily fines, in some cases—and even jail. So before you do anything to turn your home space into office space, make sure it's legal.

From imagination to concrete space

Creating a home office takes both imagination and concrete planning. You can do it alone, or you can work with an expert—an interior designer or architect. You can do it on a shoestring, or you can invest steeply (even if you don't mean to).

Start with our scenarios for some basic office design ideas or just jump right into the licensing process.

Go slowly, though. You don't have to create the whole home office in just seven days.

JUMP START: Moving into Your Home Office

Your task is to create a home workspace that will work for you and your business. Here are the steps to get started:

STEP 1: GET LEGAL

The first step is to find out what you have to do to run your business legally from your home. Regulations vary widely from state to state and town to town. But in general, you may need some or all of the following permits and licenses:

A HOME OCCUPATION PERMIT This permit is sometimes called a secondary use permit. You usually get it from your city's planning department or city hall. You may have to demonstrate that you conform to zoning requirements for your neighborhood and that you're not going to engage in any activities that will be dangerous or bothersome to your neighbors. Expect to answer questions about equipment and materials that you use, the number of employees, the number of clients or customers who will come to your home, and the volume of goods or commodities that you plan to store (if you're selling merchandise). This is usually a one-time permit. It may take a few weeks to get it.

A BUSINESS LICENSE This license gives you the right to conduct business in your community. You may need to get a license from your state, county, or local government—or some combination of those. Business licenses may be one-time licenses, or they may be annual. You typically pay a fee, sometimes proportional to your yearly business income. Look in the government listings of your phone book under "Business Licenses." If you don't find an entry there, call your local city hall or chamber of commerce.

A DOING-BUSINESS-AS (DBA) PERMIT If you use a business name other than your own personal name, you must register it. If you don't, you won't be able to open a bank account under your business name, and you won't be able to cash checks made out to your business. To register your name, you usually fill out some forms and pay a fee to the appropriate jurisdiction, often the county. (Look in the government pages for a listing for "County Records.") Sometimes you publish a Fictitious Business Statement in your local newspaper. Most small local papers are set up to help you with this process. You just take them a copy of the form you get from the county, and they take care of the appropriate legal wording in the published notice. After the notice has run for the required length of time, they send you and the county a copy of the notice and a statement of the dates the notice ran. You generally need to renew this permit periodically.

These licenses will get you up and running, but you may also need a reseller's license if you plan to sell products that are subject to sales tax. Many trades, from contracting to private investigation, also require special licenses. Check the state or county government listings in your phone book for licensing agencies.

If you rent your home, you should reread your rental agreement. Some landlords don't permit you to conduct business from their residential properties. If you want to be completely safe, let your landlord know your plans in writing. You don't want to get all your permits paid and stationery printed and then find out you have to move because your landlord isn't happy with your new business.

Even if you own your home but belong to a home owner's association, check your association's rules on home businesses. Your association could shut you down, too.

Now the real question: Is anybody going to know whether you have the proper licenses or not, especially if you do business under your own name? Maybe not. And some communities simply don't try to enforce the licensing laws unless they get a specific complaint. But it's usually easier to be legal than not. It costs a little more, but the fees support your own community— fire services, police services, libraries, schools, streetlights—all those things that make your neighborhood a nice place to work. Why not just do it and get it over with?

If you don't conform to zoning regulations, you have some options:

Apply for a variance. You'll have to go before the planning board or city council and present a request to be treated as an exception. Your neighbors will probably be notified. It may be useful to go around your neighborhood and introduce yourself and let your neighbors know what you're up to before you apply.

Try to change the zoning regulations. You'll have to invest time in a somewhat lengthy political process, but if you're settled in the neighborhood and you like to be active in your community, you may well be successful.

WHAT IF YOU CAN'T GET A PERMIT?

Rent space part-time in an office suite. Use this space for meetings and other activities that may violate zoning regulations for your home. Also use it as your official business address.

Move. If you're committed to working at home, moving may be the simplest, most efficient solution. And it may give you an opportunity to find the perfect home-office house.

STEP 2: AUDIT YOUR SPACE

One of the first things a space planner does is make an inventory of your space needs. Whether you hire a space planner or do your own planning, you'll need to be able to answer these questions:

- What are the main tasks you'll perform?
- How much space do you need for each of these tasks?
- How much storage space do you need?
- What kinds of furnishings do you need?
- What kinds of lighting do you need?
- What electrical requirements do you have?
- Do you have special ventilation requirements?

Once you know what you need, take a walk around your house and inventory what you have. Look at your house as if it were empty—just a lot of corners waiting to be filled. Don't look at rooms; look at spaces. Imagine yourself working in them, meeting in them, looking for stamps in them. How do they feel?

Then use the tables and charts on the next few pages to help you match what you need with what you have. If you don't already have your Macintosh, be sure to look at Chapters 2 and 5, too. They will help you figure out what kind of equipment you're going to need before you settle on a workspace.

The phone rings.

"Andy, the person we're looking for, will coordinate and spearhead a major new offensive, leading a team of highly skilled professionals into previously uncharted and potentially volatile territory—"

Andy rocks forward in his chair. Phone cradled between his shoulder and his ear, he bends over, reaches down, ties his daughter's shoes.

"You mean the Internet, sir?" he says.

"Yes, Andy, the Internet."

"You want C++ skills this time?"

"Yes."

"And client/server systems background?"

"Yes."

"How many years of experience?"

"A minimum of five. And Andy, I don't need to remind you that discretion, as always, is of the utmost importance."

"Of course, I'll get right on it."

The phone line clicks. Andy turns to his Mac, calls up the HyperCard stack his whiz-kid brother put together for him, finds his candidate in a matter of seconds. A few more seconds and the candidate's résumé is sparking across the phone lines.

"Come on, Ashley," Andy says to his four-year-old. "Time for our coffee break. Let's take a walk over to Grandma's."

ANALYSIS

Andy Fine runs an executive search and recruiting firm from his home. But he's also a "home office mom" for his four-year-old daughter.

Andy has set up his home office in his family room. He chose it over a small, dark, spare bedroom at the back of a long hall. He doesn't have many home clients, but when he does, he doesn't want them in the bowels of his house.

The family room has other benefits. It's a large room with good daylight. It's also a good place for Ashley to play when she isn't at daycare or napping—about two hours out of the working day.

Andy has arranged his office area so he can keep an eye on Ashley while he works but can also clearly point out *his* space and *her* space. The major expense was the built-in, wrap-around wall system, which Andy built himself. The system created a wall where there had been only a kitchen counter before.

The wall system includes a desktop area along its entire length, with some storage below and bookshelves above. Most of the bookshelves have cabinet doors, as does all the storage space below. (The lower cabinets all have childproof latches.)

Andy's solution illustrates the kinds of compromises that people with home offices often have to make. Much of his business is conducted over the phone. His ideal office wouldn't have kid noise in the background. However, in his role as Ashley's caretaker, he has other demands. His office gives him an easy way to meet those demands while working. And because his time with Ashley is limited, the family-room office is actually quiet for much of the day.

 S O L U T I O N S

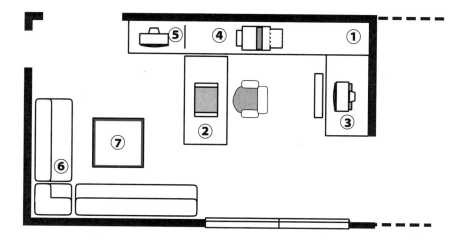

1 A deep, wrap-around, built-in book-shelf separates the family room from the kitchen. Cabinet-style doors above provide ample storage space for office supplies. Desktop space runs the entire length of the bookshelf.

2 A traditional desk creates a U-shaped office area, without cutting off the view of the family room.

3 A monitor sits on the desktop area in the bookshelf, away from the glare of the patio doors. The keyboard is on a lower pull-out tray. The computer is on a shelf below the desktop.

4 A printer, fax/copier, and digital scanner are easily accessible on the desktop. Pull-out file drawers below keep client résumés organized.

5 The family television also fits easily into the built-in bookshelf and swivels to face the sectional. Cabinets below provide storage space for printer paper and other office supplies.

6 The sectional preserves family space for conversation or television viewing.

7 A cube with doors serves as a coffee table and storage area for Ashley's toys.

OTHER DETAILS

■ Indirect overhead lighting above the bookshelves provides soft ambient light.

■ Task lights on both the computer desktop and traditional desk focus on the details at hand.

■ A cork floor reduces static electricity and is soft enough to give when Ashley falls. It's also easy to clean when she spills her afternoon juice.

■ An electrical panel beneath the computer desktop has cabinet-style doors that hide messy cords and keep them safe from a curious kid.

The sign flashed crimson, neon roses reflecting in pools of water on the street below. From her fourth-story loft, Susie Hu watched and waited.

An 8:30 appointment on a wet November night.

She'd rather be tasting a bit of brew in the Rose City Ratskeller. But a job was a job, and this one promised a big bonus. Two percent of the appraised value of the vase, if she could track down the scamp of a husband who made off with it—and prove its pedigree. Plus her hourly fee, of course.

She watched the Honda ease up the block, back slowly into the parking space vacated just moments earlier. An auspicious sign. It was always a good beginning when a new client found a parking space right away. The woman got out of the car, paused to get her bearings, then crossed the street. Moments later, Susie was buzzing her in.

While she waited for the knock at her door, Susie turned to her Mac, opened a file, typed a name and date. Nora C. November 13.

Thirteen might just be Nora's lucky number.

ANALYSIS

When Susie Hu set off on her own as a private investigator specializing in recovering lost and stolen objects, she didn't think a residential neighborhood was the right setting for her fledgling practice. But she didn't have a lot of money to invest in both living and office space.

Some friends had bought a loft in the downtown business district and remodeled it. That gave her the idea for her own home office.

She built her office as the front end to a long narrow loft space. She wanted a space that would convey professionalism and elegance, without a hint of her private life nearby.

But she also wanted the office to be friendly enough to serve as an entryway for more intimate gatherings.

And she knew that she would need to be as professional and capable on the road as in her office. So she bought a van and outfitted it to be her office on wheels.

THE VAN

Susie's van is fitted for work on the road with a desk and built-in cabinets for a second fax/copier that she operates from her cell phone. A gasoline generator provides power for heat and light and recharging her PowerBook and portable printer, both of which she takes with her on her travels. She keeps a duplicate library of some of her best reference CDs—things like the Power Finder PhoneDisk and Street Atlas USA. Her big dream, though, is to outfit her van with an ETAK computerized navigational system—to get her where she's going even when she doesn't know where that is.

 S O L U T I O N S

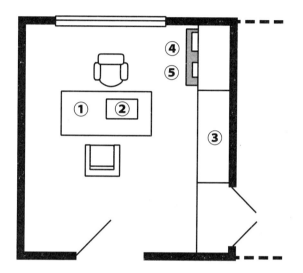

1 Susie's desk is right in the middle of the room. She sits on one side and her clients sit on the other. That's the way she wants it. It lets them know that she's all business and completely in control.

2 Susie keeps her PowerBook on her desk when she's not traveling with it. It's her only computer, and she's never without it.

3 A wall of sliding doors conceals bookshelves and the entry to her living space—a double door that opens wide for friends but locks securely whenever Susie retreats behind it.

4 Susie's telephone, fax, and answering machine are set up on a pull-out cart that she can keep close beside her while she's working and tuck away when visitors come.

5 Her printer has its own shelf on the pull-out cart, so Susie doesn't have to get up from her chair to get her printouts.

You know your parents are really losing it when the first thing he says to her in the morning is "Do we have a red toner cartridge for the printer?" and the first thing she says is "I need a picture of a pelican swallowing a pike."

I'm like: Mom! Dad! It's your anniversary. Can't you at least give each other a hug before you turn on the Macs?

He's like: Is that right? Darcy, is it our anniversary?

She's like: I don't know. Is it on your To Do list?

He's like: I don't think so. I have—let's see—get the sample pages of Wescott's science text book to them by noon—get your illustrations for Seaside's menus to them by 3:00—bug Grady's about paying their bill. And I guess I have to get another red toner cartridge, too.

She's like: You promised Seaside the menus by 3:00 today? You didn't tell me that.

I'm like: Time out! Dad, could you, like, put the empty toner cartridge down somewhere other than the dining room table? In case you didn't notice, I'm trying to set it. I'm trying to make you guys a special breakfast for your anniversary.

He's like: Oh, sweetheart, that's so—did you see the specs for the Wescott book? I thought I left them on the table when I went to bed last night—

She's like: I have no idea what a pike looks like. How can I draw a pike if I don't know what it looks like?

I groan. Welcome to desktop life.

ANALYSIS

Dave and Darcy Delacruz run a desktop publishing service out of their two-and-a-half story home. Originally, Dave did all the page layout, while Darcy did illustration and design.

When they first started the business, Dave and Darcy made a crude partition in the two-car garage with bookcases to separate the car side from the work side. It was cold in the winter and hot in the summer. And working all day under fluorescent lights was depressing.

They survived a year—largely by moving their equipment to the dining room table—but it was hard on family life. Still, they established a client base and gained the confidence they needed to do a real remodel on the garage.

Then things started booming. Dave was spending more of his time managing the business and had to hire two part-time employees to do the routine layout tasks. They took over the two workstations in the garage, and Dave found a new niche for himself by moving the washer and dryer to the garage and taking over the laundry room. Now he's conveniently close to the production team but can also close the door on them when he needs privacy.

Darcy has moved up to the attic. It gives her more working space and fewer distractions. By opening windows in the attic, she also gets good natural North light, which her artist's eye demands.

 S O L U T I O N S

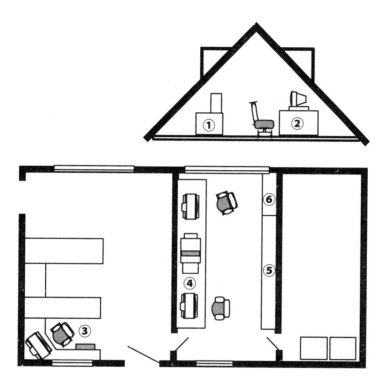

1 A row of flat files keep large camera-ready boards, large illustrations, and art materials in good condition. Bookcases above are stacked forward to fit under the slanted ceiling.

2 A long worktable gives Darcy drawing space as well as room for her computer and printer.

3 Dave cut a custom desktop from plywood to fit in the former laundry room. A file cart on rollers and wall-mounted shelving meet his immediate storage needs.

4 The long custom desktop in the garage has room for two workstations and a shared printer, as well as drawers and shallow shelves.

5 A wall-to-ceiling bookcase, which is organized with magazine files and cardboard letter boxes, provides ample open storage.

6 A window seat provides a place to step away from the computer screen and rest the eyes and mind for a while. The window replaced one of the garage's door panels.

His business card reads like a trip through the galaxies, but that's only because he lives on Andromeda Way in Mars Hill and happened to name his company Ecliptic in honor of the steadfast path of the sun through the skies. In most ways, his life is completely down-to-earth.

"Ecliptic," he says, tapping his chest like a "StarTrek" captain answering a call from his crew. In Sam's case, he's activating the headset for the cell phone that's clipped to his wheelchair.

"Sam," says the contractor, "we got the landscaping in today on the Wildwood model. You got time to come out and see it? It's a beauty."

"Terrific. I've been working on the Web page all day. All I need is a couple of quick photos, and we'll be ready to announce to the world."

"You're gonna have to double your phone staff after they get a look at this one."

"No way. There's only room for one of me in this office. But I may have to give my Mac some extra disk space to handle all the incoming calls. I just hope I can keep up with the orders and inquiries. I've got a couple more to get out today, and then I'll hop in the van and head out there. See you in, say, 40 minutes?"

"Right you are, Captain."

ANALYSIS

Sam Post runs a mail order business out of his home. After the accident—a C7 spine injury that ended his days of climbing on rooftops and crawling under floorboards—

Sam finally got that architect's degree he'd always intended to get someday.

He paid his dues as a junior associate in a firm, struggling for a year to get his wheelchair through a door that was barely wide enough for him to pass. Then he decided to go it on his own.

His angle? House plans on disk. Twenty-four models and growing. And with every electronic convenience, all born of his experience with automating his own environment.

Sam thinks of himself as a mobile professional even when he's in his own office— which is a large area carved out of the former kitchen-dining-family room. It's laid out with one long wall of desktop/storage and a minimum of furniture and other wheelchair obstacles. He calls that his base office.

He calls his wheelchair his mobile office. His lap tray holds his PowerBook, powered by a 12-volt inverter cable that plugs into his wheelchair battery. With a wireless modem and his cellular phone, he can go anywhere in the electronic world—including an Internet World Wide Web site that serves as one of his storefronts.

His other storefront is a desktop computer that runs his phone answering system. A second desktop computer serves his printing and backup needs. With infrared docking, he can print without being cabled to the printer.

With this arrangement, he's free to work wherever he happens to be—a freedom he takes very seriously.

S O L U T I O N S

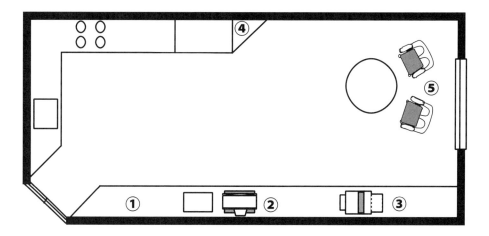

1 This long, low unit provides maximum open space in the room. It has lots of open shelves below—no drawers or cabinets that require special wheelchair maneuvers.

An L-shaped or U-shaped workspace would have given Sam handier access to his desktop equipment if he wanted to stay in one place all day. But he didn't. He didn't want to feel penned in. He wanted space to meet with contractors and other business associates and to pace as he was working. So his lap tray became his main workstation.

2 While Sam's main computer is a PowerBook that he keeps on his lap tray, he needs a desktop computer dedicated to answering his phones.

3 Sam has a second desktop computer for daily printing tasks—including letters and mailing labels. The PowerBook's infrared technology makes it easy for Sam to transfer files from his laptop to his desktop for printing without connecting any cables or sitting still while the printer prints.

4 Another low, easily accessible bookcase keeps Sam's reference books close at hand.

5 A couple of big chairs and a side table provide a comfortable meeting area for business associates.

OTHER SPECIAL FEATURES

- Remote-controlled light switches, intercom, and window blinds.
- Optically-controlled sliding patio doors.
- And of course, a bottled-water dispenser with hot and cold spigots, just like in his old office downtown, but easier to reach.

"Let's just come in and get warm and have a cup of tea, shall we?"

Ellen Gant opened the door for them and they filed in like Madeline's mates, all in a row, all dressed alike, more or less. Except for the one with the blue spiked hair and pierced eyebrow. And the other one with the cowboy hat and boots and the habit of chewing her fingernails. And...oh, well, they'd all get sorted out soon enough.

Ellen took their coats, hung them on the brass coat rack, lifted the tea cozy off the silver pot, and poured into five Old Country Rose teacups, one for each of the four young women, another for their mother.

"So, all four weddings in the same month, eh?" Ellen flicked a silver curl away from her forehead, hoping for just the right attitude. Something between Katharine Hepburn and her own grandmother, who had worked a paper press well into her seventies—manufacturing, coincidentally, wedding albums.

"Yes," said Mrs. McIntyre, "we thought we'd get them all out of the way at once. What do you think? We thought they could all be more or less the same—"

"Except for the dresses—" said Blue Hair.

"And the music—" said Cowboy Hat with bits of fingernail in her teeth.

"Then you'd actually only have to plan one wedding," continued Mrs. McIntyre, "and we could have a discount. What do you think?"

Ellen flicked her curl again and turned to the Mac, which was quietly conducting Vivaldi to scenes from Monet's garden. She clicked to interrupt the sonata and garden scenes and start up a little masterpiece of her own, An Album of Weddings. "I'm sure we'll find something here that you'll all like."

ANALYSIS

Ellen Gant works as a wedding consultant. When her husband died and left her with a too-small pension, she decided to sell the family house, buy a small condominium, and invest the profit. And when a friend offered to pay her to help "put together one of those wonderful weddings like you did for your daughters," Ellen decided to make a business of it.

Ellen needs a romantic, elegant, and comfortable setting to meet with her clients. She also needs a computer to manage the multitude of details involved in planning a wedding. Her living room fits the bill.

Rather than trying to make her home more like an office, she tries to make her business more like a friendly visit for tea with an aunt who has impeccable taste. No need to hide the kitchen or dining room from view—they become part of the stage set.

But Ellen is also a fine businesswoman and, with the acquisition of her Mac, an adventurer into the realms of multimedia. It was easy enough to get video clips of her best weddings and not much harder to put them together into a presentation catalog for her would-be clients—one that she can play for them like a good movie on her home entertainment center.

 S O L U T I O N S

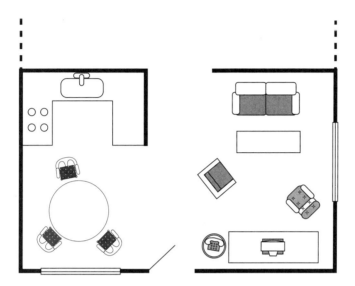

1 Ellen's home office is her home entertainment center. In place of a television, she has a large Mac monitor. In addition to a VCR, the unit holds a color ink-jet printer.

Below the monitor is a pull-out desktop for Ellen's keyboard. The entertainment center also has bookshelves for a variety of wedding references—including not only books of etiquette but also books on wines, cakes, fabrics, and flower arrangements. A few drawers keep messy stuff hidden from view

while clients are watching the screen.
2 A plant stand does double duty as a telephone stand.
3 The coffee table is a work surface, too—a place for clients to look through albums of wedding stationery, fabrics, and other samples that they need to be able to touch. Shelves underneath the table provide storage for these albums.
4 When Ellen needs to spread out, her dining room table works fine as a desktop.

TABLE 1.1   WORKSPACE INVENTORY

TYPE OF SPACE	PURPOSE	EQUIPMENT
INFO TASK SPACE	Computer tasks Phone tasks Reading	You need desk space—one or two desks or a long, low countertop or table. Put them in almost any room in the house, but look for the not-so-obvious possibilities—in closets and hallways, under stairs, in a loft, or in a window bay.
MEETING SPACE	One-on-one meetings Group meetings	An extra chair may be all you need for one-on-one meetings. For groups, look for a pleasant corner to put a small table and comfortable chairs, or make a conference table the center of your workspace. Or use your dining room table or even your living room sofa if you don't need a tabletop for paperwork.
DEMONSTRATION SPACE	Client presentations Supplier presentations	You may need a portable demonstration table, easel, chairs that you can move around to accommodate an audience. Find a good blank wall as a background—one where you can hang things. If you plan to project slides or video or use your computer as an audio/video screen, be sure you can make the space comfortably dark.
ASSEMBLY SPACE	Collating Paper cutting Mailings Product assembly	This is workbench space—garages, attics, basements may be good choices. Make sure you have good telephone access, good ventilation, and good materials storage space close by. Your kitchen may work (especially if your business is catering), but for most work, even the cleanest kitchen has too much grease potential.
STORAGE SPACE	Materials management Library Product display	Again, look for unexpected nooks and crannies. Organize storage by how often you access it. Keep things you use daily close at hand. Move long-term storage into attics, garages, or basements. In-between stuff can go in your linen closet or spare kitchen cabinets—easy to get to, but not necessarily right at your fingetips

TABLE 1.2 TYPES OF STORAGE

TYPE OF SPACE	PROS	CONS
SHELVES	Quick, easy, visual access. Often the least expensive storage medium.	Can look cluttered. No private storage.
BUILT-IN	Custom-fitted to space. Clean, neat look. Don't take up extra space in room.	Not movable or extensible. Usually require major construction. Expensive.
WALL-MOUNTED	Don't take up floor space. Often the least expensive option. May be extensible.	Require assembly. Need adequate structural support in walls. May damage walls. Once installed, not easily moved.
FREESTANDING	Movable and extensible. A great variety of styles and prices.	Take up floor space. Although movable, they may be heavy, and you may have to empty them before moving.
PORTABLE	Very movable. Can be used when needed and rolled out of sight when not needed. Suitable for very limited space.	May be unstable for certain uses. Difficult for people with disabilities to handle.

TABLE 1.2   TYPES OF STORAGE   (continued)

	TYPE OF SPACE	PROS	CONS
	CABINETS	Uncluttered, private storage.	Less accessible. May require extra space for cabinet doors to open.
	BUILT-IN		
	WALL-MOUNTED		
	FREESTANDING		
	PORTABLE		

TABLE 1.2   TYPES OF STORAGE (continued)

TYPE OF SPACE	PROS	CONS
DRAWERS	Uncluttered, private storage. Good for organizing — and finding — lots of small items. Deep storage	Less accessible. Requires extra space to open.
BUILT-IN		
WALL-MOUNTED		
FREESTANDING		
PORTABLE		

TABLE 1.3 BODY-FRIENDLY FURNISHINGS

	REQUIREMENTS	LOOK FOR	COST	OTHER OPTIONS
CHAIR	Thighs should be parallel to the floor. Feet should rest flat on the floor or on a wedge with toes up—never down. Back should be straight. Curve at lower lumbar area should be supported.	Adjustable seat and back angles. Adjustable height. Firm, high-density contoured foam cushion. Fabric that breathes.	$500 to $1,500 (your most important home office health investment)	If you can't afford the perfect chair, try using foam or inflatable back supports. Use footrests to get your feet in the right position. Look in health care or office product catalogs for these options.
DESK	Work surface should be lower than most standard tables—approximately 28½ inches for someone of average height. Table surface should not be highly reflective. If you have a white desktop, use a darker blotter or other desk cover.	Solid wood rather than veneers. Veneers are often mounted on particle board or plywood that makes the desk heavy and hard to move. It also contains chemicals, such as formaldehyde, that may be toxic to some people. Older desks that have had a chance to outgas will be less toxic. Convenient storage. A good computer arrangement if you're going to use it for your computer.	Varies widely. A good item to buy used if you're trying to keep costs to a minimum.	

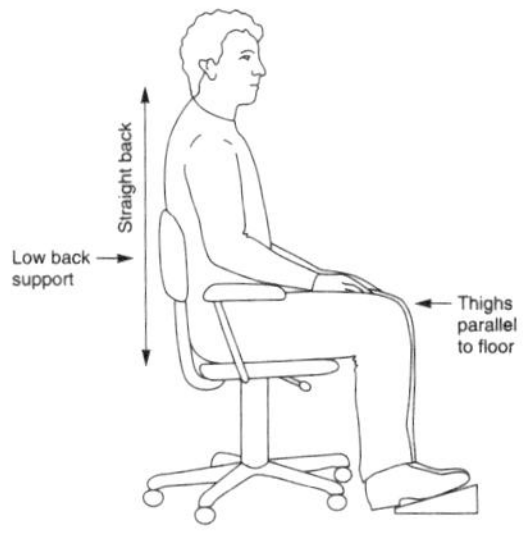

The chair illustration is labeled: "Straight back", "Low back support", "Thighs parallel to floor".

The desk illustration is labeled: "28.5"".

TABLE 1.3   BODY-FRIENDLY FURNISHINGS (continued)

EXAMPLE	TYPE	REQUIREMENTS	LOOK FOR	COST	OTHER OPTIONS
	KEYBOARD	Elbows should be level as you type—which usually means the keyboard should be 24 to 27 inches from the floor. Wrists should be straight and supported.	Low desks or desks with pull-out keyboard tray. Keyboard trays that you can attach to your existing desk. Wrist supports.	Keyboard trays from about $50. Wrist supports from $4.	Special ergonomically designed keyboards. Also, try Type Lighter—a software program that helps you use optimum fingertip pressure to avoid repetitive motion syndrome. Developed by Feldenkrais practitioner Michael Krugman.
	MONITOR	Top of monitor should be level with eyes or lower—eyes should look down on screen at an angle of 10 to 30 degrees. Screen should be 16 to 28 inches away to reduce eyestrain.	Swivel base with rotation in all directions. Add-on screens that reduce glare.	Add-on glare-reducing screens from $50 to $100. For more details on selecting a monitor, see Chapter 2.	

TABLE 1.4   LIGHTING

TYPE OF LIGHTING	WHAT YOU WANT	WHAT YOU DON'T WANT
NATURAL LIGHT	Diffuse North light is best. Window coverings should let you control the amount of light that comes in at different times of day. Vertical blinds often give the most control.	Bright sunlight either directly behind or directly in front of your computer. Strong glare from windows on either side of your workstation. Highly reflective surfaces, including blinds, mirrors, and desktops.
AMBIENT INDOOR LIGHT	Good indirect light, using fixtures that are designed to reflect off of walls and ceiling. Warm, balanced incandescent light.	Lighting fixtures that create hot spots in the room, such as chandeliers and many other types of ceiling fixtures.

TABLE 1.4   LIGHTING (continued)

TYPE OF LIGHTING	WHAT YOU WANT	WHAT YOU DON'T WANT
TASK LIGHTING	Light that you can direct toward reading materials on your desk, but away from your monitor.	Lamps that create hot spots in your peripheral vision or glare on your computer screen.
	Architect-style lamps that can be clamped to your desk and angled give you the most control and don't interfere with desk space.	Lamps that take up a lot of desk space.

STEP 3: TAKE A TRIAL SPIN IN YOUR OFFICE SPACE

Don't go out and buy a bunch of new furniture right away. Give yourself some time in your new workspace—anywhere from a couple of weeks to a couple of months—to feel out what you need.

If you can, start by emptying the space completely. If it's a spare bedroom, get rid all the old sci-fi books and the high school track team trophies and the old fold-out couch. If it's a kitchen nook, get rid of everything that has anything to do with eating.

Now just bring in what you absolutely need to get to work—something to put your Mac on, a chair to sit in. It doesn't have to be the perfect desk right now. Of course, if you've got a perfect desk, use it.

As you find a need for other furnishings—chairs, storage, work tables, whatever—bring them into your workspace. While things are still pretty simple, try out different arrangements. Watch how the light changes in the course

---

ARE YOU WIRED FOR HIGH TECH

On the scale of major appliances, computers and their peripherals don't have enormous power needs. However, you don't want your computer on the same circuit as your washing machine, for example—every time the washing machine changes cycles, your screen image will flicker and bounce up and down. Your printer is also a fairly heavy feeder, so don't plug it into the same circuit as your microwave oven and then heat up your lunch while you're waiting for your prints to come.

If you have lots of disk drives and modems and other peripherals, you're going to need lots of outlets. It's best to avoid extension cords. But if you need one, use a power strip with a built-in fuse and surge protector. If you're rewiring for your work, you might want to dedicate one or more circuits especially to your computer equipment. That way, your work won't be subject to other household activities.

Always, always use surge protectors for all your equipment. They protect the electronic circuits from damage due to power surges or brownouts. They're inexpensive and well worth their cost to protect your Mac investment.

of the day. Watch how often you get frustrated because something isn't where you need it when you need it. Notice what distracts you when you're working.

Let your body tell you whether this is a good workspace. Don't let visions from a glossy magazine override what your day-to-day experience tells you.

Also use this trial period to visit your friends who have home offices. Ask them what works for them and what doesn't. Gather as many tips as you can.

Be sure to set an end date for your trial period. You may arrive at the end date and realize that you've got exactly the office you need. Don't spend another dime. But if you're not happy, make a plan and make some changes. Even if you're already overwhelmed with work, set up a schedule for revamping, a little at a time if necessary. You don't want to get trapped in an office that isn't working well because you're too busy working to change it.

STEP 4 : DO SOME DESIGNING

Now you're ready to design your space. Are you going to do it yourself or are you going to get professional help?

Get professional help if you're too busy to do it yourself, if you're not a professional designer but you want a *Martha Stewart Living* look, if you have special physical needs that require expert attention, or if you just want company. (After your first couple of months on your own, you may be feeling the home office isolation blues.)

Start with an interior designer or space planner unless you know you need major structural changes. Interior designers offer a range of services from simple consultation to complete remakes of your room. Some specialize in home offices. If you don't want to invest in a lot of new furniture, find an independent designer who will work with your current furnishings. You should be able to hire an independent designer for two to three hours ($50 to $100 per hour) to give you basic advice.

If you plan to refurnish your workspace completely, you may want to work with a designer from your favorite furniture store, perhaps even an office furnishings store. Such designers will, of course, be most interested in

---

The best way to find a designer or architect is to get a recommendation from a friend whose taste you like and whose judgment you trust. If none of your friends remodeled or has redecorated recently, you need to rely on the professional associations:

American Society of Interior Designers (ASID)
Referrals: 1-800-775-2473

American Institute of Architects (AIA)
Internet Web site: http://www.aia.org

**HOW TO FIND
A DESIGNER**

selling you their furniture, but they may charge you less for their consultation time. And they are usually backed by the store's reputation in case anything goes wrong.

If you're going to be knocking walls out and rewiring and making other
structural changes, you'll need a contractor and maybe an architect. If you
have a very clear idea of what you want and know a bit about construction,
you can probably work very successfully with a contractor. If you don't, an
architect is probably a better choice.

Now, the other option: do it yourself. You need to take some measurements. Room dimensions. Window sizes. Door widths. Draw a floor plan
and maybe some elevations. (An elevation is a drawing of a wall, with its windows, doors, electrical outlets, and other structural features.)

Next fill your drawings with the furniture you think you want. You'll also
need to measure the furniture so you can see if the pieces you want actually
fit in the space you have. If the furniture doesn't fit in the space where you
think it belongs, find another piece of furniture. You can do this task with
pencil and paper. Or if you have a little time and want to make the most of
your Mac, you can use an interior design application to do it.

See "Power Play" later in this
chapter for step-by-step
instructions for designing
your own office on your Mac.

STEP 5: TAKE OCCUPANCY

Now all you have to do is implement your plan. If you can afford the time
and money, it's better to do it now, all at once, while your office is still young
and flexible. If you can't, just make a plan. Start with the essentials (which
may be just a good filing cabinet). Mark your Mac calendar with a date for
the next purchase and block out the time you'll need to integrate it into your
office. That way you won't always be waiting for a time when business is
slow—which will probably never correspond to a time when you have the
cash for the task at hand.

UPSIZING: Meeting Your Growing Needs

Okay. You've been in business for five years and you're thriving. But the original workspace is just getting a bit too small. What do you do?

One option, of course, is to move out of your home into commercial office space. But if you've been working at home because you *like* it, you don't want to leave. Here are some other options:

The restaurant office

If the crunch is your clients, consider using a restaurant or hotel as your office away from home. It may be less expensive to take clients out to lunch or dinner a couple of times a week than to rent an office, furnish it, pay the utilities, and pay for cleaning help. The restaurant can be as simple or elegant as the situation calls for, and your clients will probably feel as if they're getting special treatment.

Choose restaurants that are quiet and have good working space and where the management doesn't object to long conversations over the last cup of coffee. Develop a relationship with the staff so they know you and your needs.

If you need a larger meeting space, you may want to rent a banquet space or a meeting room in a hotel. Most hotels rent large and small meeting rooms for business meetings and have basic business equipment, including overhead projectors, sound systems, and fax machines. Our favorite chain is Marriott Courtyard, which caters to business travelers. If you have out-of-town clients, such chains provide a convenient and professional environment for your work together. (Some airports also have meeting facilities, by the way.)

The storage locker

Your workspace may fit you but not all the stuff you have to store. If you're in a paper-intensive business and need to keep records for all your projects or clients, you can quickly bury your home life in cellulose. You may also find that in order to buy inventory and materials in the volumes necessary to make them profitable, you're turning your living room into a warehouse. If you have to move products off your bed at night in order to go to sleep, you need a storage solution.

Fortunately, off-site storage is usually easy to come by. And it's not too expensive. You can rent storage lockers for $30 to $300 per month, depending on location and size. Things to check for? Security. Environmental controls. Access. Can you get to it any time you need to, or only during certain hours?

Some suggestions. Take a little time to organize the storage space for easy access. Set up shelves and drawer space if necessary. This is really an extension of your office. You should be able to walk into it and find what you're looking for as easily as you could in your home office. Clip a pad of paper to the back of the door and log the stuff you store. Eight months from now, you may not remember whether you stored the art boards for Whack-O Rollerblades or gave them back to the client. A quick glance at the log, and you'll know before you start sorting through eight months worth of art boards.

Off-site storage has a secondary advantage. If something happens to your home—fire, flood, earthquake (shudder)—your work isn't necessarily destroyed. For this reason, it's a good idea to keep a second set of backup disks off-site, too.

For a rundown on good backup practices, see "Jump Start" in Chapter 4, "System Smarts."

The remodel

You may simply need to make your home bigger. Now's your chance to create the office you really wanted all along. Just the right lighting. The right number and placement of wall outlets. An outside entrance. A view to inspire.

This book is not about remodeling. We, the authors, have never remodeled a house. We know a lot of people who have, though. No one has ever told us "The remodel went just the way we thought it would." No one has ever told us "It was a breeze."

Don't assume that it will be easier for you because you work at home and can keep an eye on the progress. It will be awful for you because you don't have any place to escape to. Some families rent second homes while they remodel. You will probably want to rent a second office for a few months. Just fold it into the cost estimate for the remodel.

Or take a sabbatical.

The move

If you don't want the hassle of remodeling, or if your home is already as big as your lot can handle, or if you don't own your home, it may simply be time to move.

You're looking for both a home and an office now. Make sure you look in neighborhoods where you can have your home and office on the same turf. Make sure your real estate agent knows that office space is a priority. You're probably not looking for another back bedroom or a garage to convert. A separate cottage might be nice. Or you might settle for a large master bedroom with walk-in closets if it has a separate entrance and there are three more reasonably sized bedrooms.

You might also consider something less conventional. A duplex, for example. A lot of duplexes have a one-bedroom unit attached to a larger unit. You can use the small unit for your office until you retire, and then you can rent it for income. Or sometimes, you can find two small houses that share a lot. Or if you're not attached to suburban lawns, check into commercial properties that might be remodeled (see warning above) as joint live-work spaces. Lofts and warehouses usually have huge spaces that haven't been carved up for conventional lifestyles. So you can make the space fit your office rather than the other way around.

Are you a renter? Consider two apartments in the same building or complex. A friend of ours has kept two studio apartments for years. The upstairs apartment gives her the privacy she craves, and the downstairs apartment gives her a place to focus on her work. You may not really need an extra kitchen, but you can turn it into great storage space if you're not using it for anything more than a cup of hot tea and an occasional handy snack. The square footage is probably a lot more than a two-bedroom apartment, at not much more cost.

The second home

Let's say your business does well. Quite well. But it's lapping up your living space like a hungry dog. Let's say you're also spending a bundle on getaway vacations to private houses that cost as much for a week as you pay for your mortgage for two months.

Why not just buy one of those houses yourself?

Choose one house to be the office house. Plan to spend something like four days and three nights there each week. Keep the living spaces comfortable, but minimize the family space. Move all the off-season clothes and paraphernalia to the home house. Most of the recreational stuff, the family *objets d'histoire*, the gourmet pantry and cookbooks all go, too. But you can still crawl directly from your bed to your Mac half the time, and keep in touch with it via your PowerBook and modem the rest of the time.

POWER PLAY: Designing Your Office

If you grew up as an architect's daughter (which one of us did), you probably draw floor plans in your sleep. If you didn't, you can use your Macintosh to learn how.

Start by choosing your tool. You can invest about $50 in Design Your Own Home: Interiors. Or spend $300 for the high-end, compellingly 3-dimensional design possibilities of Virtus. Or just use a draw program.

This example uses ClarisDraw. It comes with lots of predrawn furniture libraries, and you can quickly and easily create more. Its main disadvantage is that it doesn't provide automatic elevations from your floor plan. However, even the automatic elevations in Design Your Own Home: Interiors are not entirely automatic.

What you need
- ClarisDraw with its ClarisArt libraries
- A good measuring tape
- Time: About 4 hours

First, measure...
Start by measuring the space you want to design. It may be a single room, or two adjoining rooms, or an entire section of the house.

1. Measure the enclosing walls.

Measure as accurately as you can from corner to corner, at the floor. If you have floor trim all around the room, measure above the floor trim. Measure the ceiling height. You can do a quick sketch on paper and jot the dimensions down there. Or you can just label the walls like this:

North	24' 2"
East	13' 6"
South	24' 2"
West	13' 6"
Ceiling	8'

2. Measure any doors or archways.

Measure their height and width and the distance from one corner. Measure the opening only, but make a note of the width of the door frame. Label them by wall or by number or both. For example:

North	5' 6"	no frame	10" from Northwest corner
West	2' 4"	with 2" frame	10" from Northwest corner
East	6'	no frame	0" from Southeast corner
Height	6' 6"		

3. Measure windows.

Measure the actual window size and the distance from the floor and one corner of the room. Note of the width of the window frames. Label them by wall or number or both. For example:

East 1   10' x 6' 6"   1' 8" from Southeast corner

4. Measure any other structural elements, such as divider walls, half-walls, columns, islands, closets, and electrical outlets.

Measure their height, width, and length, and their location relative to one or more walls.

5. Measure any furniture you plan to use.

If you plan to use furniture you already own, measure its height, width, and depth and add it to your lists of measurements.

Yes, this step is a little tedious. But it's all fun from here on.

Choose a scale

You'll be working to scale. If you're measuring in feet and inches, a scale of *1 inch = 4 feet* is probably easiest to use.

1. Start ClarisDraw and save the new document as Floorplan.
2. Choose Rulers from the Layout menu.
3. Click option 3 to set a scale of .25 inch equals 1 foot (or 1 inch equals four feet).
4. Click OK.

You can click the ruler to move the zero point— so you have plenty of room around your drawing.

Each quarter inch equals one foot

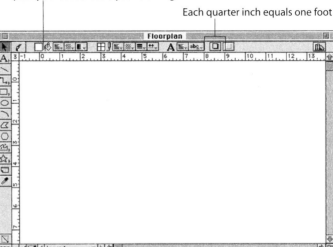

Draw a floor plan

A floor plan gives you a top-down view of your space. Use your measurements to draw it.

1. Select the line tool and choose a line weight from the line palette.
2. Draw the walls.

Use the rulers to draw them to scale. Leave openings for doors. You don't need to leave openings for windows.

3. Choose Open Library from the File menu and open the Architecture library.
4. Select a door style for your first door and click Use.

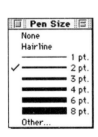

Put the door where you want it. You can drag to change its size. You can also choose the Rotate or Transform commands from the Arrange menu to make the door open in the right direction.

5. Repeat step 4 for each door and window in your drawing.
6. Use the line tool or rectangle tool to draw other structural elements.

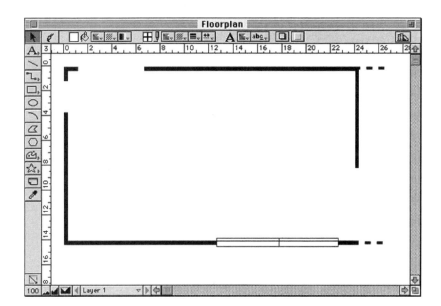

Draw the elevations

Elevations are drawings of one wall of a room. They're usually drawn flat, without perspective. You don't need them if you're just going to move furniture around your floor plan. But if you plan to build a bookshelf into the wall or turn a closet into an office cubbyhole, elevations are essential.

1. Open a new document for each elevation you want to draw and save it as North, South, East, or West.
2. Use the drawing tools to draw the walls to scale and to place doors, windows, closets, and other structural elements.

Draw the door frames and window frames. A two-inch frame can make a big difference if you're trying for a perfect fit between two windows.

This is where programs like Design Your Own Home or Virtus Walk-Through Pro can save you time. They'll automatically create the elevations for you—in 3-D. Of course, you still have to tweak windows and doors to change their height and position above the floor.

Choose your furniture

ClarisDraw comes with furniture images—both standard and office. They're in the ClarisArt libraries, which you need to custom install when you install ClarisDraw. Most of them give you a top-down view of things, so they work fine for floor plans. A few front views are included. If you're doing elevations, you'll probably need to draw your furniture.

1. Go back to your floor plan and choose New Layer from the layer pop-up menu at the bottom left corner of the screen.

Adding a layer is like putting a piece of transparent paper over your floor plan—you can scribble on it as much as you want without messing up the floor plan underneath.

2. Choose Open Library from the File menu and open the furniture libraries you want.

You may also want an appliance library if you're sharing space with the laundry room or kitchen.

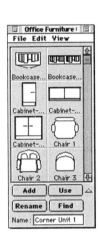

3. Select a piece of furniture and click Use.

Move it around to try it out in different places. Drag the size handles to match the actual size of your own furniture. Or make it fit to figure out what size you might actually like to buy or build. Use the Rotate and Transform commands to turn it around. Use as many pieces of furniture as you need.

4. Use drawing tools to create your own furniture.

If you don't find the furniture you need in the library, you can draw your own. It's easy to create simple pieces of furniture using the basic shape tools. Use the Group command in the Arrange menu to group several selected objects into a single piece of furniture.

5. Select your new piece of furniture and click Add if you want to save it in one of the libraries.

Create specs
You're almost done. But you might as well turn all those design decisions into hard numbers before you print.

1. Choose New Layer from the layer pop-up menu.

Now you've got a third layer. You're going to create your specs on this layer.

2. Choose the line tool and choose Autosize Line from the arrow palette. When you draw with the Autosize Line, ClarisDraw automatically calculates the length of the line and displays it.

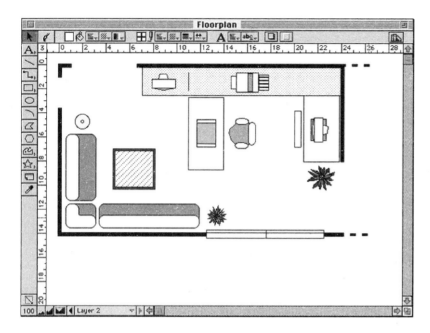

3. Draw lines to indicate the lengths of walls, windows, and any furnishings you want to show.

So that's it. You now have some basic architectural drawings. Go ahead and print them out. If you want to hide a layer—for example, if you don't want the specs to print—choose Layer Manager from the View menu, select the layer you want to hide, and click the Hidden box. Do this before you print.

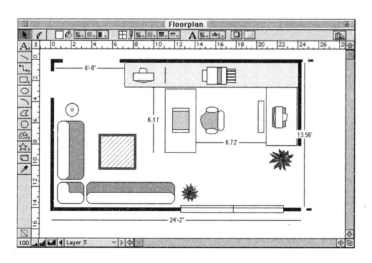

Here's a quick peek at what you can get with special-purpose architectural design programs.

Design Your Own Home: Interiors creates basic floor plans that look like this:

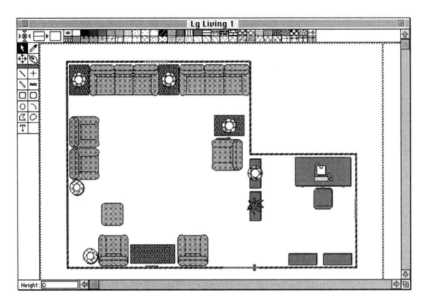

It—sometimes—turns them into elevations that look like this:

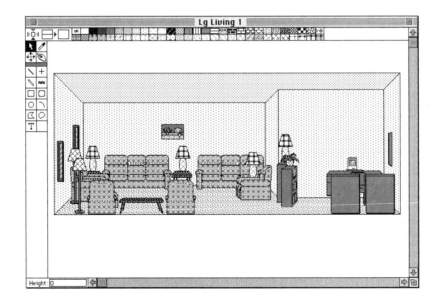

**3–D
OFFICE
DESIGN**

The elevations can be a little unpredictable. Some pieces of furniture have more than one view, but others don't. So you can have furniture in your North view that disappears in your East view. Also, the libraries are surprisingly limited for a dedicated program—and they're not as easy to use as the ClarisArt libraries.

If you're really serious about design, Virtus WalkThrough Pro is the tool to drool over. Here's a floor plan in Walkthrough Pro:

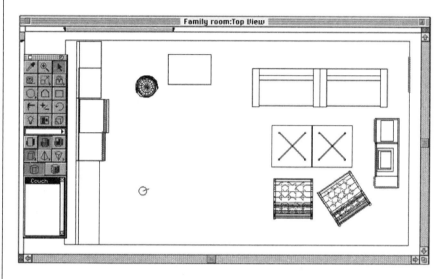

Here's the 3-D view. You can move through the room and view it from any perspective.

With WalkThrough Pro , you might just be tempted to start a new home business in interior design.

3-D OFFICE DESIGN

ON THE HORIZON:

The View from Your Home Office Window

As you gaze out your home office window and ponder the future, you can be sure of one thing: In the future, more people will be doing what you're doing.

Home offices are a trend. At present, a third of the U.S. workforce is self-employed. By the year 2000, more than half of the population could be working at home. Such a trend is bound to impact your workspace. More services will be available to people setting up home offices; more finely tuned furnishings will appear on the market; more facilities will offer better options for small business meetings. In short, you'll have more ways to spend money on your office. More important, zoning laws will probably change to keep up with the times, but not necessarily in all areas. Some staunchly residential areas may simply become more fanatical in enforcing the existing codes.

Beyond the numbers trend, technological changes could reshape your workspace. The "wireless home" may make your office space a lot more flexible. Infrared beams—like the ones you use to blink your TV off and on—can already bounce your keystrokes from your keyboard, off a couple of walls, and into your computer's processor. Think of it as electronic racquetball. Add a big flat-panel display on the wall instead of your little 14-inch monitor, and you begin to see the possibilities. If you became good enough, you could line yourself up for a shot from anywhere in the house. Who needs a desk?

You'll have to take a personal stand on videoconferencing, too. It's coming to homes everywhere. People are going to want to see you in your office. The question is whether or not you want them to, and if so, how much of your home life you want to include in the picture. If you thought the sound of children playing in the background was a distraction, imagine the sight of them. If you're considering a big remodel, you might want to plan for it by positioning your computer so that it gazes nicely on a plain pastel wall that brings out the color of your eyes. We're not exactly kidding.

Other changes? Check out the rest of chapters.

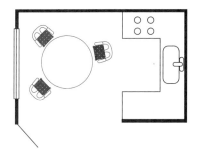

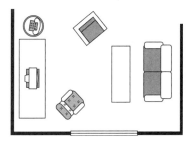

CHAPTER TWO

THE TOOLS OF YOUR TRADE

How to choose the right Macintosh and peripheral equipment for your business

Things change fast. If you now own a Macintosh, the model is (sigh!) probably already at the brink of obsolescence. You can read the rest of the book and come back to this chapter when you're ready to think about a new model.

If you don't already own a Macintosh, you're (sigh!) no better off than someone who does. By the time you make your decision and put your money on the counter, your Mac will already be verging on obsolescence, too.

You can't win by stalling, either. A friend of ours has been trying to make up her mind which Mac to buy for more than a year. Friends keep telling her how great the next series is going to be. Other friends tell her that the prices of the old models are going to drop drastically as soon as the newer models hit the streets. So she keeps waiting.

You can't afford to do this. You just have to make up your mind to buy a system—one that will do the job for, well, at least a year or two. Here's what you should consider.

Speed and space in the CPU

You measure the raw worth of your computer in megahertz and megabytes.

Megahertz is a measure of speed in millions of cycles per second. Think of it as heartbeats per second. The heart of every computer is its microprocessor, and different microprocessors beat at different speeds. Until recently, all Macintosh computers used the Motorola 680X0 series of microprocessors. Now, the Power Macs use the faster Motorola RISC processors. They cycle at about 60 to 200 megahertz and faster.

Megabytes measure memory and disk storage in millions of characters. There are two kinds of memory: ROM and RAM. ROM is read-only memory. It holds the core personality of your computer. From a practical point of view, you don't care much about ROM. You do care about RAM, which is random access memory. This is what your applications eat. And their appetites are enormous. (Picture Homer Simpson at a pie-eating contest.) Your applications won't even come to the table if you don't have enough RAM—let alone play nice with one another at the picnic.

Disk storage is where your data and applications live when they're not feasting. You can think of disk storage as your electronic file cabinet. And you never have enough drawer space.

So here's the basic strategy: Get as much speed and RAM as you can possibly afford. RAM, though not cheap, is your best—you know—bang for the buck. Choose it over other neat features like stereo speakers or a second CD-ROM drive. This is not hype. Your Macintosh sets the pace for your work, and you don't want it holding you back.

Don't worry too much about disk storage. You're not going to have enough. No matter what. You'll just have to add more—which you can. You can upgrade your internal hard drive or you can attach one or more external

See Step 2 under "Jump Start" for help with calculating your speed and memory needs.

For details, see "Upsizing" in this chapter.

WHAT'S IN A POWER MACINTOSH?

The power in a Power Macintosh comes from its RISC processor. RISC stands for Reduced Instruction Set Computer. It's a faster processor than the old 640X0 processors. It uses a smaller set of machine instructions, and it executes them very fast.

Some old software doesn't work on the new Power Macs. If you have a disk full of old software, upgrading to the Power Mac will mean also upgrading your store of software. But if you've kept up to date with most of your applications—getting new versions as they're released—they'll probably work on the Power Mac. And most new versions of Macintosh software are designed especially to take advantage of the RISC processor's speed.

drives. And whichever you choose, it will be cheaper when you get ready to add it than it is now. Guaranteed.

Size, resolution, and depth of the monitor

The monitor is what you look at. It is the display, the screen. In some models, it's built into the computer. For others, you buy it separately. In either case, check the size, resolution, and depth.

The size is measured in inches, diagonally, across the screen. This measurement can be misleading. Manufacturers measure the physical dimensions of the tube. The actual image size you can display may be as much as two inches less. Larger sizes save you time because you don't have to do as many acrobatics to see different parts of your work. You can see more windows at once, or more text without scrolling, or more graphics without reducing and enlarging the image. It's all right there in front of you.

Resolution is measured in horizontal and vertical dots called pixels (picture elements). It determines how fine your image is—the more dots, the finer the image.

Bit depth measures the number of colors one dot can display—and therefore the total number of colors you can have on the screen. Here's what you get for your bits:

- 1 bit = black and white
- 8 bits = 256 colors
- 16 bits = thousands of colors
- 24 bits = millions of colors

In addition to these basics, you may want to look for a couple of special features. Some monitors come with built-in stereo speakers. They can be handy if you're planning to use your Mac as a multimedia development or presentation tool—or even if you just want to use your CD-ROM drive to play your music CDs as you work. However, you'll get better quality if you

---

Apple offers a line of multiple-resolution monitors. With these monitors you can change your screen resolution as you work. For example, if you do a lot of page layout work with facing pages, you can increase the resolution to show both pages on the screen at the same time—at a smaller size but without any loss of detail. Multiple Scan is also useful if you do a lot of drafting or design work on large schematics.

Multiple Scan is not the perfect alternative to a larger monitor, however. When you switch to the higher resolution, everything gets smaller. It's harder to read. You also trade away colors—you can't display as many colors at the higher resolutions.

(By the way, other manufacturers also offer multiple-resolution monitors.)

PRODUCT FOCUS

MULTIPLE SCAN GIVES YOU MULTIPLE RESOLUTIONS

use the stereo output jack with an amplifier. (You can get a small, inexpensive amp and speakers for about $180 from Radio Shack.)

You may also want a power saver monitor—with a screen saver built into the hardware. It automatically turns the monitor off if you don't use it for a while. You can save about $60 a year this way.

See Chapter 4 for more information about the Views control panel.

If you have trouble seeing what's on the computer screen, try one of these options:

Larger monitors with magnified views You can buy an off-the-shelf, large-size monitor and use the Views control panel to change the font size and spacing in the Finder menus and lists that appear on your screen. You can often choose magnified views in individual applications or choose larger font sizes in documents. Some manufacturers also provide large-size monitors designed especially for people with visual problems. Sources: Power R and PDS Video Technologies

Magnification lenses You can get an inexpensive plastic fresnel lens that fits over your screen and magnifies the view up to twice the normal size. You can also use a software lens—a utility that uniformly enlarges everything on the screen from 2 to 16 times the standard size. Apple ships the CloseView utility with all its computers.

Large print processors You use these to enlarge parts of the image on your screen. You typically need two monitors and a joystick. You select the text you want to enlarge on one monitor with the joystick, and it appears enlarged on the second monitor. These processors only work with text. Source: TSI/VTEK

Speech synthesizers If you can't see the screen at all, you can use a speech synthesizer to get some help from your computer. This device speaks to you when you have a choice of operations, such as whether to save changes to a file or save without changes. Quality varies, as do prices. Sources: Street Electronics Corporation and Access Unlimited-Speech Enterprises

Talking software You can get talking applications for everything from word processing to database management to games. Some of these are designed to completely support people who can't see at all. You can also get utility programs called screen readers that turn nontalking applications into talking applications. Source: Raised Dot Computing

Tactile output systems These systems display the contents of the screen in Braille or as an exact tactile representation of the screen. The Braille processors only convert text. The other type of processor displays everything on the screen. Source: TSI/VTEK

WHAT TO DO IF YOUR EYES DON'T WORK

Braille printers These printers print the contents of text documents in Braille. You generally need Braille conversion software, too, or special word processors with built-in Braille converters. Sources: American Thermoform Corp., Enabling Technologies, and Duxbury Systems, Inc.

This information was adapted from Independence Day *by Peter Green and Alan J. Brightman, Ph. D. Allen, TX: DLM, 1990.*

Keyboards, mice, trackballs, pads...

You need to talk to your computer. You usually use a keyboard and a mouse. But there are other options, too.

The keyboard comes in two basic versions: standard and extended. Get the extended keyboard. It has function keys, a keypad, and several arrow keys. These extra keys will pay for themselves in the time they save. You can assign macros to them—miniprograms that do several steps with just one keystroke. And if you're used to doing five-finger exercises on a calculator, you can use the keypad to take advantage of your skills. (The arrows are mostly for people with mouse-o-phobia.)

Mice, which move the pointer around on the screen, also come in two basic versions: mechanical and optical. The mechanical mouse has a rolling ball that needs to be removed and cleaned periodically. It has a tendency to get gummy and balky, but it's inexpensive, and it works, more or less, on any surface. Optical mice use a light beam and a reflective mousepad with a grid. They're a little fussy about spatial orientation, but they move oh, so smoothly, and your hand learns quickly how to keep them happily aligned with the mousepad grid. Because they have no moving parts, they're basically maintenance free.

THE GREAT MOUSE BUTTON CONTROVERSY

A three-button mouse using only one button

The other options? Trackballs. Touch pads. Even voice recognition. Trackballs and touch pads take the place of a mouse. Their advantage is that

Need to input lots of existing text? Want to capture a scene in bits? See "Digital Input" in Chapter 9, "The New Information Game."

they use a small and fixed amount of desk space. (The mouse has a tendency to wander all over the place.)

Voice recognition is currently a limited option. You can train Apple's PlainTalk to perform commands for you—you just say something like "Close the window." But you can't actually enter data in a file or tell your drawing program which triangle you want to select and fill with bright purple. Also, your PlainTalk agent can be a little slow on the uptake, misunderstanding your commands or mistaking your cheery voice on the telephone for an instruction to do something. Nevertheless, this technology is growing. Before long, you may find yourself carrying on all sorts of useful, work-related conversations with your Mac.

If physical problems make it difficult or impossible for you to use a standard keyboard, try a different kind of input device. Here are some of the options:

Keyguards These are for people who have trouble pressing one key without accidentally pressing lots of others. The guards are actually shells that fit over your keyboard. They have holes over each key, so you can only press one key at a time, either with your finger or a pointer. Sources: TASH, Inc., and Prentke Romich Company

Key repeat eliminators Most keys automatically repeat if you hold them down. If you have trouble preventing keys from repeating, you can turn off the key repeat with the Keyboard control panel (see Chapter 4).

Headpointers and mouthsticks With these, you can poke the keys you want. The headpointers are headsets with a pointer attached at the forehead. The mouthstick fits in your mouth. Sources: Fred Sammons, Inc., and Zygo Industries, Inc.

Keylatches You position these devices on your keyboard to hold down special keys, such as the shift, command, and option keys while you press another key. Sources: Tash, Inc., and Apple Computer, Inc.

Switches and screen keyboards You can use a combination of a switch and a screen display of the keyboard for input. The switches may be activated by fingers, toes, eyebrow positions, or other subtle movements. You can use them to select and activate keys on the screen. Sources: Don Johnston Developmental Equipment and Prentke Romich Company

Morse code systems Morse code is a way of representing characters as short and long signals. You can use a dual-switch device to send these codes to your computer. Source: Don Johnston Developmental Equipment

Expanded keyboards With these large, flat panels you don't need fingers to choose a key. You can use a toe, for example. You can also customize the keyboard for keys you use frequently. Sources: Unicorn Engineering Company and Don Johnston Developmental Equipment

WHAT TO DO IF YOUR HANDS DON'T WORK

Miniature keyboards These are designed for people with very limited hand movement. You can reach all the keys with minimal movements of the fingers on one hand. Source: TASH, Inc.

This information was adapted from Independence Day *by Peter Green and Alan J. Brightman, Ph.D. Allen, TX: DLM, 1990.*

Printer options

You need a printer, too. It gets the stuff you do out of your computer and into the world. Here again, you have lots of choices, and this is the arena where your dealer is most likely to give you the wrong advice. These are the considerations:

Ink-jet vs. laser The first choice is how to get ink on the paper. Ink-jet printers spray dots of ink. Laser printers use conventional copier methods—electrostatic charges fuse toner to the paper. Ink-jet print is not as sharp as laser print, and it takes longer to spray a page. It's also not as cheap as it seems at first blush. The printers themselves are less expensive to buy, but more expensive to maintain. You have to replace the ink-jet cartridges frequently. Of course, you have to replace toner cartridges in laser printers, too, but not nearly as often. Your cost per page is significantly lower with laser printing. If you want a high-end image or if you print a lot of long documents and complex graphics, laser printers are the best buy.

Color vs. black-and-white Most color printers are ink-jet printers. Color laser printers are still quite expensive. So if you want to print color in your own office, your choice is so-so quality color vs. high-quality black-and-white. This is probably not the choice you would like to make. Color can be a powerful presentation tool—for flyers, overhead slides, direct mail letters, schematics, diagrams, and more. But you have to weigh the color impact against the fuzz-out factor. If you need—or just desperately want—color, your best strategy may be to buy both a color ink-jet printer and a laser printer.

QuickDraw vs. PostScript vs. PrintGear Different printers have different ways of drawing the page they print—given the information they get from your computer. For years, PostScript was considered the high-end method, providing better quality and performance. Today, PostScript is still the high-end page description language. It's used for the fastest, most expensive printers. But it's no longer really an issue of quality. QuickDraw and Adobe's new low-end PrintGear both deliver quality equal to PostScript. They just don't deliver it quite as fast. So it boils down to questions of volume and patience. If you have a lot of the former, get a PostScript printer. If you have a lot of the latter, you'll pay less for QuickDraw or PrintGear.

The bottom line on printers: don't scrimp here. This is literally your public image. It's also a huge potential time sink. Use bricks and boards for your bookcases if you need to, but get the best printer you can. Apple has traditionally positioned its lower-end ink-jet and laser printers as small office/home office printers. So dealers may steer you in that direction. But make sure you get the performance you need.

Obviously, your printer choice depends on your business. Check out the scenarios in this chapter for more considerations.

For more on using color in your information products, see Chapter 9, "The New Information Game."

HOW COLOR
PRINTING
WORKS

Whether you use your desktop printer or go to a professional for off-the-press color, the basics of color printing are the same. All the colors in the rainbow are created from just three colors—and sometimes black. The three colors are cyan, magenta, and yellow.

Your color ink-jet printer comes with three or four cartridges. Four are better than three because one of them gives you a true black, not a composite black, and your text looks an awful lot better in true black.

Some printers have cartridge packs: you have to replace the entire pack whenever you run out of one color. You'll save money over time if you buy a printer with cartridges that can be replaced separately.

Yes—a modem

For all the details on modems and other means of computer-based communications, see Chapter 6, "Weighing In on the Web."

A modem belongs on your list of basics—at least for now. It connects your computer to the telephone, which can connect you to the so-called information highway. You want access to this highway, so you need a modem. There are dozens of models. Look for these terms: Hayes-compatible and 14.4Kbps or 28.8Kbps. That's what you need.

On models and other mysteries

Like cars, computer equipment comes in lots of different models with different names and numbers. Making sense out of these models is a full-time job. They change frequently and on no discernible schedule.

For your Macintosh computer, think in terms of portable vs. desktop computers. Then think in terms of high-end, midrange, and low-end. The high-end Macs are the fastest and cost the most. However, they don't go up in price every year. The low-end models get cheaper, but the high-end models stay about the same. So don't think you need to buy a high-end Mac now or be squeezed out of the market. It's not like real estate.

For the rest of your hardware, review the scenarios in this chapter. In most cases, we give generic recommendations. Your Apple dealer can translate these into actual models in the current line.

Andy Fine wants a Macintosh that supports him at what he does best—bringing people together. He wants the computer to be a background companion, not a high-mainte- nance relationship.

His computing needs are simple. But his hardware needs are more than basic.

He has this problem with résumés— hundreds of them to keep track of. He does- n't want to do it by hand. To get help from his Mac, he needs a way to get the résumés into the Mac. He needs an OCR (optical char- acter recognition) scanner.

He also needs a printer that can pro- duce a slick newsletter, which is his main marketing tool. He doesn't want it to look like the *Family Reunion News*.

High-quality faxes are a must, too. He receives a lot of résumés via fax and then refaxes them to corporate clients. They need to look good, even after all that time on the telephone wires.

His strategy: Spend a little less on the computer and use the savings to buy extra power for the peripherals.

THE BASIC SETUP

A low-end Power Macintosh
15-inch monitor
Extended keyboard
A low-end laser printer
Visioneer PaperPort Vx scanner
External hard disk for backup
Modem

OTHER NECESSITIES

Two telephone lines: one for incoming calls, the other for fax, modem, and outgoing calls
Answering machine for incoming line
A plain paper fax machine

S O L U T I O N S

Susie Hu needs an office she can take on the road. She needs to be as well equipped in her van as she is in her loft. So portability is her first consideration.

Her second consideration is data access. She needs to be able to tap into data anywhere in the world—fast. She uses the networks. She also takes frequent spins on CD-ROM disks, plying the optical grooves for phone numbers, street addresses, maps of city sectors...

How about all that spy stuff? Well, sometimes she does need to snap an incriminating photograph. Or at least an illuminating one. And the pictures usually need to find their way into her reports.

Printing? Faxing? Yeah, sure. Quality? Professional, but it doesn't need to dazzle.

THE BASIC SETUP

A midrange Macintosh PowerBook
PowerBook printer
Apple CD-ROM drive
Internal Global Village fax modem

OTHER NECESSITIES

Two telephone lines: one for incoming calls, the other for fax, modem, and outgoing calls
Answering machine for incoming line
Cellular phone
Pager
Basic fax machine
Casio QV-10 digital camera

 S O L U T I O N S

The Delacruzes put a premium on creativity and variety in their work. So when they outgrew their one-Mac shop, they decided not to specialize in a particular kind of publishing but to invest in equipment and software that could respond to lots of different jobs—with top quality.

They are actually a four-person shop now, with four workstations networked together. Even though the two assistants are part-timers, the Delacruzes need the flexibility to have them both working at the same time to meet deadlines. Also, they expect the part-time positions to grow to full-time positions before too long.

Because their product is print, the Delacruzes need high-end printing capability. They need color laser printing for color proofs. With their own in-house imagesetter, they can produce film for projects with the shortest of fuses. A high-end laser printer with built-in fax capabilities is the fast and economical workhorse for all their black-and-white proofs.

At the front end of the process, the Delacruzes need flexibility, too. They have a flatbed scanner for digitizing photographs and hand-drawn art, as well as a digital camera for digitizing 3-D objects that Darcy turns into 2-D illustrations.

Even small jobs may require big files in the desktop publishing business—with color and complex graphics. To handle those files, the Delacruzes have both optical and magnetic disk drives and a high-speed modem for sending document files via telephone directly to printers anywhere in the country.

THE BASIC SETUP

High-end Power Macintosh for Darcy's graphics
Low-end Power Mac with a built-in DOS compatibility card for Dave
Two midrange Power Macs for two part-time assistants
17-inch monitor with built-in color management for Darcy
15-inch monitor for Dave
Two 20-inch monitors for the assistants

PERIPHERALS

Color laser printer for Darcy
1200-dpi imagesetter
600-dpi laser printer with fax
Modem
Graphics tablet
Apple color scanner
Apple QuickTake color digital camera
Gigabyte removable optical disk drives
SyQuest removable magnetic cartridge drive
Digital audio tape (DAT) drive

OTHER NECESSITIES

Four telephone lines with Panasonic integrated phone system
Fax/copier

 S O L U T I O N S

Sam Post needs a computer that can power not only his applications but also his lifestyle.

In this case, it's actually three computers—a portable PowerBook and two low-end desktop models.

The portable has both the speed and memory to support a lot of time and a lot of activity online. The high-end PowerBook gives Sam the mobility he wants. With a special 12-volt inverter cable, he can plug it into his wheelchair battery instead of swapping battery packs every couple hours. With built-in infrared technology and an infrared connector, he can zap information from his laptop to one of the dedicated computers—to update his customer database and to print labels, press releases, financial reports, and other documents.

In addition to the PowerBook, Sam needs two desktop computers for dedicated tasks. One is his answering service. It uses a GeoPort Telecom Adapter to take all his customer calls, giving product information, automatically faxing details to callers, and recording the customer contact information. It also supports PlainTalk for speech recognition, so Sam can give it commands without touching its mouse or keyboard.

Sam got a little help with the cost of this system. Under the Americans With Disabilities Act (ADA), the government pays up to $13,000 toward the cost of doing business to a person with a disability—a great investment in the economic productivity of someone like Sam Post.

THE BASIC SETUP

High-end Macintosh PowerBook, with a 12-volt inverter cable to plug into wheelchair battery (available from Apple)
Two low-end Performa Macintosh computers
Black-and-white PostScript printer
Apple Geoport Telecom Adapter Kit
Fax modem
Wireless modem card for the PowerBook
Farallon AirDock infrared connector

OTHER NECESSITIES

Cellular phone
Two phone lines: one for wireless modem jack and one for the dedicated answering system
Apple QuickTake color digital camera

S O L U T I O N S

ELLEN GANT   FOUR WEDDINGS AND A MAC

In Ellen Gant's business, image is everything. Her Mac is a dream screen—a place to create a reality, if only for a day.

To build her dream screen, Ellen needs multimedia support. She needs lots of speed, lots of memory, and a Mac that can handle audio and video.

When it comes to printing, Ellen counts on color. If a client likes an on-screen flower arrangement, Ellen wants to be able to print a color copy for the couple's personal planning portfolio. It doesn't have to be magazine-quality color. It just has to be lovely.

So Ellen's strategy is to invest most of her equipment dollars in a high-end audio-video Mac. For everything else, she can be choosy but modest.

THE BASIC SETUP

High-end AV Power Mac
17-inch monitor
Apple Color StyleWriter
Modem
Apple QuickTake color digital camera

OTHER NECESSITIES

One telephone line
Answering machine
Fax machine
VCR

S O L U T I O N S

JUMP START: Getting All the Pieces in Place

Let's say you're just starting out with your Mac home office. You don't even have your Mac yet. You don't know where to begin. Well, begin here.

STEP 1: CALCULATE YOUR REQUIREMENTS

Your computing needs depend on what you're going to use your computer for—which applications you'll use and for what projects. Chapter 3 helps you make sense out of the thousands of Macintosh applications. Once you know which applications are for you, use this table to determine your speed, memory, and data storage requirements.

TABLE 2.1 SPEED, MEMORY AND STORAGE

APPLICATIONS	SPEED**	MEMORY*	DISK STORAGE**
FINANCE	➤➤	4MB–8MB	●
WORD PROCESSING	➤	2MB–8MB	●
GRAPHICS			
Drawings	➤	2MB*–8MB	●
Paintings	➤	2MB–4MB	●●
Illustrations	➤	3MB–5MB	●
Photographs	➤➤	6MB–11MB	●●●
3-D rendering	➤➤➤	8MB–64MB	●●●
DESKTOP PUBLISHING			
Mostly text	➤	4MB–12MB	●
Complex graphics and color	➤➤➤		●●●
MULTIMEDIA			
Audio	➤➤	1MB–2MB	●●●
Video	➤➤➤	16MB–64MB	●●●
COMMUNICATIONS	➤	1MB–4MB	●
DATABASES	➤➤	2MB–8MB	● (text only)
PERSONAL INFO MANAGERS	➤	2MB–4MB	●
SECURITY	➤	1MB–4MB	●
BACKUP	➤➤➤	4MB	●●●

 * Memory requirements are suggested memory allocations for representative applications.
** Arrows and dots indicate relative speed and storage requirements, where one equals small requirements and three equals large requirements.

You'll almost always use more than one application at a time. For example, you might have several utilities, a PIM, a word processing application, and your desktop publishing application running at the same time. So you need to add their memory requirements together. However, you probably won't run *all* your applications at the same time. (Whew!) Also, you can easily add memory later.

Other things to count: slots and ports. **Slots** let you add capability to your Mac. You may not care about them now, but the more you have, the more you can grow. **Ports** are all those sockets on the back of your Mac. You plug things like your keyboard, mouse, and modem into them. You can also plug printers, external hard drives, CD-ROM drives, scanners, cameras, and other useful devices into them.

Ports come in different flavors with not-so-tasty names: ADB, serial, SCSI, and so on. Fortunately, Apple designs them to be more or less idiot-proof—you can't plug a cable into the wrong port. You usually get a good selection of ports. The ones to watch for are the serial ports. You need at least two for your printer and modem. Lots of other useful devices use this port, too, so you may end up buying a special switch box to switch among devices as you use them.

Finally, there's the question of the floating-point unit (FPU). It handles special types of computation that are essential to some applications. In the 640X0 Macs, the FPU was a special chip. In the RISC Macs, it's built into the processor. The problem: Some applications can't find the new built-in FPU. They keep looking for the old chip. The solution: Use a program called SoftwareFPU until your applications are updated to recognize the RISC FPU in your Power Mac.

STEP 2: DESIGN YOUR IDEAL SYSTEM

The next step is to put together your ideal system—the components that meet your needs. To do this, compare the product specifications with the figures you came up with from Step 1. Also compare product prices with your bank balance. You can get the information you need from several sources:

Apple, the company Apple regularly publishes a complete listing of its products in a pocket-size book called *Apple Facts*. This book lists the specifications for each product, as well as key features that distinguish the product from others in the line. You can purchase this book for $3. Call 1-800-825-2145 with your credit card in hand. You can also get info by fax (1-800-510-2834) or by recorded phone message (1-800-776-2333).

Apple dealers These guys get a lot of product information directly from Apple. Whether they read it or not depends a lot on the scope of their store. Stores or chains that are devoted to Apple products will probably have the most up-to-date, accurate information about Apple's product line. They probably

See "Upsizing" later in this chapter for details about RAM upgrades and software utilities that extend your memory.

Not all slots are created equal. See "Upsizing" in this chapter for details.

For more information about ports and plugs, see Step 5 below.

SoftwareFPU is a shareware program. See Chapter 3, "The Right Applications," for more about shareware.

PRODUCT FOCUS

DO YOU NEED DOS OR WINDOWS COMPATIBILITY?

Do your clients all have DOS machines? Is there a special custom Windows application that you'd really love to use? You can have your Mac and Windows, too.

System 7 reads PC disks straight out of the box. No special setup required. Some big applications, like Microsoft Word, can also read files in either Mac or PC file format and translate them as needed. So you can plug in your PC disk, open a Word file, and get right to work. When you're finished, you can save in either PC or Macintosh format. DataViz also offers a package of translators for several PC programs—so you can work with their files.

Apple makes a DOS compatibility card for some Macintosh models. This card has a 486DX2 processor. It's just like having two computers in your Mac housing. You can run any application that works with MS-DOS 6.2 or Windows 3.1, switching between those environments and the Mac environment as easily as you switch applications.

Insignia Solutions offers a software solution to the same problem. It's called SoftWindows, and you can use it to run Windows and its applications. It's not as fast as the hardware solution, but it works on a wider range of Macs.

One thing to note: you won't find this kind of compatibility on the PC side of things. If you need to be able to work in both environments, you have two choices: get a Mac, or get a Mac and a PC. Need we say more?

have demo models up and running, so you can try them out for yourself. A sales clerk for Somebody's Electronic Everything Warehouse is less likely to be model-savvy.

The press If you don't already know the Macintosh press, now's a good time to make its acquaintance. Monthly magazines like *MacWorld* and *MacUser* regularly publish detailed reviews of both hardware and software. *MacWeek* gives you the industry insider's view, which can be a little overwhelming. *Mac Home Journal* focuses specifically on computing issues in the home—business, educational, or entertainment. *Home Office Computing* is also a good source for home office information, but it's not Mac-specific.

Consultants If you don't want to do the research yourself, call a consultant. Look in the Yellow Pages under a heading like Computers—System Designers and Consultants. These people can do everything from answering basic questions to buying your system, installing software, and teaching you how to use it. You don't *need* someone else to set up your Mac. It's not that hard. But a consultant can quickly and exquisitely tailor your system to your needs, saving you lots of learning time. Of course, you pay for this service.

There are hundreds of user groups all over the world. See "Resources," for more information.

User Groups User groups can be formal or informal, big or small, local or national. They all have the same mission: To help Macintosh users make the most of their computer. Monthly meetings, newsletters, and networking are all part of the user group scene—and they're a great way to keep up to date, learn new skills, and get answers to niggling questions about your Macintosh hardware and software. If you have specific questions or just want to get a range of opinions from a lot of experienced users, attend a user group meeting. You may even meet your personal Mac guru—someone who will willingly spend hours on the phone with you helping you figure out things like why your Mac can't find your printer or which keys to press when your application freezes (⌘-Option-Esc).

STEP 3: COMPROMISE

Now that you've figured out exactly what you want and where to get it, you're ready to compromise. Why? Because Apple sells configurations, not components.

For example, if you're interested in a midrange Power Macintosh, you might have these choices:

- a Mac with a 120-MHz processor, 16MB of RAM, and a 1GB internal hard drive.
- a Mac with a 132-MHz processor, 16MB of RAM, and a 1GB internal hard drive.
- a Mac AV with a 132-MHz processor, 16MB or 32MB of RAM, and a 1GB or 2GB internal hard drive, plus an audio and video port.

The good news is that you can usually customize these basic configurations—for a little extra money, of course. For example, you can usually buy extra RAM at the time you purchase your computer and have it installed before you take it home. Sometimes you can even bargain for a hard drive upgrade, but don't be surprised if your dealer is reluctant. Besides, it's easy to add on external hard drives, and they're cheap as dirt.

For more about disk drives, see "Upsizing" in this chapter.

The Performa series of computers is a set of standard Macintosh configurations designed for the home computer user and, to some extent, the small-business user. They have fewer upgrade options than Apple's professional line, with less power and memory to begin with. They may not include a floating point unit (FPU). On the plus side, they come with over $1000 in software already installed—typically Quicken for personal finances, ClarisWorks for most basic computer tasks, CD-ROM encyclopedias, games, and more.

The Performas are a great choice if your computer is not the focus of your business—for example, if you use it as a support tool for a more people-oriented job like catering or counseling. You're not likely to push it past any of its limits, and by the time you're ready to upgrade, you may actually want to get a newer computer rather than expand the one you have.

By the way, the Performa line includes both the 640X0 and RISC-based Power Macintosh models. Get a Power Macintosh model. You'll have better software options.

WHAT'S A PERFORMA AND IS IT RIGHT FOR YOU?

STEP 4: FIND A SOURCE

Only Apple authorized resellers can sell you your Apple computer. To find the one nearest you, call 1-800-538-9696, extension 525. Of course, it doesn't actually need to be near you. Several dealers sell Macs by mail.

See Step 5 under "Jump Start" in Chapter 3 for a list of mail order catalogs for both hardware and software.

Mail order stores offer rock-bottom prices. You may also be excused from paying state and local taxes. But you have to do everything yourself. Don't expect to get installation and problem-solving support from a mail order house. Also, if something doesn't work, you have to pack everything up again and ship it back, paying the shipping charges.

With retail stores the keyword is support. The staff know the problems you're likely to encounter and will spend time explaining them before you head home with your boxes. If you have trouble while you're setting up, you can call them and ask questions—as many as you want. And if something still doesn't work, you just drive back to the store with your boxes and swap them, then and there, for new components.

Then again, you may not be buying an Apple product. Companies like Daystar, Power Computing, and Umax Data Systems also manufacture Macintosh computers. They use the same architecture, have the same user interface, and run the same software. And even if you buy a genuine Apple Macintosh, you may want to use other sources for components such as monitors, printers, keyboards, and modems. Again, magazines like *MacWorld* can help you compare features, specifications, and price.

Not sure whether to buy or lease new equipment? See "Power Play" in this chapter to help you make your decision.

SHOULD YOU BUY APPLE ONLY?

Apple Computer makes high-quality, elegantly designed products, with a worldwide system of dealers and service people to support them. The company message is that Apple technology makes all the pieces work together the way they should, right out of the box, without special adjustments or adapters.

This is a good argument for buying Apple brand components. You can use one dealer, one repair service. Nevertheless, you should know that you may get better buys or special features from other manufacturers. You should shop around, especially for smaller components, such as disk drives and modems. Hewlett-Packard has a strong line of desktop printers that work with a Macintosh—and sometimes outperform the Apple printers.

Ultimately, your decision may be an aesthetic one. This equipment is going to be in your home, like a stereo or like your kitchen appliances. If you're the sort of person who likes a matching washer or dryer in your laundry room, you may want matching components in your home office. If you don't care about appearances or can't find what you want in the Apple line, a third-party solution may work best for you.

STEP 5: SET IT ALL UP

This is the easy step. Believe it or not, it's much easier to set up your equipment than it is to figure out what you need. It's almost plug-and-play: plug in a few cables and you're ready to play...er...work. Just follow the instructions that come with your Mac.

A hint. If you've never used a Macintosh (or any other computer), it's well worth your time to do the Macintosh Tutorial. It includes exercises for working with your mouse, which may feel clumsy and awkward at first. Do the exercises and give it a few days. Soon you'll be dragging with your mouse as if it's always been attached to your hand.

Another hint. There are lots of special tools on the Distribution disk that comes with your Macintosh—such as QuickDraw GX, PlainTalk, and PowerTalk. You won't see them mentioned in your printed guide, but you can find out how to use them in the online Macintosh Guide.

(Both the Macintosh Tutorial and Macintosh Guide are in the help menu. Click the question mark in the upper right corner of the screen to choose them.)

A possible stumbling block in your setup is your printer. To print, you need the right printer description documents (PDD). When you choose the Print command, the system goes looking for the printer description. If it doesn't find one, you can't print. If you have a current system version, chances are you also have printer descriptions for all of Apple's current printer models. If you buy from another source or if you're using an old system version, you may have to install the printer description file that comes with the printer before you can print.

PPDs are extensions that go in your Extensions folder. See "Tour Stop 2: The Extensions Folder" in Chapter 4 for details.

If you got all your components from Apple, you should have all the cables with all the right connectors to put your Mac together. Be sure to match the cable connector to the port. Most Apple models have picture IDs for the ports, but in case you want to know the generic names of the ports—for example, to order an additional cable when the dog chews yours to threads—here's a summary of the main types:

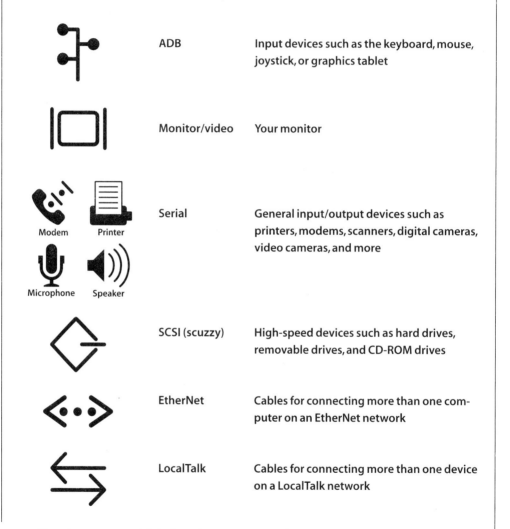

	ADB	Input devices such as the keyboard, mouse, joystick, or graphics tablet
	Monitor/video	Your monitor
Modem Printer Microphone Speaker	Serial	General input/output devices such as printers, modems, scanners, digital cameras, video cameras, and more
	SCSI (scuzzy)	High-speed devices such as hard drives, removable drives, and CD-ROM drives
	EtherNet	Cables for connecting more than one computer on an EtherNet network
	LocalTalk	Cables for connecting more than one device on a LocalTalk network

**CABLES,
CONNECTORS,
AND SWITCH
BOXES**

If you have more serial devices than serial ports, don't despair. You can get a switch box to extend the capability of your serial port. These boxes cost about $20 and may have two to several channels. You plug the box into your serial port. Then you plug each device—your modem and digital video input, for example—into a channel. When you want to use one of the devices, you use a switch or dial to switch back and forth between channels.

UPSIZING: Expanding Your Capacity to Grow

So you already have a Mac. It seemed fine when you first started out, but now it seems sluggish. You expect more from it. Your newest applications demand more from it. You find you're waiting a lot. Maybe you're desperately moving stuff on and off your hard disk. You're ready to expand.

RAM upgrades

If you want to improve performance, the best way to spend your money is on RAM. You can never have too much RAM. Today's programmers don't even try to write small applications. They want to give you features, and they want to give them to you fast. So they write big programs that require a lot of memory to run. And it's only going to get worse.

The good news is that you can add RAM to your computer or your display. Computer RAM gives you speed and the ability to run more applications at the same time. Video RAM gives you more colors. While RAM is probably your best computer buy, it isn't cheap. The going rate is about $30 per megabyte. Don't wait around for the prices to come down, either. They probably won't.

Apple doesn't tell you that you can install RAM yourself. They suggest that you take your Mac to a dealer and have the dealer install it for you. And indeed, installing RAM requires a certain amount of mechanical aptitude. You have to open up your Mac and, depending on the model, remove disk drives or other previously working parts. Also, the modules of the RAM chips—called SIMMs and DIMMs—tend to be fragile. They're held in place by clips that may break off if you don't handle them with care.

Nevertheless, you can save a lot of money buying your RAM by mail and installing it yourself. A great source is TechWorks (1-800-704-0189), which not only gives you a good price but a very thoughtful installation kit, including an instruction manual and an antistatic strap.

The Doublers

If you can't afford more RAM just now or if you've maxed out your memory, you can trick your Mac into using its memory more efficiently with utilities that take over some of the memory management functions. These utilities are all *doublers*—RAM Doubler and Speed Doubler from Connectix, and DiskDoubler Pro from Symantec.

Here's what RAM Doubler does: When you run an application, your Mac sets aside a certain amount of memory for the program and its documents. (You can select the application icon and choose Get Info from the File menu to see how much memory it sets aside—and to change it.) However, the application doesn't use all this memory all the time. So RAM Doubler checks for unused memory, gathers it up, and makes it available to other applications that need it. The result: You can run more applications more efficiently. However, the more RAM you have to begin with, the more efficient RAM Doubler is. If you're running on 4 megabytes, doubling to 8MB isn't going to buy you nearly as much as doubling 32MB would.

Speed Doubler has three components: speed copying, speed trashing, and 680X0 emulation. The first two components help you copy faster and empty your trash faster, regardless of which Macintosh you own. The third component makes your Power Mac more efficient. All Mac models before the Power Mac used a processor known as the 680X0 (where X equals some number like 2 or 4, depending on the version). The Macintosh system and most applications were designed to run on this processor. The Power Macs use the RISC processor and need to emulate a 680X0 to run the system software and any old-style applications. Apple provides a built-in emulator with System 7. Speed Doubler provides a better one.

Disk Doubler Pro is actually three separate programs: DiskDoubler, Copy-Doubler, and AutoDoubler. CopyDoubler does the same thing as Speed Doubler, but without the 680X0 emulator. DiskDoubler and AutoDoubler both double the capacity of your storage disks by compressing your files to half their size. DiskDoubler does it manually on a file-by-file basis. AutoDoubler does it automatically for all your files.

A few words of caution: RAM Doubler interacts with all your applications in memory—and not always politely. As a result, it can make your system unstable. If you're using AutoDoubler, you can expect any virus-scanning programs to run slower because they have to decompress all the compressed files to check them. AutoDoubler also makes it more difficult to recover files if they're damaged.

Slots and cards

As mentioned earlier, your Mac comes with slots. You can put cards in these slots to make your Mac do more tricks. For example, you can get a modem card to give your PowerBook a built-in modem if it doesn't have one. Or you can get audio and video boards to digitize sound and video if you didn't buy an AV Mac. You can add graphics accelerators to speed up the screen display when you're working with all those millions of colors, or you can add an MPEG board for video speeds of 60 frames per second. Special-purpose boards can also tailor your Mac to a variety of technical and scientific tasks.

There are different kinds of slots: NuBus, PCI, and PCMCIA. Different Macs have different slots:

- Older Macs have NuBus slots. They're slower.
- Newer Macs have PCI slots. They're faster.
- Some PowerBooks also have PCMCIA slots. They're super convenient.

For more information about utilities and how they make your system more efficient, see Chapter 4, "System Smarts."

For details about file recovery, see Chapter 12.

You can only use cards that match your slots, however. If you're not sure which slots you have, check your owner's guide.

You get cards from the same places you get other hardware: your local retailer or a mail order dealer. And unlike RAM chips, cards are easy to install yourself. For NuBus and PCI cards, you have to take the top off your Mac, but the slots are easy to access. You just plug the cards in. You may also have to remove a protective cover on the back of your Mac to add a special connector and cable. But if you've ever assembled a kid's toy, you can handle this.

PCMCIA cards, also known as PC cards, are even simpler. They're like credit cards. You just plug them directly into your PowerBook to get the services you want. They won't make your Mac spit out cash, but sometimes data is just as good. You can get wireless modems, pagers, and even disk drives on PCMCIA cards.

More drives

So things are starting to feel a little cramped in your Macintosh. That free-space indicator in the upper-right corner of your folder window keeps falling into the KB range instead of the MB range. Maybe you have to get rid of a couple of old documents every time you sit down to work. Maybe you're working, slowly, from floppy disks. Or you're avoiding getting new applications because you just don't have room for them on your internal hard disk.

What should you do? Add some external drives. These are your choices.

TABLE 2.2 TYPES OF DRIVES

TYPE OF DRIVE	DESCRIPTION	CAPACITY	TYPE OF ACCESS
MAGNETIC FIXED DRIVES	These are just like your internal drive. You plug them into your computer via a cable, and they show up on your screen like your internal drive. They have a fixed amount of storage. You get another drive when you fill them up. They provide good, cheap, general-purpose disk storage. (The maximum that the Mac can address is 4GB. The high-end is currently 1GB or larger.)	300MB to more than 10GB	Read and write
MAGNETIC REMOVABLE	These plug into your Mac like a hard drive, but then you can pop removable cartridges in and out of them. Removable cartridges hold 100 times as much as floppy disks or more. They work as fast as most hard drives. Excellent for storing applications you don't use all the time, for backing up files, and for exchanging large files.	100MB to 1GB	Read and write

(continued)

TABLE 2.2 TYPES OF DRIVES (continued)

TYPE OF DRIVE	DESCRIPTION	CAPACITY	TYPE OF ACCESS
OPTICAL REMOVABLE DRIVES	These are just like the magnetic removable drives, but they use an optical or magneto-optical technology to record data. They are excellent for storing long documents and very large images that you need to send to someone else, and are essential for multimedia files.	1GB to 4GB	Read and write
DAT DRIVES	These drives use those small-size, high-capacity digital audio tape (DAT) cassettes. They're removable, of course. A good option for backing up your system.	1GB or more	Read and write
CD-ROM DRIVES	You know. These use laser technology and are wafer-thin disks with lots and lots of data. They come built into almost all Mac models these days. But you might want an extra if you need to use two disks at the same time—for example, to keep a disk of clip art and one of stock photos at your fingertips.	600MB is the current standard. 1.4GB is imminent.	Read only

For more information about the EZ Drive and backup strategies, see Chapter 4, "System Smarts."

Having trouble with a SCSI device? Is your Mac ignoring it? See Chapter 12, "File Recovery," for some tips.

Our recommendation: Get the CD-ROM built into your Mac. Even if you're not interested in all those Microsoft digital collections of everything under the sun, the CD-ROM will save you lots of time and mind-numbing disk swapping when you're installing applications. (You can now install lots of the big applications directly from a single CD instead of 20-something floppy disks.) When your internal drive starts to get full and your backup floppies start showing up in your nightmares, get a SyQuest EZ Drive. It's fast, reliable, affordable, and expandable—you can just keep adding cartridges as your data files proliferate.

Whatever you choose, you plug it into the SCSI port. Of course, you may already have something plugged into your SCSI port. No problem. You can add up to seven SCSI devices. You just plug the first one, say a hard drive, into your Mac, plug the second one into the hard drive, and so on. This is called a SCSI chain or—sometimes—a daisy chain.

When you add a SCSI device, you have to give it a SCSI ID number. All SCSI devices have a switch that you can use to set the ID number. It's usually a rotary dial. You just dial in the number you want. Of course, it has to be a number that's available. The Mac recognizes up to 8 SCSI devices, numbered 0 through 7. The number 7 is always assigned to the central processing unit (CPU), and the number 0 is always assigned to the internal hard drive. If you have an internal CD-ROM drive, its SCSI ID is probably 3. That leaves 1, 2,

4, 5, and 6 for you to assign to your plug-in devices. You can assign them in any order. The IDs don't have to match the actual physical order of the devices.

THE TERMINATOR

There's one big gotcha that can get you when you're stringing your SCSI devices together—the terminator. The SCSI chain has to be terminated at both ends to keep the electrical signals from bouncing back and forth endlessly through the chain. All Macintosh computers are automatically terminated at the CPU, but you have to provide the terminator at the other end.

What exactly is a terminator? It's just a plug that you put in the SCSI port of the last device in the chain. It usually comes with your device. Sometimes, it may actually be built into a device. That's not an advantage. It forces you to put that device at the end. And if you have more than one device with a built-in termination, you have to remove it from all but one. See your manual for details.

Trading up

At some point, all the cards and slots and drives and RAM you can buy are not going to get you what you want. At some point, you're going to have to get a new computer.

The trigger to trade up will usually be one of three things:

■ New software is making higher demands on your computer, and it's not responding. Familiar operations take longer than they used to, and all those new features don't make up for the time you spend waiting for them to show up on the screen.

■ You've changed the mix of your work, and *you're* making higher demands on your computer. Your original PowerBook works fine when you're just composing short bursts of advertising copy for your clients. But now someone is paying you to write a 300-page training manual with 20 style formats, and the old PowerBook can barely turn the pages.

■ The world has changed, and you're missing out on some of the good stuff. Like video clips and real-time audio from the online news services. Like multimedia marketing strategies that could distinguish you from your competitors. Like 3-D communications possibilities you can't even imagine but would sure like to try. Like a client who just wants someone with a machine that can read both Macintosh and Windows files.

Trading up is a bit of a euphemism. You may find someone to buy your current Mac, but don't be surprised if you can't. Depending on how old it is, you may not even be able to donate it to a school. (But you should try.) The alternative to getting rid of it is to use it as a second computer. It's always good to have an old one around in case your shiny new model gets the flu right in the middle of your busiest week of the year.

If your old Mac is a Power Mac, you can turn it into a full-feature phone answering service. See "Power Play" in Chapter 5.

POWER PLAY: Making the Lease/Buy Decision

Let's say you don't have the cash for new hardware purchases. Maybe you're just starting out, and you don't want to deplete your savings at the very time you're giving up your steady job. Maybe you want to invest the cash you have in product development or marketing rather than equipment.

Your smartest move may actually be to finance your equipment. You have three options: you can use your credit card (which is probably crazy), you can get a traditional loan, or you can lease the equipment.

Which is more expensive? It depends on the terms, of course. If you know the terms, you can calculate the least expensive way to meet your hardware needs. The key is to determine the present value of the purchase—the value of future payments today.

To calculate the present value, you need to know the following information about possible loan and lease terms:

Cost of funds. This is the interest rate for your loan.

Net purchase price. This is the amount you would need to buy the equipment with cash today.

Loan down payment. This is the down payment significantly changes the present value of the deal. Experiment with different down payments.

Loan term. This is the scheduled time to repay the loan, in years.

Lease payment. This is the monthly amount you pay to lease the equipment.

Lease term. This is the period for which you agree to make monthly payments, in years.

Purchase price at the end of the lease. Many lease contracts include a final balloon payment to purchase the equipment outright. You may or may not want to purchase the equipment. Computer equipment loses its value so quickly that in three years you may not be able to sell yours for the amount of your balloon payment.

If you already have a Mac (at work, at home, or at a friend's house), you can use a spreadsheet program to calculate the present value of your deal. If you also have ClarisWorks and the ClarisWorks Small Business Template, you can do it in about five minutes.

What you need

- ClarisWorks, version 2.1 or higher
- ClarisWorks Small Business Solutions Pack
- Values for your lease and loan terms
- Time: 5 to 10 minutes

First, install the template

The template is in the stationery folder on your Small Business Solutions Pack. If you haven't already installed these templates, you can do so now. You can install them all or just the Buy vs. Lease template.

1. Open the ClarisWorks Stationery folder in your System folder. If the folder doesn't exist, just create a new folder called ClarisWorks Stationery.

2. Insert the Small Business Solutions Pack disk and double-click the Templates folder.

3. Drag the Buy vs. Lease template into the ClarisWorks Stationery Folder.

Open the template

The template is now available whenever you start ClarisWorks or open a new document.

1. Start ClarisWorks, or choose Open from the File Menu if ClarisWorks is already running.

2. Click Use Assistant or Stationery and choose Stationery from the pop-up menu in the Open box.

3. Select Lease vs. Purchase Analyzer and click Open.

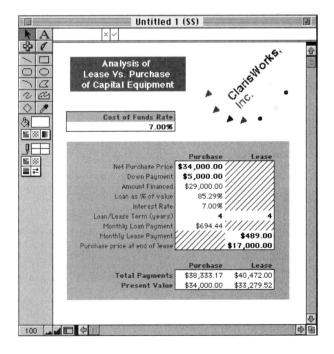

Enter your numbers, get your results

The template already has some numbers in it. You're going to substitute your own.

1. Choose AutoCalc from the Calculate menu if it's not already checked.
2. Select each number shown in bold and type your own value, followed by a carriage return.

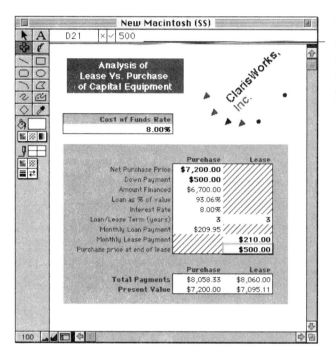

When you type a number, it appears here. Press Return to display it in the template.

ClarisWorks automatically calculates the total payments and the present value. Even though the payments may be higher, the choice with the lower present value is the least expensive choice.

Of course, many other factors figure into the buy-vs.-lease decision. For example, lease payments are considered direct expenses on your tax sheet. Loan payments for equipment are depreciated over the projected life of the equipment. Also, lease loan payments are considered debts on your balance sheet, while lease payments are considered operating expenses. These differences may be significant for your overall financial plans. In addition, lease contracts often include complete repair and maintenance provisions—with immediate replacement of the equipment if necessary.

For more information about financial strategies for your business, see Chapter 10, "Fast-Track Finances."

If you don't have the ClarisWorks Buy vs. Lease template—or even ClarisWorks—you can create your own spreadsheet to do the analysis. Here are the formulas from the template:

	Lease/Buy Spreadsheet (SS)		
A1	× ✓		
	A	**B**	**C**	**D**

	A	B	C	D
1				
2				
3				
4				
5				
6				
7			**LOAN TERMS**	**LEASE TERMS**
8				
9	Cost of Funds Rate	YOUR DATA		
10				
11				
12				
13	Net Purchase Price		YOUR DATA	
14	Down Payment		YOUR DATA	
15			IF(C18<>,C13-C14,0)	
16			C15/C13	
17	Interest Rate		B9	
18	Loan Term (years)		YOUR DATA	
19	Monthly Loan Payment		IF(C18<>0<-PMT(C17/12,12*C18,C15,0,0),0)	
20	Monthly Lease Payment			YOUR DATA
21	Purchase Price at Lease End			YOUR DATA
22				
23				
24	Total Payments		IF(C18<>0,C19*C18*12+C14,C13)	D20*D18*12+D21
25	Present Value		IF(C18<>0,-(PV($B$9/12,12*C18,C19,0,0,))+C14,C13)	-PV($B$9/12,D18*12,D20,D21)
26				

| 100 |

Make sure your spreadsheet uses the same format for the IF (logical true) and PV (present value) functions.

**THE BUY
VS. LEASE
FORMULAS**

ON THE HORIZON:
Faster, Smaller, and More Compatible

On the hardware horizon, things are going to get faster and smaller—but the prices will stay the same or drop. Computer screens will be dancing with full-motion video and 3-D rendering. But the most important change may be the result of an agreement among hardware vendors rather than any break-through in technology.

Apple, IBM, and Motorola (the company that makes the PowerPC RISC chips) have all agreed upon a computer architecture called the Common Hardware Reference Platform (CHRP, pronounced *chirp*). Any CHRP computer will be able to run lots of different operating systems: the Mac OS, S/2-PPC, Windows NT, AIX, Solaris, Novell Netware, and others that haven't been invented yet.

What does it mean? Your software won't be so dependent on your hardware. You'll be able to run Mac software on any manufacturer's CHRP computer. You'll also be able to run Windows, Unix, and other environments on the same machine. Daystar, Power Computing, and Radius have all agreed to produce CHRP computers, and so have lots of PC companies. So you'll have lots of choices. The Mac OS is what will make you feel like you're using a Macintosh, not the Apple hardware.

There are benefits. Operating systems from different vendors will start to work together, so will the applications for those operating systems. In addition, CHRP parts will be available off the shelf. Apple Macintoshes currently require specialized, custom chips—usually made by only one vendor. When that vendor has supply problems, Apple can't produce enough computers to meet the demand. But with off-the-shelf parts, there'll be lots of sources. Bye-bye, supply problems.

The other big influence in the world of hardware is the meteoric growth of the Internet. With so much information available online, you can expect a movement toward a small, cheap, network computer. This won't be a personal computer in the form you've come to know. It will derive all its data and computing power directly from the Net. It may not have any offline storage of its own. The ideas for the network computer are just now surfacing, so it's anyone's guess as to what form it will take. The one thing you can be sure of is that you can never be sure where technology is going to take you.

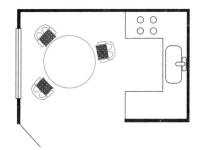

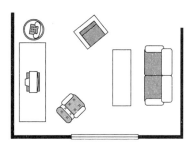

CHAPTER THREE

THE RIGHT APPLICATIONS

How to make software choices that

will make you money

This chapter is about balancing acts—because that's what choosing your Macintosh software is all about.

When you buy software, you're buying intelligence. It's a little like gathering a bunch of consultants in your home office every day to tell you how to do your work. Except you don't have to listen to them chatter all day long. And you only have to pay the consulting fee once.

You can buy intelligence for just about every type of problem you can imagine—the current list of commercial Macintosh software tops 7,000 products. There's a catch, though. You need a certain amount of skill to take advantage of all this digital intelligence. And you need a certain amount of time to gain that skill.

That's where the balancing acts come in.

Act 1: The integrated package vs. special-purpose software

In this act, you find yourself caught between the friendly forces of the all-in-one packages—often known as "the works"—and the alluring power of the dedicated applications.

The works packages are integrated. They offer everything in one application. All the commands and tools you need are available in a single program. You can compose text, draw diagrams, express yourself in a whimsical little painting, calculate hard numbers based on information in your online database, and then mail it all to a remote computer without ever switching applications.

These integrated packages offer you consistency. You can count on things. Like how the commands are arranged in menus. How the tools work. Which keyboard shortcuts do what. Everything is designed to work with everything else. This consistency makes the software easier to learn and your work easier to do. It also makes the buying decision easier. You compare the two leading packages and make your decision. Done.

Unless you want a little more power.

For example, suppose the heart of your business is a networked customer database that your three part-time employees use to record hundreds of phone orders each week. You use the database to generate sales reports, track inventory, create specialized mailing lists, and develop customer profiles. The database that comes with your integrated package just may not be up to all those tasks.

Single-purpose products—from database and spreadsheet applications to page layout and illustration software—give you power. They give you depth. They give you features you may not even know you need. They turn you into an MBA, a Ph.D., a mogul, a wizard. All in a few, er, months.

Which brings us to Act 2.

Act 2: Features vs. simplicity

The fastest way to compare two software products is to compare their features. Features are things that you can do with the software—or things that make the software do a better job of the things you do.

Software companies often list the features on the back of the box to help you out. Computer magazines often write reviews of several software products, comparing their features in tidy tables. Products with more features are generally more powerful.

So do you automatically buy the package with the most features? Not necessarily. Features are things you have to learn to use. The more things you have to learn to use, the longer it will take you to learn the product. Or you'll learn to use a few key features and save the rest for sometime, you know, when business is slow. You could have just gotten the less-powerful—and probably less-expensive—product.

Even if you master all the features, they may be overkill. You don't need a high-end illustration package to produce a classified ad in the local paper. Features may seduce you into doing more than is necessary for the job—and spending more time than you need to. Simplicity is sometimes the most important feature.

At times, of course, you may need all the power of the more full-bodied, complex applications. Then you have yet another choice to make.

Act 3: Doing it yourself vs. hiring a professional

People fall into two categories.

In Category 1 are those who jump right in and do everything themselves, from things like replacing all the wiring in their house and changing their own car oil to creating their own business cards, brochures, financial forecasts, and accounting databases.

In Category 2 are those who find it much more efficient to focus on the things they do really well, making enough money to hire others to do the things that they can't even begin to imagine doing.

People in both categories can make the wrong choice in Act 3. The do-it-yourself folks are likely to buy lots applications—often the full-featured ones—and spend too much time and resources on tasks that a consultant could do better for less. The hire-a-professional crowd is likely to overlook some very simple applications that could save a lot of money that would otherwise go to an expensive consultant.

The right balance

So how do you decide? Here are some guidelines:

- If you're using your Mac primarily for basic office operations, get an integrated package. Today's integrated packages are sophisticated. They have more than enough power to turn your Mac into a whiz-bang office assistant.
- If you're a professional in a certain field—for example, if you're a professional illustrator—get the special-purpose software for that field. It's designed to take advantage of all the power of Macintosh computing and keep you competitive in your field. You can afford the learning time because you're going to be using the software daily. And by using it daily, you'll quickly scale the learning curve.
- If you don't have the skills you need to do a task, figure out how often you need to do it. Once in a while? Hire a professional. Often? Consider spending the time to develop the skills with a new application.

That's the general advice. The rest of the chapter is more specific. By the time you finish, you should have an overview of the types of applications you need for your home office, how to get them, and how to install them. Then the rest of the book can help you figure out exactly which applications you want and how to use them.

ANDY FINE   MISSION: INEVITABLE

Andy Fine is a people person. He's on the phone all day. He's likely to meet fifty to a hundred new people each week. He needs to keep track of them—who they are, what they need, what they can do, and when he needs to get back to them.

Most of his written communications are quick and simple. He doesn't need a lot of text-formatting options. Just a clean, professional look—in a hurry.

But once a month, he sends out a news-letter to his clients, and then he needs design support.

The core of Andy's application suite is a contact manager, a scanner with OCR software for reading text, and a custom Hyper-Card database. A low-end page layout program and a personal financial package meet his other major needs.

CONTACT MANAGEMENT
■ ACT! for managing contacts—with day-by-day schedules for returning calls—and for simple word processing

DESKTOP PUBLISHING
■ Adobe Home Publisher for fast, simple newsletters

DATA MANAGEMENT
■ OmniPage Professional OCR software for reading résumés from an optical character recognition scanner
■ HyperCard—one card per résumé, with a simple script for skill searching

FINANCES
■ Quicken for tracking both personal finances and simple business accounts

COMMUNICATION
■ America Online for daily business news and occasional e-mail

UTILITIES
■ QuicKeys for quick access to contacts
■ CopyDoubler for data backup
■ Now Utilities for simple system enhancements
■ Disinfectant for virus protection
■ Suitcase for font management

SECURITY
■ After Dark password protection for quick, simple kidproofing

 S O L U T I O N S

SUSIE HU, P.I. THE CASE OF THE LOFTY GOAL

Susie Hu spends most of her day gathering information—by phone, via online information services, and in personal meetings. She needs quick ways to keep notes and turn them into reports. Nothing fancy, just professional.

She needs to keep a running log of her expenses and her time. She needs to turn that log into client reports with a minimum hassle.

An integrated package makes sense for her. ClarisWorks is a good choice because she has a medium-power, medium-capacity Mac. ClarisWorks gives her the biggest punch for her computing power.

CLARISWORKS
- Text documents for preparing client reports and marketing materials
- Custom database documents for managing contacts and keeping case notes
- Custom spreadsheets for tracking hourly charges and expenses as well as personal finances

COMMUNICATIONS
- Compuserve Navigator for Compuserve searches
- Netscape Navigator, NewsWatcher, and Anarchy for Internet searches

UTILITIES
- StuffIt Expander for decompressing online documents in lots of different formats
- SAM for virus protection
- QuicKeys for automating operations, including backup

SECURITY
- FolderBolt for locking folders and encrypting sensitive files

 S O L U T I O N S

As with their hardware, the Delacruzes have opted for flexibility with their software choices.

For publishing, they have two standards. For high-design, complex documents that typically go through lots of customer reviews and revisions, they prefer Adobe PageMaker with its traditional paste-up model. For most of their book projects, they use QuarkXPress, which has become a de facto *industry standard.*

For compatibility, they also need industry-standard software for word processing, illustration, and photo enhancement, with special plug-ins for special-purpose work.

On the management front, Dave has developed his own custom process for tracking tasks, materials, resources, and customer communication—all in a custom spreadsheet. He also prefers the spreadsheet for estimating jobs, although he needs an accounting package with a payroll module to manage the company's finances.

A few efficiency utilities as well as lots of fonts and an application to manage them complete the Delacruz software library.

PUBLISHING
- Adobe PageMaker for brochures, catalogs, and other high-design projects
- QuarkXPress for book-length projects

WORK PROCESSING
- Microsoft Word for producing and reading industry-standard word processing files

GRAPHICS
- Adobe Photoshop for fine-tuning photographs for reproduction on laser printers or commercial presses
- Kai's PowerTools and KPT Convolver for special effects in Photoshop
- KPT Bryce for creating landscapes
- Adobe Illustrator for original art
- KPT Vector Effects for special effects in Ilustrator
- Adobe TextureMaker and Specular Texture Scape for creating special textural effects in illustrations
- Ray Dream AddDepth2 for interpreting 2-D drawings and text as 3-D objects
- Adobe Streamline for quickly turning photographs and art into line drawings

 S O L U T I O N S

- Adobe Fetch for cataloging all kinds of graphics files
- ClarisDraw for simple line drawings and diagrams
- Fractal Design Painter for special desktop painting effects

COMMUNICATIONS
- MacCIM for communicating with clients via the Compuserve network
- Proprietary communications software for direct phone-to-phone data communication with commercial printing firms

MANAGEMENT
- Microsoft Excel for project management

FINANCE
- MYOB for account management, including client invoicing and payroll management

UTILITIES
- Now Menus for custom menus and worksheets
- AppleScript and QuicKeys for automating operations such as file conversion
- Suitcase for font and resource management
- StuffIt Deluxe for compressing large data files
- Speed Doubler for better system performance
- Retrospect Remote for backup to a DAT drive
- SAM for virus protection

SECURITY
- System 7 built-in file-sharing software

SAM POST   CYBERWORK

Sam Post runs an online business. He solicits customers and takes orders on the Internet. He uses online services to keep up with the latest in electronic convenience technology, to participate in discussions about architectural standards and community planning, and to share his environmental know-how with other disabled individuals.

So he needs an efficient way to manage his e-mail. He also needs an efficient way to manage his phone orders.

Then there's basic development. Sam uses a professional program for computer-aided design (CAD). But he also gets extra design and marketing mileage from a 3-D virtual reality design tool.

Finally, there's the basics of day-to-day business: a financial package that can help with inventory management, as well as software for correspondence, for producing online product information, and for simple ads in home improvement magazines.

Speech recognition software and Apple's built-in scripting language give Sam space-age command of his work environment.

COMMUNICATIONS
- Pleiades Front Office for automatic phone-answering and fax-back service on a dedicated desktop Mac
- Claris Emailer for automatically retrieving messages from all the online services
- Netscape Navigator for navigating the Web

DESIGN AND DEVELOPMENT
- Virtus WalkThrough Pro for visualizing interior spaces and providing walkthrough marketing from a Web page
- A professional CAD system for drafting and developing architectural specifications

MARKETING
- Adobe PageMill for developing Web pages
- Microsoft Works for basic text and graphics support
- PhotoFlash for cataloging digital photographs of model homes, as well as "idea" photographs

FINANCE
- MYOB for account management, customer tracking, inventory management—even mailing labels

UTILITIES
- Apple PlainTalk for speech recognition
- AppleScript and QuicKeys for automating operations, including data backup
- Now Utilities for setting up worksets and other system management features
- The doubler programs for system efficiency
- Suitcase for managing fonts, sounds, and other resources

S O L U T I O N S

Ellen Gant manages events—which means she needs to coordinate schedules and people.

She also creates scenes—lovely scenes. And she needs a way to capture these scenes and communicate them to her clients, both for marketing and planning purposes.

Ellen keeps the event-management tasks simple with an organizer that integrates contact management and calendar scheduling. She invests her creative time and energy in simple but powerful multimedia presentations, with lots of graphics and video clips from all her weddings.

EVENT MANAGEMENT

■ Claris Organizer for scheduling events and keeping track of wedding suppliers and facilities

MULTIMEDIA

■ Adobe Persuasion for Mac-based presentations
■ Adobe Premiere for video editing
■ Macromedia SoundEdit 16 for editing sound clips

FINANCES

■ QuickBooks for tracking reimbursable expenses and billing clients

UTILITIES

■ QuicKeys for automated backup and quick-starting client presentations
■ Now Utilities for WYSIWYG menus and automatic saving
■ Suitcase for managing fonts and sounds
■ Speed Doubler for faster handling of large multimedia files
■ AutoDoubler for automatically compressing large data files
■ SAM for virus protection

EVERYTHING ELSE

■ ClarisWorks for correspondence, for text and graphics support for multimedia presentations, and for spreadsheets to track food, beverages, seating, flowers, and other wedding requirements

SOLUTIONS

JUMP START: Stocking Your Desktop Workspace

OK. You've got a lot of software to sort through. To zoom in on the right applications for your home office, try following these steps:

STEP 1: SORT BY TYPE

Start by figuring out which kinds of software you need. Here's a checklist in which we've taken the liberty of checking a few things you can't work without.

- ☑ Financial applications—for accounting, business planning, budgeting, estimating, invoicing, taxes, and other generally frightening tasks
- ☑ Word processing applications—for everything from simple correspondence to book-length reports
- ❏ Graphics applications—for illustrating products, processes, ideas, your financial past, the market of the future, and everything in between
- ❏ Desktop publishing applications—for combining the fruits of your word processing and graphics applications into refined, elegant, and perhaps complex pages for ads, brochures, newsletters, pamphlets, reports, and more
- ❏ Multimedia applications—for marketing your work in virtual worlds with slides, 3-D, animation, and video
- ❏ Communications software—for getting and sending electronic mail, schmoozing with others in your field, tracking down data of all kinds, and grabbing software updates
- ❏ Database applications—for organizing information into categories that you can then quickly search and sort
- ☑ Personal information managers (PIMs)—for keeping track of all the people you know (or should know) and your plans for spending time with them
- ☑ Security and backup applications—for protecting your applications and data from accidents and malice
- ☑ System utilities—for making your applications, as well as your system, work faster and better

STEP 2: COMPARE FEATURES

Now you know what kinds of applications you need. That probably narrows the choice down to a few dozen. To narrow further, you can begin to compare features.

Remember that the application with the most features isn't necessarily the best product for you. Try to find the product that fits you. We'll help by pointing out what to look for. The charts on the following pages walk you quickly through all the categories, starting with the integrated packages.

These are overview charts. They don't cover all the products in the Mac universe—just a few examples of those that are easily available or that we think are particularly notable. The charts also don't go into detail about the applications. We do that later in the book.

TABLE 3.1 INTEGRATED APPLICATIONS

WHAT THEY DO	THE PRODUCTS	BASIC FEATURES	SPECIAL FEATURES
Integrated applications offer you lots of different types of documents in one application. When you choose a document type, you get the menus and tools associated with that type.	ClarisWorks	Word processing Drawing Painting Spreadsheets Database Communications	Outlining Stationery and Assistants Sections in text documents Graphics in database documents Adjustable rows and columns in spreadsheets AppleScript support Zoom in/out in all modules
Think of it as one-stop shopping for all your computing needs—or at least most of them. Note that while both the Works packages have a communications module; this is not software you'll need unless you want to communicate directly from your computer to another computer via a phone line. Today, most communication is accomplished via commercial services or Internet service providers.	Microsoft Works	Calendar Word processing Drawing Painting Charting Spreadsheets Database Communications	Drag-and-drop text editing Special effects with Adobe Photoshop plug-ins Thumbnail view for sorting slides Wizards

TABLE 3.2 FINANCIAL APPLICATIONS

WHAT THEY DO	WHAT TO LOOK FOR	EXAMPLES
Accounting packages help you manage your books—income, expenses, investments, invoices, payroll, and inventory, depending on the package.	Orientation: Is it geared toward personal or business financial needs?	ACCOUNTING QuickBooks Quicken MYOB
	Special features: Can it handle your special accounting needs, such as a multiple-user ordering system or payroll tasks?	
Spreadsheets can help you manage your books, too. But they're most helpful for financial analyses—to calculate ratios that measure your viability and profitability.		SPREADSHEET ClarisWorks Microsoft Excel Microsoft Works
	Ability to customize: Can you track your information in the form that's easiest for you?	
Tax preparation software uses the numbers from your accounting packages to automatically prepare your tax forms.	Compatibility with other programs: How easy is it to use your tax preparation software with the data in your accounting package?	TAX PREPARATION Kiplinger TaxCut MacInTax MacInTax for Business

TABLE 3.3 WORD PROCESSING APPLICATIONS

WHAT THEY DO	WHAT TO LOOK FOR	EXAMPLES
Word processing applications create text: memos, letters, reports, newsletters.	Ease of control over text formats: How does it create and apply styles?	AT THE HIGH END Microsoft Word WordPerfect
They make it more or less easy to: ■ Change the text fonts, styles, and sizes ■ Set up columns and tables ■ Include graphics and data from other applications ■ Check your spelling ■ Reuse formats ■ Set up footnotes, indexes, and tables of contents ■ Create outlines	Compatibility with other document formats: Can it open files from other applications and can other applications open its files? Quality of text: How much control do you have over the line spacing and letter spacing? Tables and columns: How easy is it to construct them? Control over graphics in documents: How easy is it to import, move, crop, or resize them?	AT THE LOW END Scorpio QuickLetter INTEGRATED PRODUCTS ClarisWorks Microsoft Works
The high-end products give you more options for doing all these tasks.		
The low-end products do only a few of these tasks.	If you work with large documents, pay special attention to how well the application handles sections, page numbering, indexing, and tables of contents as well as complex styles.	

TABLE 3.4 GRAPHICS APPLICATIONS

WHAT THEY DO	WHAT TO LOOK FOR	EXAMPLES
Drawing programs create simple graphic objects that you can color, fill with patterns, resize, and group. They're particularly good for mechanical drawings, diagrams, floor charts, forms, and drawings that require a lot of text.	Formats: Can you read and save files in a range of graphical file formats?	FOR DRAWING ClarisDraw Pro ClarisWorks Microsoft Works
	Text: Can you easily include text and format it?	
Illustration programs create complex object-based illustrations. Paint programs create pixel-based illustrations. Both are good for all kinds of expressive arts, including product illustrations. They generally require more art skills and experience than drawing programs do.	Plug-ins: Can it make use of industry-standard plug-ins for special effects? Does it come with its own plug-ins?	FOR ILLUSTRATION AND PAINTING Adobe Illustrator Canvas ClarisWorks Color It! Fractal Design Painter Macromedia Freehand
	Layering: Does it support multiple layers for text and graphics, for example? Are the layers easy to use?	
Image processing programs work with photographs and other images that have been scanned. They can create spectacular special effects but are also useful for simply getting a clean, clear image for printing.	Color matching: What kinds of tools does it provide for previewing printed colors on-screen or matching colors from industry-standard color systems such as Pantone?	FOR IMAGE PROCESSING Adobe Photoshop Canvas Macromedia XRES
	Learning tools: Does it provide adequate instruction to make use of the sophisticated tools?	FOR 3-D RENDERING infini-D Macromedia Extreme 3-D Ray Dream Studio
3-D rendering programs build 3-D objects in a 3-D world. You can move 3-D objects in space and view them from different angles. Objects can have shadows and you can control lighting and shadows.	Previewing and undoing: Can you try out effects and preview them without destroying your earlier work?	StrataVision 3-D Stratus Studio Pro Blitz

TABLE 3.5 DESKTOP PUBLISHING APPLICATIONS

WHAT THEY DO	WHAT TO LOOK FOR	EXAMPLES
Desktop publishing programs create pages with lots of different elements: ■ Text ■ Illustrations ■ Photographs ■ Line art You usually create these elements in other applications and then import them into your desktop applications. Then you can work with them individually to move them around and change their size, color, and orientation on the page. You have lots of control over text in desktop publishing applications. You can flow text from page to page or column to column. You can wrap text around objects like pictures or boxes of text. And you usually have more control over line spacing and letter spacing than in word processing programs.	Capacity: How well does it handle long documents? What are the page limits for a single document? Multiple documents: Can you open more than one document at a time? Multiple page designs: Can you set up more than one master page for a single document? Flexibility of workstyles: Can you use both analytical tools and direct manipulation? For example, can you both type 80% to reduce the size of a drawing and drag the drawing to fit the space you have? Accurate color: Does the program have built-in color matching tools for predictable print results, both on your own printer and on commercial printing equipment? Cost-to-utility ratio: Do the features justify the cost for your needs?	AT THE LOW END Adobe HomePublisher ClarisWorks Microsoft Works Publish It! AT THE HIGH END Adobe PageMaker QuarkXpress FrameMaker

TABLE 3.6 MULTIMEDIA APPLICATIONS

WHAT THEY DO	WHAT TO LOOK FOR	EXAMPLES
Multimedia applications are like publishing applications, but with time and motion built in. You can work with all the same elements as in desktop publishing, plus audio and video. You can manipulate these elements individually and let your audience manipulate them, too—for example, to run a movie or play a game. You can jump from place to place in the document, using links. The results can vary from simple slide presentations to complex interactive environments. Multimedia applications include both authoring environments and programs for creating video and audio elements.	Ease of scripting: Does the program use a special programming language or direct operations, or both? How easy is it to learn and use the programming language? Sequence sophistication: How much linking does the program support? Can it easily support both text and graphic links? Does it have tools that help you track and test the links? Compatibility: Does it work on non-Mac platforms?	SLIDE PRESENTATIONS Aldus Persuasion ClarisWorks Microsoft PowerPoint Microsoft Works VIDEO EDITING Adobe Premiere AUDIO EDITING Macromedia SoundEdit 16 AUTHORING ENVIRONMENTS HyperCard Macromedia Authorware Macromedia Director mFactory mTropolis Oracle Media Objects Storyspace

TABLE 3.7 COMMUNICATIONS APPLICATIONS

WHAT THEY DO	WHAT TO LOOK FOR	EXAMPLES
This arena is changing rapidly and unpredictably. Historically, generic communications software provided a way to communicate directly from one computer to another. Or it provided general e-mail management on corporate networks. With the appearance of online services like America Online and CompuServe, service software has largely replaced direct communications software except in situations where companies regularly need to exchange very long files. Some applications help you manage e-mail from several different sources, while others provide easy access to the complexities of the Internet.	Ease of use: Does it have a Macintosh look-and-feel? Economy: Does it save you online charges by processing most of your communications offline? Compatibility: Does it work with the service you're using (whether it's a commercial online service or an Internet provider)? Search features: Can it quickly find and display the topics you're looking for? Does it provide bookmarks or some other way to keep track of interesting information or sites on the Internet?	GENERIC SOFTWARE ClarisWorks MicroPhone Microsoft Works Versaterm SERVICE SOFTWARE CompuServe MacCIM CompuServe Navigator PERSONAL E-MAIL MANAGEMENT Claris Emailer NETWORK COMMUNICATIONS CE Mail Microsoft Mail INTERNET BROWSERS Internet Explorer Microsoft Mosaic NSCA Netscape Navigator

TABLE 3.8 DATABASE APPLICATIONS

WHAT THEY DO	WHAT TO LOOK FOR	EXAMPLES
Database applications organize information in records. They can be as simple as list managers—sorting a list of items alphabetically. Or they can be complex repositories for information that needs to be searched and sorted into sophisticated categories. There are two main types. Flat-file databases keep all the records for the database in one file. Relational databases share data among many files. For example, a relational database may use a customer file and an invoice file, relating the two together to get up-to-date addresses for mailing and up-to-date customer histories.	Ability to store both text and graphics. Ability to format pages, including the use of color. Control over the layout of information: How much customization can you do? Speed of searching and sorting. Ease of use: Do you use a form-based setup, or do you need to know a programming language? Network ability: Can two people share the same database from different workstations?	FLAT-FILE DATABASES ClarisWorks HyperCard Microsoft Works RELATIONAL DATABASES Acius 4D FileMaker Pro FoxBase Pro Helix Omnis 7

TABLE 3.9 PERSONAL INFORMATION MANAGERS

WHAT THEY DO	WHAT TO LOOK FOR	EXAMPLES
Personal information managers are like electronic DayTimers. With them, you can: ■ Keep track of phone numbers, names, and addresses ■ Keep track of your work with To Do lists ■ Schedule your work for the day, week, or month ■ Set alarms to remind you of things on your schedule ■ Create address labels to print and paste in your paper DayTimer or mailing labels for envelopes ■ Do simple word processing tasks	Ease of use: Do they fit your way of organizing your day-to-day information? Flexibility: Can you keep track of all the kinds of information you need to track? Format options: Can you customize the formats for the information you acquire? Special features like extensive search and sort functions.	GENERAL PURPOSE HyperCard CONTACT MANAGEMENT TouchBase Datebook TouchBase Phonebook ACT! Claris Organizer

TABLE 3.10 SECURITY BACKUP AND MAINTENANCE APPLICATIONS

WHAT THEY DO	WHAT TO LOOK FOR	EXAMPLES
Security and backup applications keep your data secure—from accidents, vandalism, and theft. Security applications either restrict access to your system or encrypt your data so it can't be read without a password. Or they may do both. Backup applications automatically copy your files for safekeeping onto a second disk drive or removable media. Maintenance applications diagnose and repair disk problems. You can use them routinely to check for problems before they turn into disasters, or you can use them to recover from disasters.	Ease of use: Is it easy to set up and use without an advanced degree in cryptology? Appropriateness: Do they provide more protection than you need and cost you extra time to get it? Recoverability: Can you recover your data if you forget your password?	SECURITY After Dark At Ease DiskGuard FolderBolt NightWatch Norton DiskLock UltraShield BACKUP CopyDoubler DiskFit Pro Retrospect Remote MAINTENANCE Can Opener Guaranteed Undelete Last Resort Norton Utilities Rescue Text

TABLE 3.10 SECURITY BACKUP AND MAINTENANCE APPLICATIONS

WHAT THEY DO	WHAT TO LOOK FOR	EXAMPLES
System utilities work with the Macintosh operating system to give your Mac extra capabilities.	Stability: Watch out for buggy utilities. They'll wreak havoc with your system.	MACROS AppleScript QuicKeys
Macro utilities automate tasks—so you can do complex repetitive tasks with a single command or keystroke.	Cost: Don't pay a lot for things you can get for free or for small shareware fees. Reliability: Do they do what they're supposed to do consistently?	PERFORMANCE ENHANCERS RAM Doubler Speed Doubler DiskDoubler Pro StuffIt Deluxe
Performance enhancers make the operating system perform more effectively.	Minimum configuration: Do they require a lot of special setup, or do you just drag them to your System folder and forget about them?	
Some utilities provide additional features that Apple doesn't—or they provide them more efficiently.	Transparency: Do they do their job without a lot of interference in your day-to-day work?	ADDED FEATURES After Dark Now Utilities Suitcase

WHERE TO GET THE BIG LIST

The Redgate Register of Macintosh Software is an online list of all the commercial software available for the Macintosh. It includes a brief description of each product as well as the price and the publisher's name, address, and phone number.

You can browse the register on AppleLink or America Online. You can also order their quarterly CD-ROM listing on the Internet at `http://www.redgate.com/www/redgate/home/mpr.html`.

STEP 3: TRY IT OUT

You can try out an application before you buy it.

Some software stores have workstations set up for just this purpose. You may be able to try out the full application or a demo version. The salespeople can get you started and answer your questions.

If you're shy about talking to strange applications in public places, you can often get demonstration versions of your own. Demonstration versions usually give you a scaled-back set of features. Or they have a disabled Save command, so you can try everything, but you can't actually save a document. Or they time out—you can use them for a few days or a few weeks, and then they stop working. You can get demos from your local retailer or online.

For details on getting software online, see "How to Get Updates and Bug Fixes Online" later in this chapter.

Another good way to get to know an application before you buy is to take a short introductory course. These are generally available for the big, well-known applications. Check your community college course catalog or call your local software store to see if they offer courses. If they don't, they may be able to tell you who does.

What do you look for when you try out an application? Look at the way it organizes your work. Is it intuitive? Does it make sense to you? Does it think the way you think? Look for productivity features. Is it fast? Does it have shortcuts for things you do all the time? Don't ignore the aesthetics. You may be sitting in front of this application for hours every day. Do you like it? Is it charming? A little charm goes a long way on those days when you have a killer deadline, a plumber coming at ten, a parent meeting at four, and no more coffee in the house.

In addition to the gazillions of commercial Macintosh products, you can choose from bazillions of shareware and freeware products.

Freeware is software that's free. Absolutely. No strings attached. (Copyright laws do apply, of course.) Freeware can be anything from a little utility to a well-developed, but special-purpose program that's probably only of use to about ten people in the whole world. But, hey, you may be one of those ten people.

Shareware is pay-if-you-use-it software. Shareware products—from fonts and utilities to games and programming software—can be quite useful. They're usually inexpensive, and you get to try them out before you pay for them. You're on your honor to pay if you use it.

Both freeware and shareware are usually available online or from Macintosh user groups. You can also get shareware on a CD: *The Best of the Macintosh Shareware* has over 1,500 products available for test-driving.

DON'T FORGET ABOUT FREE-WARE AND SHAREWARE

Step 4: Check the power requirements

Applications require computing power, and each new generation of applications seems to require more.

Memory is the first concern. Each application has a minimum RAM requirement and a recommended RAM requirement. The application won't run without the minimum requirement. Without the recommended memory, it may run slowly. The RAM requirements for an application are usually printed on the package.

Speed may also be a concern for some applications. Page layout, photo retouching, video editing, and 3-D rendering all require a lot of processing. If you have an older, slower Mac, you may be spending a lot of time waiting for these applications to do their work. The applications you try out at the store on a high-end, high-speed, memory-loaded workstation may not seem nearly as fast or charming on your midrange, minimum-memory Mac at home.

Also be sure to add up the requirements of your core applications. You don't want to have to close one application every time you open a new one—just because you only have enough memory to run one at a time. Don't forget to add in your system memory requirements.

For details about your system software and what it does, see Chapter 4, "System Smarts."

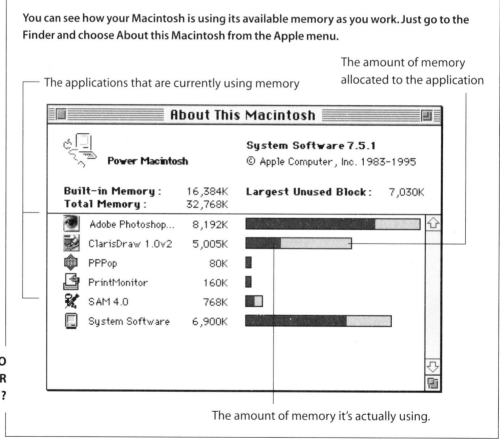

You can see how your Macintosh is using its available memory as you work. Just go to the Finder and choose About this Macintosh from the Apple menu.

The amount of memory allocated to the application

The applications that are currently using memory

The amount of memory it's actually using.

WANT TO CHECK YOUR MEMORY?

STEP 5: FIND A SOURCE

As with hardware, you have two choices once you decide what software you want—mail order or a local retail store. And as with hardware, you'll probably get better prices from the mail order houses and better support from your local retailer.

If you decide to go with a local retailer, look for stores that specialize in Mac software. Their staff is likely to be savvy enough to help you decide which application works best for you. They may also come out and install it for you to get you started (usually for a consulting fee). If you have any trouble installing it—or any trouble using it after you install it—you can call and ask questions.

If you own a Mac, you're probably already on mailing lists for half a dozen catalogs. But in case they've missed you, you can call them. Here are a few of the big guys:

Tiger Direct
1-800-238-4437
The Mac Zone
1-800-248-0800
MacWarehouse
1-800-255-6227
MacMall
1-800-222-2808

WHERE TO GET SOFTWARE CATALOGS

STEP 6: BUY AND INSTALL

Installing an application on the Mac used to be simple. You just popped in a disk, dragged an icon to your hard disk, and off you went.

It's gotten a little more complicated. Most applications are too big to fit on a single disk. So you have to use an Installer program that repeatedly tells you to insert this disk and that disk. For some of the large applications, like the integrated packages, be prepared for a long, dull stint in front of the Mac unless you're installing from a CD.

When you use an installer program, you may have to quit all your current applications and turn off any virus-checking software you have. (Installing software creates activities that virus-checkers can mistake for viruses.) Be sure to read the Read Me file before you install (or at least skim it). It tells you critical details that may not be in the user's guide—like new features and compatibility issues.

Installers put a lot of stuff on your disk:

■ They usually create an application folder with the core application and supporting files that the application needs in order to run. They usually ask you where you want to create this folder—so you can choose your internal hard disk or an external storage device. You may be able to tell the installer to put the new application folder in some other folder, such as a folder for all your applications. (And you can always move the application folder later.)

■ They may add things to your System folder: control panels and preferences that the application checks each time you start it. It isn't always obvious what these files are, but you need them to run the application.

■ Most install a copy of SimpleText or TeachText, which is the application that opens the Read Me file.

The guide that comes with the product should tell you what files are installed and where. If you're in a housecleaning mood and want to get rid of superfluous files, be sure to check your product documentation before you discard any files of unknown purpose.

A tip: After you install several applications, you will almost certainly have several copies of TeachText or SimpleText on disk. Use the Finder's Find command (in the File menu) to find all the copies. Check their dates, and then throw away all but the most recent copy.

WHAT INSTALLERS REALLY DO

For details on setting up your modem and using online services, see Part 2, "Getting Connected."

If you can't get the application installed, you can call the retail store where you bought it (if you bought it there) or the manufacturer's technical support line (if they have one). A lot of companies now offer online support, with an online bulletin board or newsgroup. Of course, you'll have to get your communications software set up before you can use them.

UPSIZING: Keeping Pace with the Industry

Applications tend to grow by themselves, regardless of what you do. Here are some ways to keep up with them—and expand your own skills.

Updates, bug fixes, and new versions

Software is released in versions. Big version changes are numbered with whole numbers like 1, 2, or 3. Small version changes, often called upgrades or maintenance releases, are numbered with decimal numbers. So version 3.2 means that you're using the second upgrade to version 3.

With big version changes, you usually get major new features or more streamlined operation. Small version changes usually fix bugs and enhance existing features.

You don't necessarily need every new version of a product, even major versions. Here's a little test to help you decide:

■ Do you regularly share the files with major clients and/or suppliers who are using the new version?
■ Do you need to use files that are more than two years old?
■ Do you really need some of the features in the new version?

If you answered *yes* to any of these questions, you should probably get the new version. Although new versions are usually designed to support files from the previous version, they may not support earlier versions. So if you skip Version 3, you may not be able to use Version 4 to open your Version 2 files.

So how do you keep up? Start by sending in your registration card when you get your application. These cards are mainly ploys to get you into a marketing database, and you may not get any free upgrades for your effort. But you probably will get a notice when new versions are available. Some software companies also publish newsletters with product tips as well as announcements of updates. Other sources are user groups, online services (where you may actually be able to get free bug fixes directly), and Internet World Wide Web pages for the software publishers.

When Apple releases new versions or patches for its operating system, software vendors often come out with patches for their software. All in all, there's a whole lot of software updating going on.

It's rare these days for a software company to send you a free bug-fix disk. Companies usually rely on their online support forums to distribute information and patches to their software.

Almost every online service has some Apple support as well as software vendor support. The best places to find Apple support are on CompuServe and Apple's own World Wide Web home pages on the Internet. On CompuServe, GO APLSUP for Apple support; GO MAUG for general Mac support. For Apple's Internet software updates, go to `http://www.support.apple.com`.

Software vendors usually have a support group under their company name. If you don't know where to look for a particular vendor's support forum, you can usually use the online service's Find or Search command to locate them. There are lots of good search engines for the Web, so you can usually find a software company's support page, if it exists.

So what kind of support will you find on the online services? You'll find patches that bring an older version of your software up to the current version. If there are support documents like dictionaries or databases that work with your application, you may find new versions of these programs. You may also find special "not supported" programs that fix unusual conditions or provide extra features.

Software companies often post a FAQ file—frequently asked questions about their products. They may also maintain a message board or post the contents of other message boards that pertain to their product. On a message board, you can talk to other users of individual products or with company representatives. Very useful.

HOW TO GET UPDATES AND BUG FIXES ONLINE

Templates and plug-ins

Templates and plug-ins are a great way to grow your skills quickly.

Templates are predesigned documents. Typical templates include:

SPREADSHEET TEMPLATES like the buy/lease decision template in Chapter 2, as well as profit and loss statements, cash flows, timesheets, and more sophisticated financial analyses.

DESIGN TEMPLATES for page layout, presentation, or word processing applications—to help you quickly produce professional-looking business stationery, newsletters, brochures, reports, and slide presentations.

CORRESPONDENCE TEMPLATES for standard types of business correspondence, including invoices, overdue notices, memos, résumés, and letters of referral.

DOCUMENT BUILDERS that help you develop an entire document, such as a business plan.

PLUG-INS are modules that work with existing software to extend their functionality. For example, several companies offer plug-ins for Adobe Photoshop to provide special effects, such as charcoal drawing or watercolors, or to simplify operations that take a lot of time and skill in Photoshop.

Templates and plug-ins are shortcuts to fast, reliable results. Even if you already know how to set up a balance sheet or design a report or manipulate an image pixel-by-pixel to create a special effect, do you really want to spend your time on that? Templates and plug-ins help you focus your attention where it's really needed. They save time, teach you new skills, and make you look good.

For more information about templates, see "Upsizing" in Chapter 9, "The New Information Game."

Classes

Everyone reaches plateaus in work. Your skills are good enough. Your applications are good enough. You're productive at what you're doing. But what if you want to expand into a new area? Or make a leap in productivity to buy you more time with your family?

Sometimes an investment in a class can be the quickest way to break through a plateau. You can find courses for Macintosh software in lots of places. Some Continuing Education programs use Macintosh applications as a focus for developing a set of skills such as multimedia publishing. Lots of private groups, including software retailers, also offer advanced seminars. And if you have associates who are interested in the same skills as you, you may be able to hire a consultant to give you an evening's worth of special tips—or an introduction to a new high-end application.

User groups and special interest groups

As already mentioned, user groups can be a great source of new learning about your Macintosh and the applications that run on it. Some user groups even have special forums on individual applications.

Special interest groups—or SIGs—are online versions of user groups. (On the Internet, they're called **newsgroups**.) They often have a more specific focus, however. You can find SIGs for most of the major applications. Some of them are sponsored by individual software companies as a way to provide technical support. Some are indepedent. Either can provide some of the most expert information available anywhere. You can just eavesdrop to pick up tips, or you can ask questions and offer your own advice.

For more information on user groups and SIGs, see Chapter 13, "Resources."

Head spinning from all this hard work? Take a "funny business" break. Some great games are available for the Macintosh, and with QuickDraw 3-D now plugged tightly into the operating system, just wait till you see what's coming.

Two of our favorite games for the Macintosh are *Myst* and *Marathon*. (No alliteration intended.) They're at opposite ends of the game spectrum, but both show off the multimedia prowess of the Macintosh.

In case you haven't already slipped into the *Myst*, this game takes you to a strange, compelling world where you wander around, gathering clues and trying to build the story of the former inhabitants. Everything is quiet, slow, serene, and beautifully rendered. Eerie and mysterious sounds permeate the place. It's a visual delight.

Marathon is a little different. You're sent to a colony ship that has recently been attacked by aliens. You move through many levels of the ship battling aliens and an aberrant artificial intelligence computer. *Marathon* shows off its superior graphics by giving you fluid motion in a striking 3-D world. It also provides stereo sound clues—a great aid in certain deadly situations.

These two games represent a range of Macintosh entertainment, from total concentration to total carnage. Be sure to include some games in your application collection. There's a little of everything available, from solitaire to surgical strike missions in an F-18. Leave a little time for play, and the work will go better, too.

FUNNY BUSINESS

POWER PLAY: Starting Up Fast with Worksets

You walk into your home office. The sun is shining. You have a bagel in one hand, juice in the other. You start up your Mac, take a big bite of bagel and watch as everything you need for this morning's project opens automatically. All the applications. All the documents. Without a single mouse-click on your part. (After all, your hands are full.)

Yes, you're really awake. It's not a trick of your dreaming mind. It's a trick called **worksets**. And you can do it two ways—with System 7 or with Now Menus.

The System 7 method
With System 7, you can use aliases to set up worksets. You can either open them automatically when you start up or keep them in a folder that you can launch whenever you need them.

What you need

- System 7
- Time: About 5 minutes

You create your workset by making aliases of all the documents you want in your workset. If you want to launch an application without using an existing document, make an alias of the application itself.

1. Locate the documents and applications you want to include in your workset. Open the folder that contains each document. If you're not sure where the documents are, use the Find command in the Finder.

2. Select each document and choose Make Alias from the File menu. An alias appears next to the original in the folder.

3. Drag each alias into the Startup folder in your System folder. Or drag them into a folder that you create for the workset.

Security Report

Security Report alias

If you put the aliases in the Startup folder, the documents will open automatically when you start your Mac.

If you put them in another folder, you have to open them manually. Just select all the items in the folder: open the folder window and choose Select All from the Edit menu (or type ⌘-A). Then choose Open from the File menu or type ⌘-O.

This method is fine for a single workset or if you only occasionally use worksets. If you find worksets a useful idea, you should graduate to Now Menus.

The Now Menus method

Now Menus provides a more powerful way to create and manage worksets. For one thing, you don't have to create any aliases. You just set up your work environment the way you want it—with all the documents and applications open—and Now Menus automatically makes the workset.

What you need

- Now Menus
- Time: About 2 minutes

With the Now Menus method, you create a clickable icon for your worksets. Here's how it's done:

1. Open all the documents and applications you want in your workset.

2. Open the Now Menus control panel and click the Create/Modify Workset icon.

This dialog box appears:

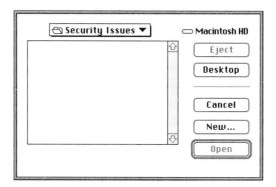

3. Click New to create a new workset.

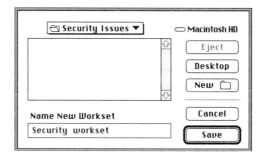

4. Give the workset a name, select the folder where you want to keep it, and click Save.

You can put it anywhere. If you put it in the Startup folder, all the documents will open when you start your Mac.

When you click Save, a window shows all the currently active applications and documents. You can use this window to add or remove applications and documents.

When you want to use a workset, you just double-click the workset document.

Security Workset

You can put this document in the Apple menu—drag it to the Apple Menu Items folder in the System folder—or in a Now Menus custom menu. If you need to edit your workset, just hold down the ⌘ key and double-click the workset icon to open its window.

Worksets are particularly useful if you need to set up a workstation for an assistant—for example, if you have a part-time person who uses your Mac to create mail-merge letters from your customer database periodically. Or you can use them to give your kids quick access to the tools they need for school reports. Or just to get you up and running when a bagel and orange juice aren't quite enough to wake you up.

ON THE HORIZON:
The Brave New World of Modular Applications

The forces of the future are pulling applications, as you know them, to pieces. Software applications have been getting bigger, more complex, more feature-rich, and more monolithic. But they're about to change directions—they're going to get smaller, be more modular, and actually be designed by their users. Welcome to OpenDoc.

OpenDoc is Apple's document architecture that will change the way you use your computer. Instead of using several complex applications—such as a graphics program, a word processor, and a spreadsheet—OpenDoc will give you a common document format with word processing, graphics, and spreadsheet parts that work together.

You'll design the document to have the tools you need. It will have content containers and parts editors. The content containers hold the actual data. The parts editors are like miniversions of the applications you're used to. But these editors will be eminently tailorable. By mixing and matching them, you'll create an application that's perfectly suited to your document.

For example, your document may be a summary report that has integrated text, graphics, and database information. When you click in the graphics frame, you immediately have access to the graphics-editing tools. The menu bar and cursor change to match these tools. You can also drag the graphic elements anywhere in the document. The elements are tightly integrated within the document, too. Changes in your database element automatically show up in the text and graphics in your document.

OpenDoc, along with the rest of Apple's system strategy, is part of an object-oriented model. In this model, the emphasis is on direct control, extensibility, collaboration, and ease of use. It's a move away from bulky massive applications to small, intelligent *applets*—where you get more control and more power with less cost and confusion. Not a bad future, eh?

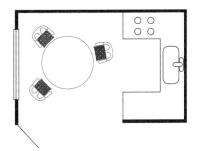

CHAPTER FOUR

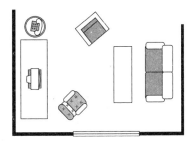

SYSTEM SMARTS

How to make System 7 work harder

for you and your business

T his chapter is a tour of your System folder—which is something like a tour of the plumbing and wiring in your house. If you're one of those people who like to rip light switches out of the wall and put rheostats in their place, you're going to love this chapter. If you're not, it will probably give you hives, but it will also give you some important information.

Tour Stop 1: The System and Finder files

Your System folder contains the Macintosh operating system, sometimes known as the Mac OS. The operating system is the go-between for your hardware and all your applications. It allocates memory and directs processes. Its heart is the System file. But it also includes, among other things, the Finder file.

The Finder is the program that creates your Macintosh desktop—the visual space you work in. With it, you can manage your applications, files,

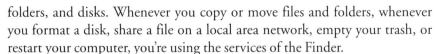

folders, and disks. Whenever you copy or move files and folders, whenever you format a disk, share a file on a local area network, empty your trash, or restart your computer, you're using the services of the Finder.

The system software comes in versions, just like application software. Each version introduces new features—and sometimes new problems. Old applications don't always play nice with new versions of the system, and vice versa. Nevertheless, you have to update your system from time to time. Otherwise you'll be left in the dark (sort of like trying to light your house with gas lamps in the 1990s).

Tour Stop 2: The Extensions folder

Extensions add capability to your system or change the way it works. They're sometimes called INITS or startup documents, because they start up before anything else whenever you restart your Mac. You can watch their icons pop up across the bottom of the screen before the Finder appears. That's how you know they're there and working.

Extensions hang out in the Extensions folder. The Mac OS puts them there. In fact, they may actually be part of the OS. QuickTime video is an example of a system extension that comes with your Macintosh. Applications may also add their own extensions to your System folder when you install them, and you may sometimes even add extensions directly. For example, the RAM Doubler utility is an extension. Printer descriptions are also extensions.

You don't have to think too much about extensions. When you copy an extension in the System folder, the OS recognizes it and asks if you want it in the Extensions folder. You never have to think about it again—unless, of course, you don't want to use it anymore. Then you just move it out of the Extensions folder.

Tour Stop 3: The Control Panels folder

Control panels give you control over parts of your Macintosh. They give you options. For example, you can use the Mouse control panel to make the cursor move faster or slower when you move the mouse. Or you can use the View control panel to change the font and size in the Finder windows—which can be particularly useful if you're having trouble with your eyes. If your Macintosh is sluggish, you can wrestle some extra processing power away from your color monitor by using the Monitor control panel to switch from color to black and white.

The system comes with lots of control panels (also called CDEVs). Some applications also install their own control panels. And as with extensions, you can install some control panels directly. Unlike with extensions, you do things with control panels. You make choices. You turn things on and off. So get to know this folder. It will make you master of your Mac.

Not sure which version you have, or how to get a new one? See "Upsizing" in this chapter.

You also have a Startup Items folder, which is entirely different. Remember the "Power Play" section in Chapter 3?

For more about printer descriptions, see "Jump Start" in Chapter 2.

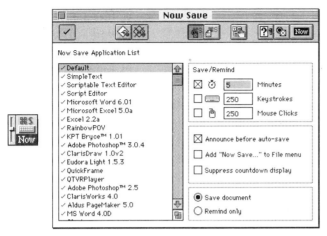

The NowSave control panel can save you from disaster. It saves your changes automatically. You choose the applications where you want to use it and tell it how often to save.

By the way, some control panels have extensions built into them. These have to start up whenever you restart you Mac. Otherwise, you can't use them. Putting them in the Control Panels folder guarantees that they'll start up. It's a good idea to keep all your control panels in the Control Panels folder—even those that don't have extensions.

Tour Stop 4: The Font folder

Fonts are art. You may think of them as those eight names in the stripped-down Font menu—Chicago, Courier, Geneva, Helvetica, Palatino, Times, Zapf Chancery, and Zapf Dingbats. But fonts are much more. They're like the musical score to a movie. They give your documents their mood, their style, their emotional undertones and overtones, their impact.

So you might want more than seven. You might also want to know a few behind-the-scenes details in case you're confronted with choices like whether to use PostScript or TrueType fonts.

Fonts come in three basic types:

POSTSCRIPT PRINTER FONTS are designed for printing, specifically on PostScript printers. Sometimes called outline fonts, printer fonts are defined by a mathematical formula rather than an arrangement of dots on the screen. This formula makes them smart enough to redraw themselves in any size, smoothly and elegantly. And they can print at the highest resolution your printer offers. However, you need at least one size of the corresponding bitmapped version in order to display them on the screen.

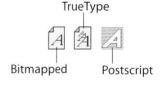

TrueType

Bitmapped   Postscript

BITMAPPED SCREEN FONTS are designed to be displayed on your screen. They come in preset sizes, and they look awful if you try to display them in other sizes. They're actually added to your System *file* when you install them. If you don't want to install all the sizes for a particular font, you can install Adobe Type Manager instead. It draws nice screen versions for any size of any PostScript printer font you have installed.

TRUETYPE FONTS are two-in-one fonts. They work both on the screen and in the printer, smoothly. They don't give you quite as much control as PostScript fonts over the fine typesetting details of letter spacing, but they also don't require a PostScript printer.

For details on adding fonts to your system, see Step 2 under "Jump Start" in this chapter.

If you do all your printing from your own home printer, the TrueType fonts are probably the simplest solution. But if you need very high-quality text or if you work with printing professionals such as typesetters and graphic arts camera folk, you should use PostScript fonts. They're the standard for high-end work. Also, keep in mind that a file you create on a system with TrueType fonts won't look—or print—the same on a system with PostScript fonts.

Tour Stop 5: Preferences

Many applications have a Preferences command. You can use it to tailor the application to your needs—for example, to measure things in centimeters instead of inches or to choose your favorite font whenever you open a new document.

Your application saves these settings in a Preferences file. It installs the Preferences file in a Preferences folder in—yup!—your System folder. (Some older applications install them directly in the System folder, so you may occasionally see them scattered about.)

Your application *doesn't* automatically remove its Preferences file if you decide to remove the application. These files are small, and they don't eat a lot, but who needs all those useless files? Some rainy November afternoon when no one's knocking on your home office door, just make yourself a cup of hot chocolate, go through the Preferences folder, and get rid of all the Preferences files that belong to old, outgrown applications.

WHEN PREFERENCES GET YOU IN TROUBLE

Sometimes applications start acting weird for no obvious reason. Sometimes the problem is the Preferences file. It just gets corrupted. Try removing it from the Preferences folder and then restarting your application. Many applications create a new Preferences file if they can't find one when they start up. But don't throw away the old one until you're sure your application has set you up with a new one.

Tour Stop 6: The Apple Menu Items folder

It's easy to forget about the Apple menu. Big mistake. You can make the Apple menu your fast-access gateway to documents and applications anywhere on your system. All you need to do is use the Apple Menu Items folder to your advantage.

Anything in your Apple Menu folder appears in your Apple menu. If you want to be able to open an application from the Apple menu, create an alias of the application and put it in the Apple Menu Items folder. If you want to open a document—such as your standard report template—create an alias of it in the Apple Menu Items folder. Then you don't have to go looking through folders to find things. You just choose them from the alphabetical listing in the Apple menu.

> For other ways to customize your menus, see Step 1 under "Jump Start."

Last Stop: The reckoning

The System folder is a little like a sorcerer's workshop, and you might fancy yourself the sorcerer's apprentice once you get started with it. Mix a few extensions with a few control panels, wave your wand a few times, and you've got your Mac performing feats of magic only you could imagine.

Well, sort of.

The things you put in your System folder can certainly make your Mac seem faster, more efficient, and more powerful. They can give you features and functions that the Apple engineers never dreamed of. But they exact a price, too. They take up memory, and they use computing power. So while they may optimize some operations, they can actually slow down the overall performance. They can also create conflicts—serious conflicts—with applications and other extensions and control panels. The more of these guys you have, the more time you'll spend debugging your system.

> Need help sorting out conflicts in the System folder? See Chapter 11, "Troubleshooting."

Some days you probably wish you could be in two or three places at one time. Maybe you wish you had a personal clone to run the stationery store while you finish the accounts payable. Sorry, this book isn't about that technology.

But you can clone your files and folders so they can be in more than one place at a time. The clones are called *aliases*, and they can save you lots of time by being where you need them when you need them. For example, your accounting package installs itself in a folder with dozens of supporting files and folders. You may install that folder in another folder called Accounting, which is actually in another folder called Applications. It's good organization, but it takes you forever to get to it.

So what do you do? Create an alias for the accounting application on your desktop. Or in your Apple Menu Items folder. To create an alias, just select an application or document and choose Make Alias from the Finder's File menu. The alias appears next to the original, with the same name *in italics*. Now, anytime you want to run the application, double-click the alias.

ALIASES—IF YOU CAN'T CLONE YOUR-SELF, CLONE YOUR FILES

Andy Fine doesn't need a lot of system enhancements. He has simple needs: with a few applications running on a Mac with enough speed and memory to handle his operations efficiently.

What he does like is a fast way to get to his contact files and To Do list, as well as his other applications.

He also needs a little protection against accidental intrusions from his four-year-old daughter.

He also wants a simple, trouble-free backup strategy, one that doesn't require a lot of maintenance.

A set of function-key macros, a screen saver, and a copy utility do the trick.

THE TOOLS

QuicKeys
After Dark
CopyDoubler
Disinfectant
Now Utilities
Suitcase

With QuicKeys, Andy can assign macros to the function keys (F1, F2, and so on) on his keyboard. Then he just presses a key to start an application or open his contacts file, for example.

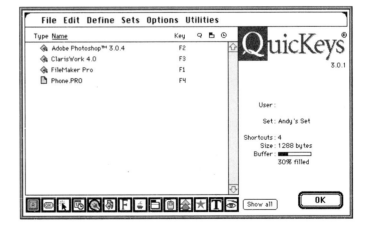

SOLUTIONS

After Dark is a screen saver. It automatically pops an animated display on the desktop when Andy isn't using the computer. The animation prevents any one image from "burning in" the screen.

With its password protection option, After Dark also gives Andy a simple way to protect his Mac desktop from daughter Ashley. If he walks away for more than a few minutes, the screen saver automatically takes over the screen. To get back to the desktop, Andy just types his password.

Andy uses CopyDoubler to make a complete copy of his internal hard disk on an external hard disk. Once a month he copies everything to floppy disks and drops the copies off at his parents' house for safekeeping.

If his main hard disk ever goes down, he can quickly rebuild everything just by reformatting it and copying the entire set of files from the external disk.

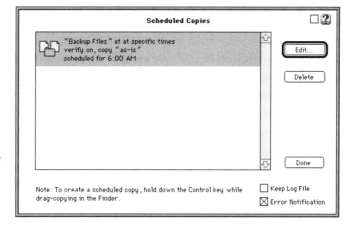

Susie Hu needs a secure system. Her clients expect it.

Unfortunately, Susie's system is out in public a lot. She takes it with her on the road—in her van and sometimes into offices and homes as she makes inquiries.

She also takes it into cyberspace—with online searches for files that may bring viruses back with them. The files bring back another problem, too. Most are compressed, and many use different compression formats.

To keep secure, Susie needs to be able to lock her folders and even encrypt some files that contain sensitive information—a feature some of her clients demand.

She also needs virus protection, and she needs an expansion utility that can read a variety of compression formats.

THE TOOLS

FolderBolt

StuffIt Expander

SAM Virus Protection

QuicKeys

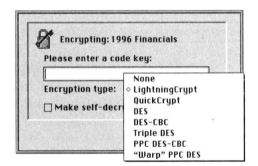

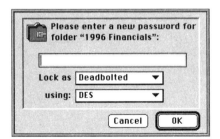

With FolderBolt Pro, Susie can lock folders with a choice of security options—including various levels of encryption. She can lock folders individually or define sets of folders that lock and unlock at the same time.

 S O L U T I O N S

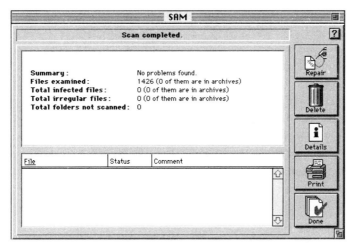

SAM—Symantec AntiVirus for the Macintosh—scans for viruses.

For the Delacruzes, effective document management is a top priority. Each project uses lots of documents—text, photographs, illustrations, and the page layout document itself. Working with these documents requires several applications. So Dave, as general manager, creates worksets for each project. Then anyone can quickly open all the documents for a project to review or to work on.

Sometimes documents are in the wrong format. Darcy may need to create 20 files in TIFF format but save them in EPS format. Dave has mastered AppleScript and has created several standard miniapps specifically for automating tasks like file conversion.

The Delacruzes also have a lot of resources to manage, including an extensive library of fonts. Again, Dave sets up font sets to be used on a project-by-project basis.

Backup is a serious matter for the Delacruzes. Their documents are their product. They take up lots of disk space, and they can't be discarded the moment the project is complete. There are also four computers to back up—a lot of maintenance. So the Delacruzes need a dedicated backup program to keep their archives in order.

Security is not a serious matter. Although the Delacruzes have four networked computers, they aren't worried about digital trespassing. They have taken care to hire people they like and trust. The simple file protection that's built into the file-sharing software in System 7 is more than adequate for their needs.

THE TOOLS
Now Utilities
AppleScript and QuicKeys
StuffIt Deluxe
Speed Doubler
Suitcase
Retrospect Remote
SAM
System 7 file sharing

S O L U T I O N S

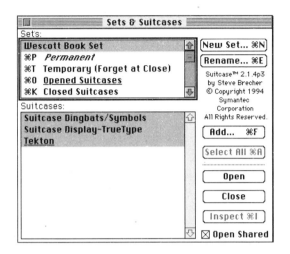

Dave can create a font set for each project—as well as worksets he creates with Now Menus.
Then other members of the Delacruz team can open the font set directly from the Suitcase window to display the fonts they need in the Font menu.

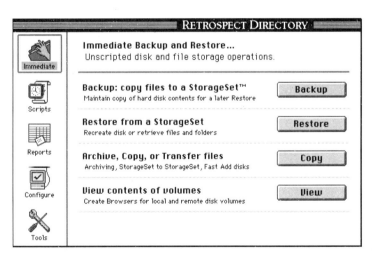

With Retrospect Remote, Dave can back up all four computers from his own computer—to a single DAT drive.

112

Sam Post likes to work at maximum efficiency. He likes to customize. He likes to test limits.

For big applications like Microsoft Works and Virtus WalkThrough Pro, he needs to make the most of his memory. For his own personal satisfaction, he needs to make the most of his computer's processing speed. So he uses software tools that double speed and memory capacity by using the built-in speed and memory more efficiently.

Sam has an AppleScript macro that automatically prints mailing labels after he enters new order information in MYOB.

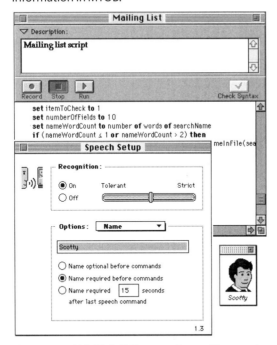

Sam also needs to coordinate three computers—a task that could involve a lot of jockeying for the right position if he didn't take advantage of speech recognition and macros. He uses keyboard macros on his laptop computer. But for his desktop printing and management computer, he uses a scripting language to create his own commands for complex sequences of operations. Then he just speaks the commands to his computer.

And of course, he's always experimenting with new tools for managing menus, windows, and documents. Here's his current set.

THE TOOLS

Apple PlainTalk
AppleScript
QuicKeys
Suitcase
Speed Doubler
RAM Doubler
DiskDoubler Pro
Now Utilities

Sam just drags the icons for the doubler programs into his Extensions folder and restarts his computer to take advantage of their efficiencies.

Sam named his PlainTalk agent Scotty. He can give it verbal commands, including AppleScript commands.

Ellen Gant has a computer that's built for the demanding applications she's running— video-editing, graphics, and presentation software.

Even so, she can't afford to ignore speed and space issues. She needs smooth, fast, flawless performance when she's making client presentations. She needs a clean, simple system with reliable speed and space enhancement.

She doesn't need a lot of system security. Her daughters are grown, and she lives by herself. She doesn't surf the Web or exchange files with her computer buddies.

Nevertheless, she has invested a lot of time, effort, and vision in her presentation files. She's not about to lose them because of a glitch in the system. So she backs up on a project-by-project basis to a removable cartridge.

THE TOOLS

QuicKeys
Speed Doubler
AutoDoubler
SAM
Suitcase
Now Utilities

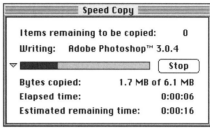

Ellen Gant uses Speed Doubler to copy all her files faster—but she clocks especially big gains for her large graphics and video files.

Ellen Gant can use QuicKeys to set up one-key access to everything from a backup script to her multimedia presentation.

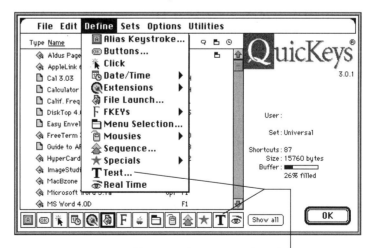

QuicKeys are organized by type. The types are listed in a menu—with corresponding buttons at the bottom of the window.

So proceed with some caution here. By all means, use the tools that make your work more efficient. They're terrific. Check our solution scenarios for some ideas about how to make your system work efficiently and securely—especially for your kind of home office. But watch for the point of diminishing returns. You don't want to spend all your time managing your Mac desktop any more than you want to spend all your time straightening up your office.

JUMP START: Tuning Up Your System

Start simple. The system folder has great clutter potential. And clutter can lead to conflicts, which in turn can lead to downtime you can't afford.

But don't overlook the basics of good system management, either. Here are the basic steps.

STEP 1: GET ORGANIZED

The first thing you want to do is get your desktop organized for action. Menus are where the action happens. So start by customizing them.

You can do the Apple Menu trick mentioned above. But the Apple menu can grow unwieldy with up to 255 items, all in alphabetical order. So you may want to use Now Menus—part of the Now Utilities package—for a grander solution.

With Now Menus you can change the appearance and content of the Apple menu as well as create your own custom menus in the menu bar. You can put applications, documents, and folders in these menus and use separators to group them. You can put them in any order you want, too. You just drag them where you want them.

For example, you might create a special Applications menu, with applications grouped by type. Then you could list template documents for each application in submenus. The result might look something like the figure at right.

This menu would appear in all your menu bars. It could be called Applications, or you could use a graphic icon for it. You can also assign ⌘-key combos to choose any of your new menu items from the keyboard.

Or you could just skip the menus altogether and set up lists in a folder window. Just create a new folder and give it a name, like Applications. Then create an alias for each of the applications you want to group together and put them in the folder.

Experiment with different views for your list of applications—this is the Small Icon view.

If you're someone who likes to find things by feel (rather than by some particular logic), try organizing your folder window spatially, like this:

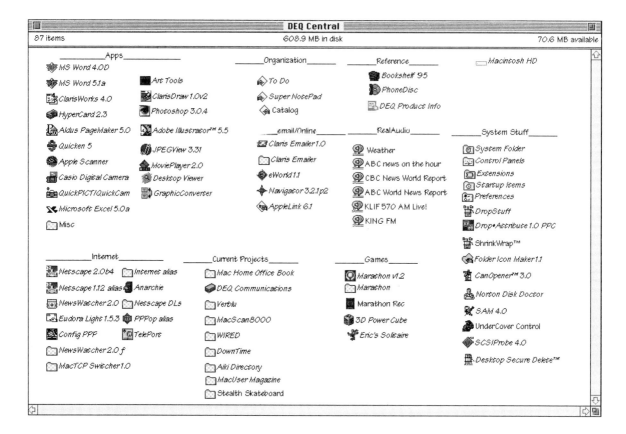

This window uses several little tricks. First, the headings for Apps, Organization, Internet, and so on are actually empty folders without an icon. To get rid of the icon, you replace it in the folder's Get Info box with a blank, white square. You create the blank in a draw program and copy it. Then you choose the folder, choose Get Info from the File menu, select the folder icon, and paste the blank in its place. You can also paste some other icon if you want to design your own icons for your folders. To create the rules in the headings, just use the underscore character. Then create your aliases and drag them where you want them. You may need to turn the Snap To Grid feature on or off in the Views control panel to get things lined up.

As your system becomes more crowded with applications and documents, finding the one you want gets harder. The system has a mighty Find command in the File menu that can search the titles of your files and folders, show where they are, and even take you right to them.

Some applications have a Find File button in the Open or Save dialog box—in case you can't remember where you put the file or folder you want. You can also use a few other tricks:

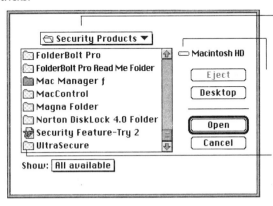

Use this pop-up menu to scroll up the hierarchy of your folders.

Click here to move up one level in the hierarchy. Or type ⌘+Up Arrow.

To quickly find a file in this list, type its first letter. (Press Tab if necessary to move the cursor here in the Save dialog box.)

If these built-in features aren't enough, you can use some utility applications to get more help. Fast Find, which is part of Norton Utilities, works like the Find command with some extras: when you find the file, it shows the file type and creator and gives you a quick view of the contents. Boomerang, which is part of Now Utilities, adds a Find button to all standard file dialog boxes, such as Save As and Open. With this button, you can find any file or folder with lightning speed.

FINDING THINGS

STEP 2: GET FONTS

Apple ships eight font families with your Macintosh. They're a good assortment for basic letter-writing, spreadsheet work, even newsletters and reports. But you can do so much more with fonts. You can express intention, style, or state of mind:

Some days are just fuzzy around the edges

This font was designed especially for the Mac by Jill Bell, a calligrapher, font designer, and friend from Manhattan Beach, California.

Keep in mind, of course, that there are **text fonts** and **display fonts**. Text fonts are designed paragraphs and pages of text—text that people actually have to read. **Serif fonts** like Times and Palatino are traditional text fonts. They have those odd little flourishes at the edges, curves or spikes or slabs that tie them to each other and to the page. They're easiest to read in pages dense with text. **Sans serif fonts** like Helvetica are streamlined, no flourishes, straight up and down. They're better for short, sleek paragraphs of text. **Display fonts** are designed to catch attention. Use them for headlines, banners, labels, illustrations—stuff like that. They have a lot of character but they're often not too easy to read, especially in large doses. So don't use your favorite fancy font for the fine points of your message.

Fonts with serifs ——— Serif fonts have flourishes called— guess what!—*serifs.*
Fonts without serifs—Sans serif fonts don't.

Okay, so where do you get these guys? Buy them on CDs from software stores and catalogs. Look for free fonts online. Get Jill Bell to design you a custom font. Then put them in your System folder.

If you're using a System version prior to Version 7.1, you need to drag the fonts directly into your System *file*. If your System file gets corrupted and you have to replace it, you need to drag the fonts into your System file again.

If you're using System version 7.1 or later, you can drag the fonts into your System *folder*. The OS automatically puts them in the Fonts folder and makes them available to applications that use fonts. Uh-oh, problem here. Fonts are always loaded. They're always using memory.

Don't worry. Suitcase to the rescue.

Suitcase is a utility program from Symantec. It manages your fonts. It loads them as you need them. It remembers which fonts you were using the last time you used your Mac and automatically loads them. You can also create special sets of fonts for individual projects.

Suitcase helps manage other resources, too. See "System Utilities" under "Upsizing" in this chapter.

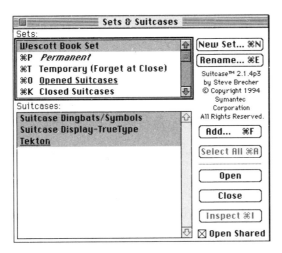

If you have more than the basic font set, get Suitcase.

Step 3: Get a backup strategy

The basic backup strategy is simple: Always back up. You're going to have many hundreds—maybe thousands—of dollars worth of software on your disk. You're going to have weeks, months, maybe years of labor in spreadsheets, reports, databases, and correspondence. You're going to have information you can't work without in your Mac telephone books and calendars. You're going to have all your accounts, including tax records, on your computer.

And some day, disaster will strike. Your Mac won't smile at you in the morning. It will just sit there, humming away as if it just got back from a frontal lobotomy. It won't know you even have a hard disk, much less what you have—er, *had*—on it. If you don't have copies of all the data on your disk, you're out of luck.

The insurance against such disaster is a good backup strategy—one that takes account of all the possible things that could go wrong. For example:

PROBLEM: A file gets corrupted.

PRACTICE: When you stop for a coffee break, make backup copies of the files you're working in—on floppy disks or a removable cartridge. If you don't take coffee breaks, take backup breaks. In other words, do this often, particularly if you're working in large files that represent hours of work. (Think of it this way: how many hours of work would you be willing to lose? Back up your files that often.) Always back up current projects at the end of the day. Also regularly back up critical data files such as your phone book and calendar—once a day or once a week if you have lots of contacts and appointments, or once a month otherwise.

PROBLEM: Your disk gets corrupted.

PRACTICE: Back up your System folder whenever you add new applications or fonts or system utilities. You can create and maintain a duplicate

> Need to recover data you forgot to back up? See Chapter 12, "File Recovery."

copy of your entire system on a separate hard drive. This is a perfect replica of your system on the date you create it. If your main drive goes down, you simply switch drives and keep working. The only time you lose is the time to reformat your main drive and restore the files, which you can do when it's convenient—not when you have a deadline looming.

PROBLEM: Your house burns down, a thief steals all your equipment, or a power surge wipes out both your main disk and your backup disk at the same time.

PRACTICE: Copy your data, applications, and System folder to floppy disks or removable cartridges and store them offsite, perhaps in a safe deposit box or just with a relative or friend. You may want to get into the habit of updating the data disks in your safe deposit box whenever you go the bank to deposit your checks. Or use it as a good excuse to send your mother a friendly package once a month. (Be sure to include postage for her to return your old disks. Or maybe she has her own backups to make and you can just swap disks.)

Repeated crashes? See Chapter 11, "Trouble-shooting."

Got that? Back up your data files every day. Back up your System folder and applications when you make big changes. Store a complete copy somewhere offsite, updating data files periodically.

Backing up takes time, of course. You don't need special tools, but they can sometimes make it easier. Here are the options:

METHOD 1: Drag and Copy This is the standard method for copying files to external disks. You select the files and folders you want to copy and drag them to the disk where you want to save the copy. The CopyDoubler utility can save you time: it copies faster and it only replaces the files that actually have changes.

Be sure to secure your disks before you store them. You can lock floppy disks by opening the little square slot in the upper corner of the disk.

When this slot is open, you can't change the contents of the disk.

MAC SMART

SECURE YOUR BACKUP DISKS FOR STORAGE

To lock removable disks, see the instructions that come with your removable disk drive.

METHOD 2: **Use a Macro** This is the poor folks' version of automatic backup—but it may be perfect for your needs even if you're not poor. You can use CopyDoubler or QuicKeys or AppleScript to specify a standard set of folders that you want to copy. You need to make sure they all fit on the disk or cartridge you specify. You can also set a time for copying automatically, but in this case, you should have an external hard disk to copy to.

METHOD 3: **Use a Backup Application** Dedicated backup applications like DiskFit Pro and Retrospect Remote, both from Dantz, automate the backup process. They can back up your entire disk, or they can ferret out the files that have changed and only update those. They can also help you restore files from your backup. If you're backing up to floppies, they'll keep track of which floppies have which files and prompt you for the right disk at the right time. If you're backing up to a hard disk drive, they'll do it all for you at the time you set. Retrospect Remote can back up several networked computers to a single disk drive.

Removable cartridges have always seemed like the right backup solution. But until recently, the drives never seemed to offer the right cost, convenience, and capacity factors for every-day use.

Now that's changed. The SyQuest EZ135 is the best of the first crop of removables that are perfect for midcapacity backups. They're also suitable as general-purpose hard drives.

These drives cost around $200. The cartridges cost around $20 each. At such prices, these drives are much more suited for today's normal system and project backups than tape or floppy backup. The disks for the EZ135 are about the same size as a floppy—just a bit thicker—and they hold 135 megabytes each. This storage capacity is going to grow, too.

This drive should be an indispensable part of your backup strategy.

THE BACKUP CHAMP

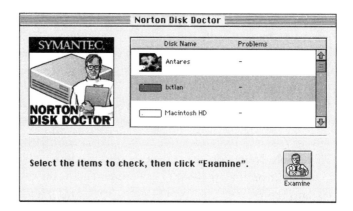

**AN OUNCE OF
PREVENTION
IS WORTH
FISTFULS OF
HAIR**

If you don't like to pull your hair out, a little preventive maintenance can help you avoid file and disk disasters in the first place. Disk Doctor, which is part of Norton Utilities, is a great tool for checking the overall health of your disk. It checks for a variety of things that can go wrong with your disk and file system. It also reorganizes things on the disk to make disk storage more efficient, so performance is better. Run Disk Doctor once a month.

STEP 4: GET SECURE

For many home offices, security is not an issue at all. For some, it is. Some clients demand security precautions. And sometimes you just need to secure your files from accidental damage by inexperienced users of your computer—like your three-year-old. For the former, you may need encryption software. For the latter, you need tools that restrict access.

Encryption software scrambles your data. Some programs scramble it better than others. Proprietary encryption routines are fast but tend to be the least secure. Programs that use the Data Encryption Standard (DES) take longer to encrypt but provide more-secure protection.

While encryption secures your files, it also jeopardizes them. If you forget your password, there's no way to recover them. None. Zip. You're dead. Also, if the file gets corrupted while it's encrypted, recovery is virtually impossible. So don't use encryption casually. Use it only when a real and pressing need exists.

Restricted access can be accomplished in several ways and at several levels, from individual files to your entire computer. Here are some of the options:

■ Use a screen saver with password production, like After Dark. If you have to leave your computer for a while, the screen saver blanks the screen and requires a password to restore it. This is a good solution if you have children or even pets in your house. It protects the work that's open on your screen from accidental keystrokes. Of course, someone could restart the computer to bypass the screen saver.

- Set up workshells. You can set up special versions of the Finder that limit access to your system. These shells might have icons for a subset of your applications and files—for example, to give kids access to their own files or to ensure that a part-time clerical helper can enter orders in your customer database but can't get to your financial and correspondence folders. To get beyond the shell, you need a password. Apple offers a product called At Ease that gives you a couple of different levels of shells.
- Lock your folders. You can set up password protection for folders with programs like FolderBolt, Norton DiskLock, and FileGuard.
- Restrict access to your online services. Most online services require a password to log onto the service. You can set up your communications software to provide this password automatically, or you can type it each time. If you provide it automatically, anybody can log on from your computer. Next time you get your monthly bill, you might discover that your 16-year-old is carrying on an expensive virtual romance with someone in a virtual coffee house. Unfortunately, if your 16-year-old is also a whiz programmer, he or she might just hack out your password protection.

For most home offices, some simple forms of restricted access are adequate protection. If you need the more sophisticated protection of security software, read the manuals carefully and take every precaution they suggest to protect your data from loss.

When you put a file in the Trash and choose Empty Trash from the Special menu, the file disappears from the screen, but it doesn't disappear from the disk. All that's erased is the pointer to the file. As you work, the operating system gradually overwrites the old data. But until it's overwritten, someone could recover part or all of it with a file recovery program.

If you're worried about this kind of hacking on your computer, you can get a *secure delete* with programs like CopyDoubler by Symantec, SpeedBoost by Aladdin Systems, and Speed Doubler by Connectix. With a secure delete, the program writes zeros over the data you delete so it can't be recovered.

SECURING YOUR TRASH

UPSIZING: Pushing the Power Pedal

Much of the power of your Macintosh resides in the System folder. When you're ready to push the power pedal, here are some things you should know.

System updates

System software, like your application software, comes in versions. If you're up to date, you're using some version of System 7.5—like System 7.5.3. Major releases add significant new features. Minor releases fix bugs, performance, and compatibility problems. In addition, you may need a **system enabler.** Enablers make the system software work on particular machines and usually have names that don't give you a clue which particular machine is involved. You usually get the enabler when you buy your Mac and don't need to worry about it.

The easiest way to find out about updates and new versions of the system software is to register your Macintosh when you buy it. Your name goes on Apple's mailing list, and you get announcements when new system software is available. If you didn't register your Mac, you can get on the mailing list by calling Apple's customer service number: 1-800-776-2333.

The alternative is to follow the news in Macintosh magazines or check with user groups and Apple dealers. Updates are free. You can get them from online services, user groups, and Apple dealers. New versions of the system cost about $100. You can get them from Apple dealers.

You don't need to change your system every time Apple releases an update or even a new version. Apple includes a Read Me file with updates—it has recommendations for who should use the update. When a new version hits the streets, your best strategy is to sit back and watch for about six months. New versions typically introduce a lot of incompatibilities, and it takes a few months for things to shake out. Even then, you may choose to keep your existing system. If you're not expanding and upgrading your applications— and if you don't need or want the new capabilities in the new system—you're better off sticking with a system that works.

If you decide to upgrade, installation is virtually automatic. An installer updates everything and restarts the Mac for you. However, you'll have to remove and then restore anything that you manually put in the System file— things like sound resources, for example.

System utilities

System utilities are applications that extend your system capabilities or help you with system housekeeping. You don't need utilities. Your Mac will work fine without them. But if you have the slightest inclination to tinker, system utilities open up a new dimension of life with your Mac.

System utilities abound. They can be complete applications or simply control panels or system extensions. They can be commercial products that you'll find in any software catalog, or they can be shareware or freeware that you find in an online forum. So how do you decide which are for you? You can experiment, keeping in mind that system extensions, in particular, don't always work together well. Or you can just use our Essential Utility Shopping List, as follows:

NOW UTILITIES This package is actually a team of some of the most useful, well-designed, and reliable utilities you could ask for. It includes, among others:

■ Now Menus for setting up your own menus and command keys.
■ Now FolderMenus for immediate access to files buried inside layers of folders.
■ Now WYSIWYG Menus for displaying your font names in their own font—so you can see how they look in the menu.
■ Now Save for automatically saving changes to documents as you work.
■ Now Super Boomerang for faster access to files and folders in the directory dialog box—with things like document menus that appear automatically when you choose the Open command.
Source: Now Software

SUITCASE If you have more than a dozen or so fonts, you need Suitcase. It gives you complete font-management tools. You can load in special fonts as you need them for different projects. You can keep your fonts in Suitcase folders, so you don't have to reinstall them when you update your System file. You can display the fonts in their own typefaces in the font menu. You can also manage other system resources, such as sounds and desk accessories, with Suitcase.
Source: Symantec Corporation

QUICKEYS If you don't want to take the time to learn AppleScript, QuicKeys is your alternative. You use it to create macros—automated sequences of commands—and assign them to keys. For example, you can assign an application to each of your function keys. Then you just press F1 to open your contacts manager or F2 to check your e-mail. You can also preset QuicKey macros to run at a certain time—to give you reminders or to run e-mail programs late at night, for example.
Source: CE Software

AFTER DARK This utility has been called one of the great time-wasters of the ages, but it's also a fine tool for many trades. It was designed as a screen saver to prevent image burn-in when you leave your computer inactive for long periods. But it also includes password protection, a desktop picture display, and an infinite variety of screen saver modules, including a virus-protection module, a QuickTime video player, a video game, and other time-wasting fun.

Source: Berkeley Systems

DLS This system extension works twice a year—it changes your Mac's internal clock from standard time to daylight saving time in the spring and back to standard time in the fall. Simple, but it's one less clock to change each spring and fall.

Source: Freeware from D. Grant Leeper. Available online.

DISKDOUBLER PRO This is the combo package with CopyDoubler, DiskDoubler, and AutoDoubler. For extending the storage capabilities of your Mac, you can't beat the compression services of DiskDoubler and AutoDoubler. As already mentioned, CopyDoubler is a handy tool for automatic copying.

Source: Symantec Corporation

RAM DOUBLER Unless you're RAM-rich, this system extension should be in your System folder. It effectively doubles your RAM by managing it more effectively—so you can open more documents and more applications at the same time. It may slow your Mac down a bit, but if you've got a Power Mac, you shouldn't notice any real problems.

Source: Connectix, Inc.

SPEED DOUBLER While RAM Doubler gives you memory at the expense of speed, Speed Doubler saves you time in operations like copying files and folders. If you've got a Power Macintosh, it will actually double performance for nonnative applications as well as for the System 7 software, which is currently nonnative. (Nonnative means it hasn't been designed specifically for the RISC processor.)

Source: Connectix, Inc.

TEMPERAMENT If you use Microsoft Word, you may notice your System folder filling up with dozens of files labeled Word Temp 2, Word Temp 3, and so on. These are temporary files that Word leaves in the System folder for various reasons. Temperament is a little jewel of a utility that checks for these temp files at startup and deletes them for you.

Source: Freeware from John Rotenstein. Available online.

AppleScript

If you really want to play magician with your operating system and applications, take the time to learn AppleScript. It's a high-level scripting environment that comes with the operating system. With it, you can write scripts that perform all kinds of complex tasks, involving several applications.

For example, you can make your applications work together by writing a script that grabs data from your spreadsheets, graphs it in a separate charting application, and then pastes it into a word processing document. Or you can automate repetitive processes like converting graphics files from one format to another—importing them into an application that can read the old format and saving them in the new format.

You simply save your scripts as mini-applications and then double-click them to run them. Of course, they only work with AppleScript-aware applications—those that understand AppleScript commands. And you have to make sure you've installed both the AppleScript extension and the Apple Events Manager extension in the Extensions folder. (They come with System 7.) *And* you have to learn the AppleScript language, which is pretty sophisticated in spite of its English-like grammar.

Want even more magic? Use the QuicKeys utility described above with AppleScript. Then you can take advantage of both QuicKeys' ease of use and AppleScript's power. In addition, QuicKeys works in all applications, even if they're not AppleScript-aware.

POWER PLAY: Backing Up to Stay Ahead

You mean well. You're going to get around to setting up your backup system real soon now.

Don't wait. It's incredibly easy, especially if you just need to back up a small number of important data files daily—like your electronic accounts, your correspondence, and a current project. CopyDoubler's scheduled copy feature can work perfectly for your regular backup needs.

What you need

- CopyDoubler (part of DiskDoubler Pro from Symantec)
- An external hard drive or removable cartridge drive
- Time: 2 minutes

Schedule the backup

If you've already installed CopyDoubler, you're ready to start. If not, follow the installation instructions that come with DiskDoubler Pro. Then decide which files you want to back up, where you want to make the backup copies, and when.

1. Select the files you want to back up.

2. Hold down the ⌘ and Option keys while you drag the files to their destination.

The destination should be your backup drive or a folder on your backup drive.

When you drag the files, CopyDoubler gives you a few copy options.

3. Click Later With CopyDoubler and then click Schedule.

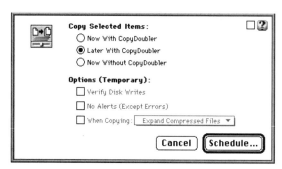

CopyDoubler displays a Schedule Setup box.

Click this option and all of the days if you want to back up every day at the same time.

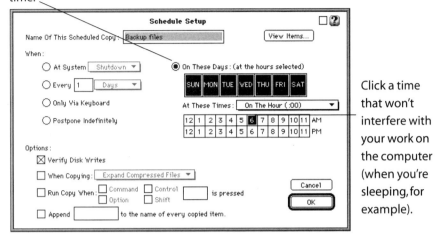

Click a time that won't interfere with your work on the computer (when you're sleeping, for example).

If you turn off your computer at the end of each working day, you can choose the option to copy At System Shutdown.

4. Click OK.

That's it. At the scheduled time, CopyDoubler automatically copies the files to the destination you indicated. It's a smart copy, too—CopyDoubler only replaces the files that have changed.

If you want to add more files to the copy list, just select them and repeat the process. You can copy them at the same time and to the same destination as the first set—or set up different times and destinations.

Change the backup schedule
Want to change the backup schedule? Here's how.

1. Double-click the CopyDoubler control panel in your Control Panels folder.

2. Click Copy Schedule.

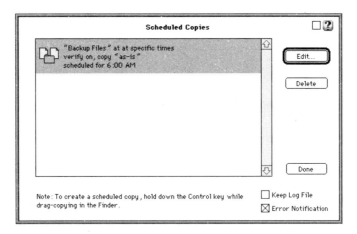

3. Select the copy set you want to change, click Edit, and enter the new schedule instructions in the Schedule Setup box.

4. Click OK.

If your backup needs are modest, CopyDoubler may do it all for you.

ON THE HORIZON: An Orchestra of Agents, Applets, and Audio-Visual

With System 7, Apple defined the basic philosophy for its operating system. Future operating systems—with the musical code names Copland and Gershwin—promise to make this philosophy sing.

You already see the foundations of the future in today's system: rudimentary agents (as in the Apple Guide), integrated communications, and high-end media. These will be refined and integrated in the next major system releases.

Copland will be document-centric with the wide use of OpenDoc technology. With OpenDoc, you're going to be able to use intelligent documents to create your own custom solutions—something like a special-purpose application for each document.

Smart software modules, known as user agents, will become your partners at work, watching over your work patterns and taking over the routine chores.

QuickTime 3D could also change the look and feel of everything you do on your computer. Imagine a three-dimensional workspace instead of a flat desktop. How will you move in it? How will you act in it? How will you find things in it? Those are the questions that Apple and Macintosh developers are already thinking about.

All this, and better performance and reliability too. System 7 isn't native code: it doesn't take full advantage of the power and speed of the RISC processor in the Power Macs. But Copland will.

After Copland comes Gershwin—with more integration, more refinement, and better performance. Look for more work possibilities in designing your own workspace. Watch for intelligent agents that will actively anticipate and respond to your needs. This is the sort of thing that Apple envisioned in its early Knowledge Navigator video. With Gershwin, it will be ready for the real world, along with seamless movement among networks, services, and databases.

Tomorrow's technology universe is being recrafted in smaller and smaller pieces that are smarter and more adaptable. If Apple can keep its vision of the future on track, we'll all end up with a high-fidelity communications environment that is malleable, cooperative, and very, very smart.

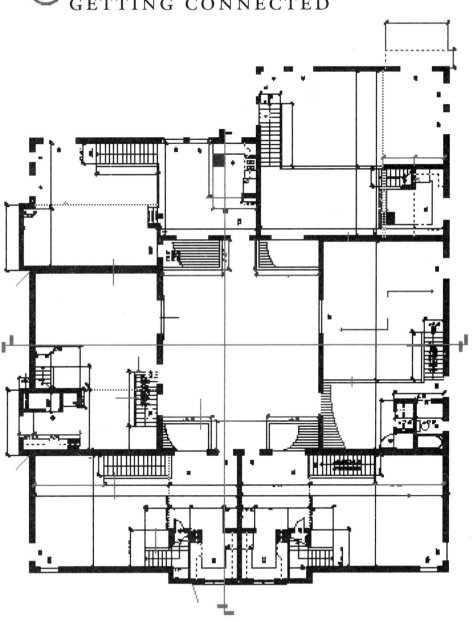

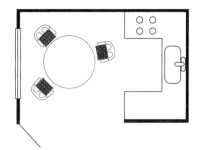

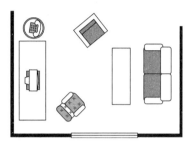

CHAPTER FIVE

TANGLE-FREE

TELEPHONY (ALMOST)

How to turn your Mac and

your phone into a professional team

S uperman has it easy. All he has to do is find a phone booth to change in. You have to juggle phone lines, jacks, connectors, pagers, fax machines, cell phones, answering machines, and a host of Macintosh options to do your superhero act in the business world.

So think of this chapter as a juggling lesson. You need a few props and a little coordination. But before long, you'll be showing your stuff in front of the TV cameras—that's the, uh, digital televideo cameras.

Telepresence

You can't do business in today's world without a strong telepresence. Telepresence is what your clients get when they call to ask if you're available for a job. Telepresence is what mail order customers get when they call to ask about a product you've advertised. It's what lets people know that they've reached a business when they reach you.

It's basically the way you answer your phone—or don't answer it. There are lots of good reasons for not answering your phone. For example, you probably work alone, and if you answered the phone every time it rang, you'd never get any work done. Or maybe you're not ready to respond to a call. Or you've just gone out to walk the dog.

You don't want to be stuck like glue to the telephone just because you have a home business. So what do you do? You have several choices:

Get an answering service. This was the solution before there were answering machines, and it's still an option if you need to have a real person available to answer calls. The problems with answering services are the problems you expect with real people. They often don't know anything about your business and can't answer your caller's questions accurately. They tend to be overworked, they make mistakes, they lose messages, and sometimes they're even rude on your behalf. And they're expensive—but not as expensive as hiring your own full-time receptionist.

For a summary of essential answering machine features, see Step 3 under "Jump Start" in this chapter.

Get an answering machine. For many home businesses, a basic answering machine is a perfect solution. Answering machines are inexpensive, although they do have to be replaced periodically. (Check your tape cassette before you pitch your answering machine, though. Lots of people think their machine has gone haywire when all they need is a new cassette.) Advanced machines do a lot more than just answer your phone. You can use them to:

- Monitor or record phone conversations
- Receive messages in more than one mailbox
- Leave memos for yourself or others
- Hold conferences between a caller and several people in your room
- Put someone on hold with music in the background

You have lots of models to choose from. Just look for the features you need—and decide whether you want digital or magnetic tape recording. (Digital recording technology in answering machines is not ideal. It wouldn't be so bad for incoming messages, but it makes your message to the world less than elegant.)

Team up an answering machine with a pager. You may need to know when someone is trying to reach you even if you're not at home. An answering machine plus a pager—or a PowerBook with a plug-in PC pager card—will do the job. For example, maybe you're a plumber. You spend an hour in your home office in the morning taking calls and returning them, setting up appointments, and arranging your day. After that, you're out on jobs. But if one or two of your best customers have an emergency, they can call your answering machine, which announces your emergency pager number. They beep you, you call them back from wherever you are, and you've saved a business relationship.

Sign up for your telephone company voice mail service. Most answering machines only take messages when no one answers. If you're on the phone and you get a call, they can't answer. The caller gets a busy signal. With a voice mail service, all your calls get answered whether you're on the phone or not. You can also set up mailboxes—which are handy if two of you are working at home on the same line or if you want to leave different messages in different boxes. For example, you might want to describe different services or products that you offer. Then customers can get information without disturbing your work. They can leave their names if they're interested, and you can call them all back at your convenience. You can even tell them when you'll call them back. The downsides? You pay an ongoing monthly fee, and you can't screen your calls. There's no blinking light and no LED to display the number of messages waiting. You have to call your mailbox to check for messages.

Turn your Mac into an answering service. You can get hardware and software that turns your Mac into an answering service. Then your Mac can take messages just like your answering machine, and even respond to them. For example, you can use Front Office from Pleiades—together with the Apple Geoport Telecom Adapter—to set up any number of hierarchical voice mailboxes, each with an outgoing message up to 8 minutes long. When customers call to inquire about your product line, you can direct them through the hierarchy to the information they need and even automatically fax them a spec sheet for a particular product. The problem with this solution is that it monopolizes your serial port—you can't use the modem for your other online work, even if you have a second line. If you want to use the fax-back feature, it monopolizes your printer port, too And if anything goes wrong with your Mac, your phone doesn't get answered. However, if you're in business for any length of time, you'll eventually need to upgrade your Mac. Then you can use your old Mac as a dedicated phone answering service.

> For step-by-step help in turning your Macintosh into an answering service, see "Power Play" in this chapter.

Telefax

In today's business world, you have to have a fax system. It's not that you couldn't wait till the day after tomorrow to get the information in the mail. It's possible you could. But many of your customers and suppliers won't. They expect you to have one. It's just part of doing business—as necessary as your telephone.

You have two basic choices to make here:

Get a fax machine. Fax machines work like copiers. You feed pages into the machine; it scans them and converts the image to signals that can be sent over your phone line. At the other end, a similar machine reads the signals and prints them out. A fax machine can also double as a home office copier—but

> Not sure what to look for in a fax machine? See Step 3 under "Jump Start" in this chapter.

you can only copy individual flat pages. You can't copy or fax a page in a book or magazine, or the back of a cereal box, for example.

Get a fax modem and fax software. You can attach a modem to your Mac and use fax software to turn your Mac into a fax machine. You send a file via the modem. At the other end of the line, it can be read by either a fax machine or another fax program. With fax modems, you can only fax things that are already in files on your Mac. If you want to fax a photograph or page from a book or your personal sketch of the Total Perspective Vortex, you'll need a scanner to digitize the image first and turn it into a file. This is obviously a bit of a hassle.

How do you decide which solution is best for you? It depends on the volume and content of your fax traffic—and how you like to work. Here's a table to help you make up your mind:

TABLE 5.1 FAX MACHINE OR FAX MODEM?

FAX MACHINES	FAX MODEMS & SOFTWARE
ADVANTAGES You get an immediate hard copy. You can send any flat page without any preparation. You get a built-in copy machine. You can get and send copies when your Mac is down.	ADVANTAGES You can read the faxes on your Mac, so you save paper. Copy quality at the receiving end tends to be better because the image isn't scanned. Fax modems take almost no space on your desk. (Internal fax modems take up none.) You can automatically add custom cover sheets to faxes and keep a log of your faxes. You can use OCR software to automatically convert documents you receive to Mac text files.
DISADVANTAGES The quality of fax copies is mediocre. The machine takes up space on your desk. If your fax machine doesn't have built-in memory and runs out of paper while you're receiving the fax, you lose part of the fax.	DISADVANTAGES If you need a hard copy, you have to print the file out on your printer after you receive it on your Mac. You can only fax documents that you have stored as files on your Mac. If your Mac goes down—or if you just shut it off for the night—you can't send or get faxes.

For considerations about telephone lines and your fax solution, see Step 1 under "Jump Start" in this chapter.

Fax modems are usually less expensive than fax machines—but fax machines aren't all that expensive either. You can get a good one for less than $200. You may decide that the best solution is actually to get both: use the fax modem to send long documents you create on your Mac, but use a fax machine to receive documents and send quick pages that aren't on your Mac. A fax machine and fax modem can share the same line. One can be the default receiving machine. To use the other, you switch to it manually.

For years we advised people to stay away from fax modems and software. Most fax modem manufacturers buy their software from third-party developers and don't support it well. The programs are difficult to use, and they don't work well with other software. We have two fax modems languishing in a drawer somewhere because we could never get them to work satisfactorily.

Then we got the Global Village Teleport Platinum fax modem. The software that comes with this modem really works. Here are some of the things you can do:

■ From any application on your Mac, you just hold down the Option key, and fax commands replace your print commands in the File menu. You can use one of these commands to Fax your open document.

■ You can easily create and use custom cover sheets.

■ You can create envelopes to send several different documents in a single fax transmission.

■ You can create an address book of individuals as well as groups—to fax your document to several people at the same time.

■ You can schedule faxes to be sent at a time you choose—when phone rates are lowest.

■ You get a log of all the faxes you send and receive, with options for easy filing and other management tasks.

The Fax command replaces the standard Print command when you hold down the Option key. It opens this dialog box.

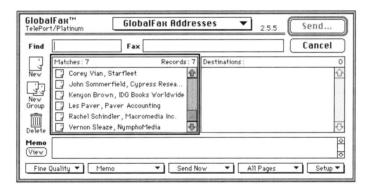

GLOBAL VILLAGE: FAX SOFTWARE THAT REALLY WORKS

Teledata

A fax is only one way to send and receive information via your phone line. You can also use a variety of communications applications—from online services like America Online and CompuServe to your Quicken electronic payment software. They are all ways to get digital data from your computer to someone else's.

To send and receive digital data via your phone, you need two things:

Modem. A modem translates the digital signals from your computer into the analog signals that your phone line uses. It sits between your Mac and

For more information about communications software, see Chapter 6. For details about electronic bill payment, see Chapter 10.

your phone, using the serial port to talk to your computer. (Of course, if it's a wireless modem, it may just beam signals to a special telephone jack.)

Software. The communications software packages the information for transmission. It talks to your modem, giving the instructions to send and receive. The software may be embedded in another application, as in Quicken. It may be an application dedicated to a particular online service or communications task. Or it may be generic communications software, like the kind that comes with Microsoft Works, for transmitting files from computer to computer.

You also obviously need phone lines. And unless you're talking directly to your target computer via those phone lines, you need some sort of network support for relaying your data to its proper destination. But that's the subject of Chapter 6.

Televideo

The technology for video telephone has been around for several decades already. The reason it's not in everyone's home is that people didn't want it in their homes enough to pay the high price tag. Besides, the audio-only telephone offers lots of benefits: anonymity, discretion, and privacy.

In the business world, however, televideo has a different standing. Business meetings are more formal than private phone conversations. They have fixed formats and protocols. They often involve a review of materials—things you have to look at. For all those reasons, concerns about anonymity, discretion, and privacy are diminished. The importance of a visual presence is greater. And televideo is a way to get that presence, even when participants in a meeting are strewn across town or across the country.

Of course, if you're working from your home, you may still have all the concerns about privacy. You may not have a spiffy conference room attached to your family room. The space next to your desk may be your laundry room, with a week's worth of laundry sorted into piles waiting to go into your washing machine. The prospect of televideo meetings with your clients may make you shudder.

Nevertheless, televideo can expand your business territory. Clients who are reluctant to hire someone a few hundred miles away might be happier with the arrangement if they could see you quickly and easily—and work together with you on graphics such as flow charts or page designs. It can also simply save you travel time and money when visual cues are essential to the progress of the meeting.

And your Mac can help. Apple has built videoconferencing technology into the Macintosh—this technology has the potential to turn your Mac desktop into a remote conferencing site where you can view a slide show that's running on someone else's computer. Or present your own multimedia slides.

Or even work jointly in a spreadsheet application with someone on the opposite coast—sort of like an electronic chalkboard with computer-smarts built in. Plus you get voice and video-in-a-window.

Apple offers a QuickTime Conferencing Kit to take advantage of this technology. It includes the QuickTime Conferencing extension, the Quick-Time Conferencing Camera 100, and Apple Media Conference software. Several other systems—such as Northern Telecom's high-end VISIT and VideoPhone from Connectix—also take advantage of this technology. Some of these solutions are a bit pricey for home-office budgets: the VISIT package costs more than your computer! But if long-distance visual communication is essential to your work, televideo can keep you off the streets and out of airports. Which may actually save you money in the long run.

Your complete telesystem

The telephone used to be simple. It's not anymore. It's a component—or several components—in a total information system that helps you work more or less effectively. Getting that system up and running reliably is crucial to the success of your business. This is not a platitude. (Well, it might be, but it's an important one.) Your business really can founder on your failure to handle your phones well. So check out Sam Post's high-end solution, and then check yourself against the steps under "Jump Start" and the options in "Upsizing." And let your Mac help you everywhere it can.

Sam Post has pushed the telephone—like all his technologies—to the limit.

He needs a professional telephone answering system to handle lots of incoming customer calls—not only to take messages, but also to provide detailed information on the individual products in his line and even fax well-crafted documents from his Mac automatically. A dedicated Mac with a Geoport Telecom Adapter and Front Office software meets this need.

He needs quick, easy, mobile access to the Internet and commercial online services from his portable PowerBook. A wireless modem that can connect via an omnidirectional jack from anywhere in his home office fulfills this function.

He needs phone service at his side for outgoing calls and selected incoming calls—from his contractors and friends who need to reach him, rather than his customer service line. A cell phone with a headset keeps his hands free to work and maneuver his wheelchair around his office while he talks.

People ask him if it's worth the investment in equipment. His answer: The alternative would be to cable himself to his desk and hire a full-time person to handle phone calls and faxes. That's no alternative, as far as he's concerned.

THE TOOLS

Pleiades Front Office
Apple Geoport Telecom Adapter
Fax modem
Wireless modem and jack
Cell phone with headset

Sam's Geoport Telecom Adapter reads incoming phone signals to answer calls and play recorded messages for callers. It plugs into the other serial port.

A fax modem plugs into the one of the serial ports for immediate, automatic fax-back service to callers.

Microphone

Printer port

Modem port

Fax modem

Geoport telecom adapter

Line 1

Line 2

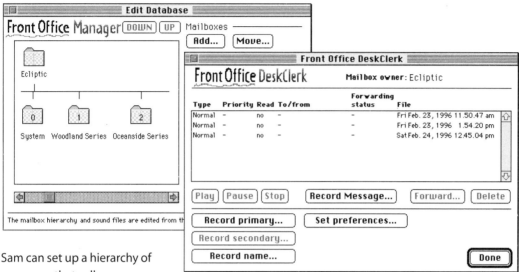

Sam can set up a hierarchy of messages that callers can navigate with their touch-tone phones.

Once a day, Sam can review the calls that have come in and respond to any of them personally, if necessary.

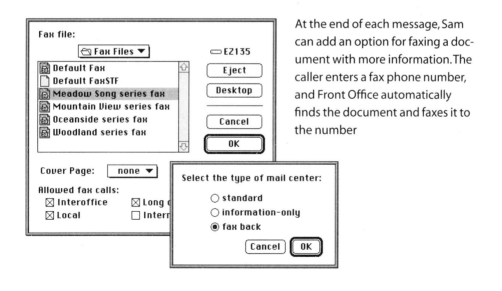

At the end of each message, Sam can add an option for faxing a document with more information. The caller enters a fax phone number, and Front Office automatically finds the document and faxes it to the number

JUMP START: Getting Wired for Business

Whether you're just starting your home business or rethinking your telephone strategy, getting properly wired can be a snarly endeavor. Here are some steps to help you plan and implement a telephone solution with a minimum of knots.

STEP 1: GET A STRATEGY

Telephony solutions don't come in an all-in-one package. You need to put together your own component system. Here's a checklist of possible components (**with essentials checked**):

- ☑ Your Macintosh
- ☑ Phone line
- ❏ ISDN line
- ☑ Phone
- ❏ Fax machine (with or without built-in phone)
- ❏ Answering machine (with or without built-in phone)
- ☑ Modem
- ❏ Video camera
- ❏ Telephone answering software
- ❏ Fax software
- ☑ Communications software
- ❏ Televideo software
- ❏ Autodial software
- ❏ Telephone company voice mail

Start by drawing some pictures. Draw a picture of how all the pieces of your telephony solution are going to fit together. There are lots of ways to hook things up, but pay special attention to how incoming calls are handled. For example, if you're using both an answering machine and a fax machine on the same line, you want your answering machine to take the call and pass it on to the fax machine only if it's not a voice call.

You may be able to get everything you need with a single phone line.

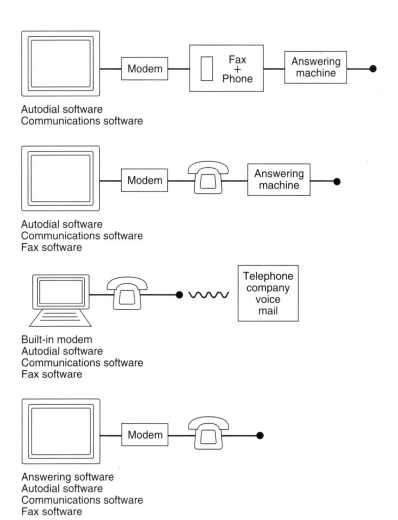

Autodial software
Communications software

Autodial software
Communications software
Fax software

Built-in modem
Autodial software
Communications software
Fax software

Answering software
Autodial software
Communications software
Fax software

Here are some single-line solutions that work:

Although single-line solutions work, they can get bogged down with heavy traffic. Remember, you've got voice calls coming and going, faxes coming and going, and possibly long online stints during which your phone is tied up.

Having two lines relieves the congestion and also offers greater flexibility for handling heavy incoming calls—which you might have if you take customer orders on the telephone. Here are some two-line solutions:

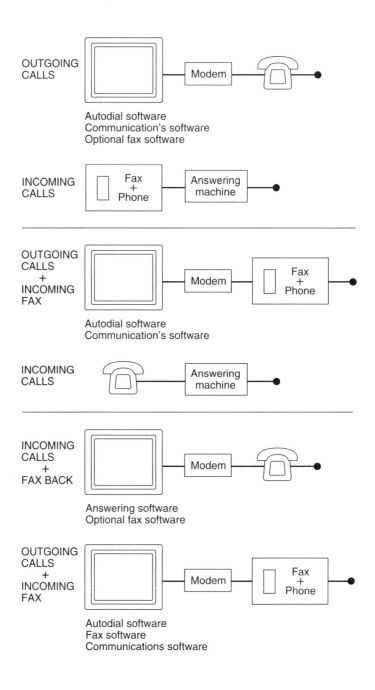

Of course, you can have more than two lines. But each line adds overhead to your operations. Two is usually enough...er, that's two in addition to your home phone.

STEP 2: GET YOUR PHONE LINES

Unless you live alone, you don't want to use your home phone for business calls. You probably won't want to take business calls in your off-hours, and you may not want to take personal calls during working hours. If you've only got one line, you have to screen all your calls to figure out which is which. Screening is tedious and sometimes detrimental to your business—and your personal relationships.

So get a line for your business. You can get either a business or a residential line. You don't have to get a business line just because you're using your phone for business. The only time you have to get a business line is if you're in a commercial district that is only served by business lines. But since you're working from home, you're probably not in such a district. If you already have residential service, you can simply add another residential line—or two or three.

Business lines cost more than residential lines. You pay a higher monthly fee, plus per-call charges. You also pay higher fees for services such as voice mail, call forwarding, or multiparty calls—about three times as high.

Although phone company services vary from community to community—and from company to company—you can usually get the same services on your residential phone as on a business phone. With a business line, however, you typically get two benefits:

- A free telephone listing under your business name in the white pages of the telephone book.
- A free one-line listing in the yellow pages under one heading.

With a residential line, you can't list your business name in the white pages or with directory assistance. But you can buy advertising space in the yellow pages.

STEP 3: GET EQUIPPED

Now you need to choose your equipment. Before you run out to your local consumer electronics store, consider these three basic alternatives:

Hardware vs. software solutions. You can get a lot of the functionality you want in either free-standing hardware or software that you run on your Mac. Hardware solutions don't tie up your Mac resources, and they work even when your Mac doesn't. Software keeps your desktop spaces clear of clutter, and it doesn't turn into landfill when it stops working.

DO YOU BELONG IN THE YELLOW PAGES

Some businesses belong in the yellow pages. Here's a good way to tell if you're one of them:

YES NO   Is there currently a heading in the phone book that describes your business accurately?

YES NO   Are there five or more listings under that heading?

YES NO   Would you yourself look for your service or product in the yellow pages?

If you answered YES to all of the questions, you will almost certainly benefit from a yellow pages ad. If you answered NO to any of the questions, you might do better to spend your advertising budget elsewhere.

By the way, there are other directory services besides the yellow pages. You can find them, ironically enough, in the yellow pages under a heading such as "Directories and Guides" or "Publishing: Directories."

All-in-one vs. multiple components. All-in-one solutions offer setup convenience and don't take up as much space as multiple components. But there are more ways for an all-in-one solution to break down, and if one function fails, you have to send the whole unit into the shop for repair.

Own vs. lease. For most telephony products today it makes sense to buy. The only exception might be high-priced, high-end phone solutions for complex, multiuser environments. These aren't typical of home offices.

Now for specifics. This table shows what to look for and what to avoid in the major components:

TABLE 5.2 BASIC TELEPHONE EQUIPMENT

	WHAT TO LOOK FOR	WHAT TO AVOID
PHONES	Touch-tone dialing Comfort—you have to hold these things in your hand. Plug-in headsets—if you need to talk on the phone and work on your Mac at the same time	Some portable phones—analog models are not secure enough for business.
ANSWERING MACHINES	Voice-activated recording Call screening Alternate outgoing messages Mailboxes	Limits on message lengths Digital recording—the technology in most answering machines isn't quite good enough yet.
FAX MACHINES	Ability to automatically distinguish voice calls from fax tone—so it can receive faxes when you're not there to push the Receive button Gray-scale capability to read photographs Built-in paper cutter Built-in memory to save faxes in case you run out of paper during reception Plain paper—if you need permanent copies that won't fade Auto-redial	Manual-only receive
MODEMS	Hayes-compatible 14.4 Kbps or faster Fax software compatibility—if you're using a fax software solution Voice adapter—if you want to use your Mac as an answering machine	

For more details about modems and what to look for, see "Jump Start" in Chapter 6, "Weighing In on the Web."

You may need portability. If you're on the road a lot, a cell phone gives you that portability. If your home business isn't a desk job, you may want a cordless phone that you can attach to your belt to take calls wherever you happen to be.

However, most cellular and cordless phones aren't secure. They use radio waves to convey signals from a base phone or a repeater station to your handset. These radio waves can be picked up on radio monitors. There are millions of ordinary people in the United States with scanners that can pick up cellular signals or portable signals or both. Some are sure to be in your community. If you don't want to have strangers listening in on your business calls, don't use cellular or portable phones. The telephone industry is trying to fix this problem. You can get digital cordless and cellular phones that transmit digital signals, which radio scanners can't pick up.

ABOUT
CELLULAR AND
CORDLESS
PHONES

STEP 4: GET SOFTWARE

The Macintosh is designed to work with your phone. Its Macintosh Telephony Architecture supports basic and not-so-basic telephone applications. Here are some of the types of software you may want to use:

Contact-management software. These applications link your telephone to an online phone book. When you look up a contact in the phone book, you can just click the phone number and your Mac automatically dials for you. It some cases, the software can provide automatic redial.

Telephone answering software. These applications turn your Mac into an answering machine. The main players are currently Pleiades' Front Office and two products from Cypress Research Corporation: Megaphone, which includes both contact-management and basic answering machine functions, and PhonePro, which uses scripts to set up the kind of hierarchical voice mail messages that you get with Front Office. These programs all require the Apple Geoport Telecom Adapter and its software. They also make serious demands on your serial ports—and may, in fact, require you to dedicate a Mac to telephone service. They make sense if you have a high volume of incoming calls that you can't afford to handle yourself and if you want fax-back capability. Otherwise a telephone company voice mail system or a basic answering machine will be more cost-effective.

PRODUCT FOCUS

IF YOU DON'T HAVE A SPARE POWER MAC

If you don't have a Power Mac that you can dedicate to your telephone system, you may be able to use an older Mac. Pleiades makes a hardware version of their product—called Digital Storefront—that works with older Macs. It takes the place of the Geoport Telecom Adapter, but it requires a built-in microphone.

If you don't have a built-in microphone, you may be able to plug a sound input device like MacRecorder into one of your serial ports and Digital Storefront into the other. Of course, that means you don't have a serial port available for the fax modem, so you won't be able to use the fax-back feature. Contact Pleiades for more information.

Communications software. This is the software that you use to send a file directly from your computer to a colleague's computer via your phone line. It encodes the file for transmission in one of several file transfer formats. Your colleague must have software that can read the format you choose. Some of these programs are general-purpose commercial products. Some are proprietary for use by clients and customers of a company. With the growth of networks, direct modem-to-modem software is becoming obsolete. You probably don't need it.

Networking software. This is the software that connects you to the world of data—worldwide. It connects you, via a modem, either to commercial networks like America Online or CompuServe or to the Internet. Each network requires its own software. If you want to take advantage of this expanding world of commerce, you need this software. In fact, a basic e-mail account on a network is almost a business essential these days.

Setting up this kind of software can be simple or it can be an exercise in hair-pulling frustration. At the simple end, you just set some basic phone codes, like area codes or other special dialing instructions. At the hair-pulling end, you're trying to configure your modem to talk to a network computer that doesn't recognize it because you don't know the right modem string and can't figure it out without a degree in network communications protocols. See Chapter 6 for some semi-soothing advice.

Of course, you want more details about networks. See Chapter 6. "Weighing In on the Web."

UPSIZING: Increasing Your Bandwidth

Bandwidth is a measure of how much information you can send and receive. You know that you haven't got enough bandwidth when you start missing important calls because you're busy with other important calls, or when you need to send a fax and talk to someone at the same time, or when you're sitting around waiting for your e-mail while you've got dozens of calls to make.

Here's how to get more.

More services

Most phone companies offer a range of calling services for a small additional monthly charge—usually about $5. Some of them are particularly useful for the home business:

Three-way calling. With this service, you can set up conference calls among three parties. This is useful if you often have to play the role of go-between for two people—for example, if you're like Andy Fine in our solution scenarios.

Intercom. With this kind of service, you can use two or more phones on the same line as an intercom, put a caller on hold, and transfer calls between phones—all of which can make it easier to work if two of you are working at home. This service may also provide the three-way calling described above.

Call return. This service automatically dials the last call you received. If you miss a call and the caller doesn't leave a message, you can return the call automatically, even though you don't know who called.

Call forwarding. This service comes in a variety of forms. If you're a bookkeeper who travels from client to client, for example, you can use call forwarding to forward your calls to the client-of-the-day. If you spend a lot of time on your phone, you can forward calls to another line in your own home when you've got your main line tied up. If your phone is in your office, but you're working in the dining room for the day, you can forward all your calls to your home line in the dining room, so you don't have to run to your office every time the office phone rings—or even miss calls altogether because your office phone is out in the garage and you can't hear it while you're working inside. You can even forward calls selectively, if there's one particular call you don't want to miss while you're in another part of the house.

Caller ID. This service identifies the phone number of an incoming phone call—unless your caller has blocked the service. This information can be useful: it can help you quickly identify repeat customers or clients and greet them appropriately. If you're using your Mac to record all your incoming calls, it can keep a record of numbers for all your customer inquiries. With the PhoneDisk CD-ROM, you can quickly convert this information to names and addresses for a customer mailing list. (It's against the law to sell such a list, however.) To use this service, you need a phone or answering machine that can display incoming numbers.

There's one phone service to avoid on your home office phone: **call waiting**. In the business world, there's simply no polite way to put someone on hold while you take another call. There's no polite way to tell one party that the other party is more important. Also, the call-waiting signal can break your network connection if you're working online. So you might as well just use a call forwarding or voice-mail solution to pick up calls you can't take while you're talking.

More lines

At some point, you may just need more lines. If you've already got one business line, don't get another. Get a residential line. Use it for all your outgoing calls. Use your business line for incoming calls—it's the one that's listed with your business name.

In addition to adding these standard lines, you may want to add some special-purpose lines:

An 800 line. If you want to give your customers a toll-free number, you need an 800 line. This is actually a service that you can add to an existing residential or business line or set up on a separate line. You pay a small initial setup charge and a small monthly fee (about $5) to your local telephone company. You arrange the toll-free service with a long-distance carrier like AT&T.

A 900 line. You use 900 lines to provide information for a fee. For example, you might provide a referral service by phone. Customers pay for this service, and you pay the telephone company. (Some people make an entire business of 900 lines.) If your service is regional, you can use a local phone company. For national services, you need to arrange the service with a long-distance carrier. The 900 service can be added to existing residential or business lines, but the charges are steep. In the San Francisco area, it's $1,100 to set up the line, plus $20 per month to maintain it. In addition, you pay the phone company $.27 for the first minute and $.11 for each additional minute. There are limits to what you can charge per minute, too: $5 for the first minute and $2 for each additional minute, up to a maximum of $50 per call.

An ISDN line. ISDN lines are 3-in-1 lines. They have two 56-Kbps data channels plus a voice channel. You can combine the two data channels to get a 128.8-Kbps channel—compared to 33.6-Kbps for the fastest modem speed on a standard phone line. In some areas, you can get an ISDN line from your phone company for about the same amount as a standard phone line, including standard installation charges. In other areas, ISDN lines are priced for large business customers—that is, high. With most ISDN lines, you also pay a per-minute charge during standard working hours, but you can transmit for free in off-hours. Other costs? The special ISDN teleport adapters (or ISDN modems) range from about $300 to $1,000, depending on features. One of these features is a special ISDN handset, which you need in order to use the voice channel on your ISDN line (you can't use a regular phone). The good news: Setting up an ISDN adapter is a lot simpler than setting up a standard modem.

A point-to-point circuit. These are dedicated data lines. They connect your modem directly to a modem at a remote site. They're useful if you exchange lots of data with a single computer (or a corporate computer network). By lots, we mean several hours of connect time per day. Unless you need to plug into a client's computer to do your work, you probably don't need this kind of line.

Multiple line managers

Let's say you've got several lines coming into your house now. You've got your fax line and a couple of voice lines for you and your spouse, who also works at home. You've got a home line that your 15-year-old has tied up all evening. Phones are always ringing all over the place, and you think you should be able to get more service from all this cable.

You're right. You can. For about the same amount as you paid for your Mac, you can buy a phone system that manages all those lines much more efficiently. For example:

- You can program the system to roll over. This is not a silly dog trick. It's a way to automatically transfer incoming calls to another line if one line isn't available. For example, if you're on your main business line, the system can automatically transfer the call to your spouse's line or the fax line, where either your spouse or a machine can take a message. If your daughter won't give up the phone in the evenings, you can program calls coming into your home line to roll over to your business line after hours.
- You can turn your lines into an intercom. You can dial a specific extension—for example, to ask your spouse in his or her office at the other end of the house if he or she knows what happened to the computer insurance policy.
- You can turn your phones into a public-address system. You just dial a code and shout "Where on earth is the computer insurance policy?" over all the phones in the house (using the built-in speaker phones).

In addition, such systems offer all the high-end answering machine features, such as multiple mailboxes and hundreds of programmable numbers for speed dialing every customer or supplier on your list. For most people, these systems are hardly necessities. But if you have multiple people working in your home and a lot of incoming calls, they can certainly make more efficient use of your telephone lines. If this is your situation, look into the Panasonic KX3280.

POWER PLAY: Setting Up Your Front Office

If you need a strong telephone presence but can't afford to be on call to your telephone 24 hours a day, you can turn a Macintosh into a telephone information system. This is not just an answering machine. It's a way to get information to a wide public—and take their messages when appropriate.

To do it, you probably have to dedicate a low-end Power Mac to the task. You also need an Apple Geoport Telecom Adapter to convert voice signals to digital data, and vice versa. You plug the adapter into your modem port and your telephone jack. It has an extra cable for a telephone handset, if you want one.

And of course, you need software. The two main products are Phone Pro from Cypress and Front Office from Pleiades. This example uses Front Office.

What you need
- Geoport Telecom Adapter
- A fax modem for fax-back
- Pleiades Front Office
- Your Mac microphone
- Time: 1 to 2 hours

First, plan your voice mail system
With Front Office, you can set up three kinds of mailboxes:

Standard mailboxes for recording incoming calls

Information-only messages for providing information to callers

Fax-back mailboxes for faxing a Mac document to the caller's fax phone number

These mailboxes can be arranged in a hierarchy to route your callers to the proper messages. At each level in the hierarchy, there's a primary announcement that tells the caller which keys to press for which options. Obviously, setting up such a system requires a little thinking.

1. Sketch the hierarchy and define the types of mailboxes. You can have up to nine mailboxes in each level of your hierarchy.

2. Assign a key code to each mailbox.

Callers get to mailboxes by pressing a single-digit code: 1 through 9. At each level in the hierarchy, you start over with 1. Decide which message gets which number at each level.

3. Compose your messages in SimpleText or a word processor.

You can type your messages in the recording window as you go, but if you have a lot of messages—or long messages—it's better to compose them ahead of time. Also, the text document can be a permanent record of your messages in case something happens to your Front Office file. Each message can be up to 480 seconds long.

Build your mailbox hierarchy

When you build your Front Office system, you're actually editing an existing system—the sample system that comes with Front Office.

1. Start Front Office and choose Edit Database from the File menu. The database is protected by a password. For the sample system that comes with Front Office, the password is demo.

2. Discard all the mailboxes and announcements except the top-level mailbox and the System mailbox.

To discard a mailbox, select it and click Discard.

3. Click Set Preferences and change the name of the system to your own company name.

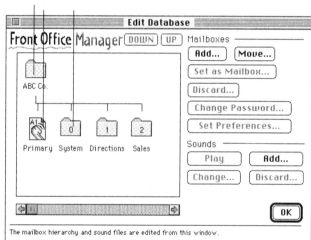

Discard all mailboxes except these

4. Select the System mailbox and click Add.

You can type a name for the new mailbox in the dialog box that opens.

5. Click Set as Mailbox and choose the type of mailbox you want to create.

6. Repeat steps 4 and 5 for each mailbox in your system.

Click the Up and Down buttons to move up or down in the hierarchy. Front Office automatically creates a place holder for your primary announcement file for each level. You can move your mailboxes around and rename them at any time. But if you've already recorded your primary announce-ments, you'll have to change them to match the new arrangement of your mailboxes.

Next, record your messages

Now you're ready to record your messages. If your Mac has an external microphone, make sure it's plugged into the microphone port and select Microphone for the Sound Input setting in the Sound control panel.

1. Select a mailbox and click Change.

A recording window opens. It has controls for recording your message and playing it back.

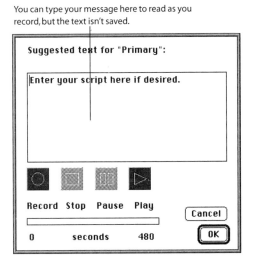

You can type your message here to read as you record, but the text isn't saved.

2. Click Record, speak your message, and click Stop when you're done.

You can click Pause if you need to stop in the middle of the message. You can also click the Playback button to listen to the message. If you don't like it, you can just click Record again and start over.

3. Click OK when you've finished the message.
4. Repeat steps 1 through 3 for each mailbox and for your primary announcement.

Remember that the primary announcement is the announcement that directs callers to press the right numbers for each of your mailboxes at the current level. Callers can always press the star key to move up the hierarchy. You may want to tell them that.

Now go online

Your system is ready to use. All you have to do is turn it on.

■ Choose Go Online from the Front Office menu.

The system is ready to take messages now. When you want to check your messages, you need to choose Go Offline.

ON THE HORIZON: Multimedia Telephones

The forces of telecommunications are blowing up a big storm these days, and when the weather settles, it's going to be harder to figure out what's a telephone, what's a computer, what's a television, and what's a meeting. Technologies from all these directions are likely to converge on the kind of multimedia conferencing that we described earlier in the chapter. It will be so easy and cheap to send images along with voice that when you don't want anyone to see you working in your pajamas, you'll transmit something like a personalized screen saver—your corporate ID in motion. Well, maybe something like that.

Your fax machine won't be left out in the cold, either. Look for new developments in 3-D fax technology. Instead of putting flat pages through a slot in a little machine, you'll pop a prototype of your revolutionary lunch pail design in something that looks like a microwave oven. Laser beams will scan it and digitize at a blinding rate of, uh, a few hours. Then the digital signals will be sent as a three-dimensional model to a computer at your tooling specialist, who'll create the tools you need to give to your manufacturer to make your lunch pail for you. But don't toss your fax machine yet. This one won't be in the affordable range for home offices for a while.

Of course, it's not exactly clear what all these home office communications devices are going to plug into. You may dial up your friendly phone lines—or an even friendlier cable line. And your animated corporate ID may actually be a Web page on the Internet with a voice link to you. But we haven't talked about the Internet yet. Maybe we should.

For more on your corporate ID, see "Jump Start" in Chapter 8, "The Marketing Plan."

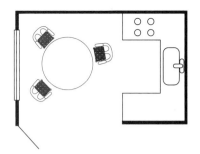

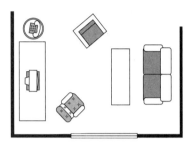

CHAPTER SIX

WEIGHING IN ON THE WEB

How to thrive on the Internet—and

take advantage of commercial and

local area networks, too

Once upon a time, long long ago, the Department of Defense decided that it would be nice to have a network of computers that could talk to each other in case the government had to conduct its business from underground bunkers scattered across the global landscape. Well, the Cold War is over, and now that network is available to all of us who want to conduct our business from comfy home offices scattered across the global landscape.

The network is, of course, the Internet.

The Internet is just a bunch of computers, all over the world, talking to other computers all over the world. There's no central Internet computer, and no one owns the Internet (although plenty of companies would like to). The network exists by virtue of a widespread agreement among lots of different groups—companies, universities, government agencies, and private individuals—to support certain kinds of communications and make certain kinds of information available in standard formats. There are committees to set and update those standards, and there are companies, such as Netscape, that are driving those committees to distraction. It's the electronic Wild West, and a lot of folks are looking to make their fortunes out there.

You may be, too. Or you may just want to take advantage of the Net's offerings as you go about your business day to day. In either case, you need a map of the territory—and some tips for getting around. That's what this chapter is.

E-mail—It beats the U.S. Mail

The Internet is, first and foremost, a way to communicate with other people. And the simplest way to do it is via e-mail.

E-mail is a way to send and get personal messages. You can send simple text messages. Or you can send messages with attachments—files that include graphics, sound, video, programs, or anything else you can put in the file. So you can send a note to a client confirming an order, or you can send a 100-page proposal with engineering drawings and photographs.

When you send e-mail, you type a quick note, an e-mail address, and a subject. You can send a file, too.

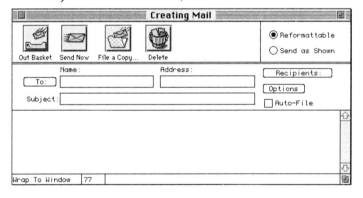

For more information about e-mail, see Step 4 under "Jump Start" in this chapter.

E-mail is virtually instantaneous. In most cases, the recipient can pick it up a few minutes after you send it. It doesn't get lost or misdelivered (except in extremely rare cases). If you misaddress it, it doesn't drop into the electronic equivalent of a dead letter box. It comes back to you, usually within a few hours. You can send the same message to one person or a thousand people for the same amount of effort and in the same amount of time. (Well, almost. You do have to add the addresses of all those people. But if you have them in an address book, you can just select them all and send the message on its way.) Automatic replying and forwarding make quick work of all your online communications.

At the moment, e-mail is informal. In most e-mail software, you can't format it. Even if you can, all the formatting goes away if you send it to someone with different software. And you don't need to spell-check it either (unless you're terribly self-conscious about your spelling). E-mail messages are quick and dirty communiqués. No one worries about grammar and other niceties.

To use e-mail, you need e-mail software. Commercial online services like America Online and CompuServe offer this software free with their service. You can also buy generic e-mail software like Claris Emailer or SnapMail2 from Casady and Greene, which work with lots of different services as well as the Internet.

Yes. Of course. You need the U.S. Mail whenever you actually need to send a piece of paper.

You need it for legal documents. You need it when you want proof that a document arrived at a certain place at a certain time. (Sometimes private services like UPS and Federal Express can meet these legal requirements.)

You also need the U.S. Mail when you want to get someone's attention. It may be hard to make an envelope stand out among a half dozen other direct mail offers. But it's a lot harder to make an online message stand out in a list of 100 messages, all with cryptic subjects.

You also need the U.S. Mail when your recipient doesn't have an e-mail address—or even a computer.

DO YOU NEED THE U.S. MAIL?

Usenet—Newsgroups with an attitude

Usenet is where you'll find newsgroups on the Internet. Newsgroups are public discussions. These discussions take place over days, months, or years. They are asynchronous: they don't happen in real time. You log on, read the new messages, leave a message or two of your own, and log off. Sometime later, you log back on and see what people have had to say about your messages. The messages may be text or binary files—graphics, video, sounds, or programs.

Newsgroups may be moderated or unmoderated. In moderated groups, a moderator reads all the messages and filters them before they're included in the discussion. The goal is to keep the discussion focused on the topic and weed out disruptive or irrelevant messages. In unmoderated groups, anything goes.

On the Internet, you can find a newsgroup on any subject you can imagine—and some that you can't. Newsgroups cover the entire gamut of topics in science, arts, politics, religion, culture, and crime. They're a vital way for people with serious interests in a subject to get up-to-date information quickly. They're also a place for the casual and criminal to congregate. Newsgroups are the wildest of the Wild West, and plenty of people who have nowhere else to wreak havoc spend their time here.

A news group is a list of messages that you can read and respond to.

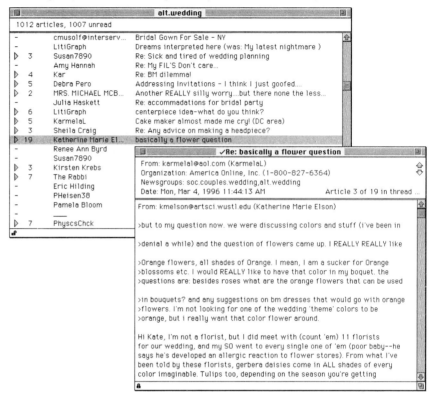

Or you can start your own topic—called a *thread*.

As a businessperson, you want the expertise and marketing edge you can gain from newsgroups. They're a direct link to people who might be interested in your products and services. They're a source of marketing information about those people. They're also a great source for technical and business information of all kinds.

If you're buying new equipment, you're sure to find a group of experts discussing the models you're considering.

If you're having trouble with your Mac or its software, you can get answers to your questions.

You can find groups of special interest to small business, too. For example, if you want to find out about the world of import/export businesses, check out `alt.biz.import-export` or `biz.marketplace.international`.

Looking for help on the Internet? Drop in on some of these newsgroups:

For Apple support

```
comp.sys.mac
comp.sys.mac.comm
comp.sys.mac.hardware
comp.sys.mac.apps
```

For computer consultants

```
alt.computer.consultants
```

For desktop publishing

```
comp.text.desktop
alt.design.graphics
```

For multimedia

```
comp.multimedia
```

For home office and small-business topics

```
alt.business.home.pc
misc.entrepreneurs
```

NOTEWORTHY NEWSGROUPS

There are thousands and thousands of newsgroups on the Internet. New groups form hourly. To join one, all you need is a general-purpose Web browser (see below) or a newsgroup reader, like NewsWatcher. It lists the newsgroups in a folder-like hierarchy and can search for topics in the text of the newsgroup transcripts. When you select a newsgroup, it displays a list of messages for the past several days or weeks, depending on how many messages pile up each day.

Like most cultures, the Internet has a number of unspoken rules of good behavior. If you're new to newsgroups, here are a couple of guidelines:

■ When you join a newsgroup, don't start yakking right away. It's just like any group discussion. You probably don't just walk into a room full of people and start talking without taking time to find out what the group is discussing and what you can best contribute. It's the same online. Read for a while before you start sending messages

■ If you have a question, read the earlier messages to see if someone else has asked it. Most expert participants in groups are happy to share their knowledge with newcomers, but they get tired of answering the same questions over and over. So check to make sure someone hasn't just asked your question.

NEWSGROUP NETIQUETTE

Real-time chats—Almost like being there

Real-time chats are like newsgroups with one important distinction—they happen in real time. People agree to meet on an Internet Relay Channel (IRC) at a particular time to discuss a particular topic. After that, it's pretty much a free-for-all.

Some people love chats, and some people hate them. The pace is maddeningly slow—10 characters per second (or your typing speed, whichever is slowest)—and hectic at the same time. You wait and wait for messages to appear, and then by the time you've composed your response, you find that the group has moved on to another subject. If you like your conversations tidy and well ordered, this is not the place for you. If you like the feeling of being in a room with a lot of people at the same time all moving in slow motion, this is as close as you'll get on the Internet.

(Don't imagine, however, that just because you've got a bunch of people together in an electronic room, you can get them to make some big important decisions. IRC rooms are not conference rooms, and it's nearly impossible to bring a group of chatters to consensus on just about anything.)

Digital libraries—Online access to documents and software

Digital libraries, like their real-world counterparts, are repositories of information. They come in two varieties:

- File transfer protocol (FTP) sites
- Gopher sites

These sites are actually computers that store files—text and binary files that someone else created and that you can get. This is where you go when you need software updates. It's where to look for shareware and freeware, as well as thousands of documents on topics like how Arctic weather patterns affect crop exports in Southeast Asia.

FTP and gopher sites store and retrieve files differently. So you need different software applications to use them. For example, Peter Lewis's Anarchy is a popular shareware program for trudging around FTP sites. TurboGopher is a good choice for gopher sites. You can also use Web browsers (see below) to get files from FTP sites.

World Wide Web—A new way to see the world

The World Wide Web started out as a modern, slicked-up digital library. Two things make it more than that:

It's a universal multimedia environment. With it, you can create pages of graphics and text, with sound and video—and others can view them more or less the way you created them on any computer anywhere on the Internet, anywhere in the world.

You can use a program like Anarchy to view the contents
of an FTP site.

Name	Size	Date	Zone	Machine	Pa
📁 text	–	3/3/96	1	ftp.amug.org	
📁 vir	–	3/3/96	1	ftp.amug.org	
📁 _Anti-Virus	–	7/6/95	1	ftp.amug.org	
📁 _Application	–	7/6/95	1	ftp.amug.org	
📁 _Art_&_Info	–	2/21/96	1	ftp.amug.org	
📁 _Communication	–	7/6/95	1	ftp.amug.org	
📁 _Compress_&_Translate	–	2/21/96	1	ftp.amug.org	
📁 _Configuration	–	7/6/95	1	ftp.amug.org	
📁 _Data_Management	–	10/26/95	1	ftp.amug.org	
📁 _Development	–	7/6/95	1	ftp.amug.org	
📁 _Disk_&_File	–	2/21/96	1	ftp.amug.org	
📁 _Education	–	10/28/95	1	ftp.amug.org	
📁 _Font	–	7/6/95	1	ftp.amug.org	
📁 _Game	–	7/6/95	1	ftp.amug.org	
📁 _Graphic_&_Sound_Tool	–	2/21/96	1	ftp.amug.org	
📁 _Info-Mac_Help	–	7/6/95	1	ftp.amug.org	
📁 _Information	–	7/6/95	1	ftp.amug.org	
📁 _Newton	–	7/6/95	1	ftp.amug.org	
📁 _Periodical	–	7/6/95	1	ftp.amug.org	
📁 _Printing	–	7/6/95	1	ftp.amug.org	
📁 _Recent	–	7/6/95	1	ftp.amug.org	
📁 _Science_&_Math	–	2/21/96	1	ftp.amug.org	
📁 _Text_Processing	–	7/6/95	1	ftp.amug.org	
📁 _User_Interface	–	7/6/95	1	ftp.amug.org	

It's a hypermedia environment. You can turn any text or graphic into a link to some other page that you yourself create—or to any other site on the Web.

These two features—multimedia and hypermedia—have changed the Internet from an arcane landscape into a playground for all the people who brought you mass media television and radio: big corporations, advertising companies, and creative professionals. But this playground is also accessible to small companies with their own marketing savvy and creativity.

For ways to make the World Wide Web part of your marketing plan, see Chapter 8.

One of the technologies that's responsible for this transformation is a markup language called HTML (hypertext markup language). HTML is a standard way to code text, graphics, and other media—a standard that makes it possible for any HTML reader to display the information pretty much the way you intended, on any computer on the Net.

Not exactly, though. The HTML reader—aka the *Web browser*—may interpret the code using its own fonts, substituting black and white if it doesn't support color, or ignoring pictures if it can't display graphics. You don't have complete control, but new extensions to HTML promise more in the future.

For details on setting up your own Web site and Web pages, see "Power Play" in this chapter.

Fortunately, you don't have to know a lot about HTML to browse Web pages or to create your own. With Macintosh software like Adobe PageMill, you can use the familiar Mac tools to build pages. The software does all the encoding for you. You also need access to an Internet computer. You can buy this access from an Internet service provider.

You can't enter the world of network communications without learning two new words: *client* and *server*. These are relationship words. Like husband and wife. Or parent and child. Or buyer and seller.

In this case, the client is your computer. It's the client of a network service—either a commercial online service or an Internet service provider. To use the service, you need client software that runs on your computer.

The server is the particular computer—or more accurately, its software—that you connect to when you use a network service. In fact, you may connect to several different servers—one for your e-mail, another for newsgroups, a third for your Web site. And of course, as you surf the net, you're actually being connected automatically to lots of different servers, all through your main server.

Telnet—Getting dumb

If you really want to get into the belly of the beast, Telnet can take you there. Telnet is a way to talk directly to any remote computer via a phone line.

Why would you want to do this? Well, you might want to change your e-mail password, for example. To do so, you might need to log into the computer where you have your Internet account and use the UNIX `passwd` command.

Or perhaps you consult with big companies who want you to have access to some proprietary software running on their corporate computers.

With Telnet, you turn your computer into a *dumb terminal* to log onto another computer on the Internet. In this terminal mode, you have to speak to the computer in its own language—which may be UNIX, DOS, or some other command-based operating system. Of course, the remote computer could be a Mac, too. Lots of Internet machines are, in fact, Macintosh computers.

You need terminal software to use Telnet. Some of these programs are avail-

Lots of folks are rushing to get their own Web sites. And with good reason. It's a fine way to build a presence in a community that has millions of citizens. However, a Web site isn't the right solution for everyone. You can have an e-mail account on the Internet without a Web site. You can participate in newsgroups without a Web site. You can browse other Web sites without your own.

So when do you really need your own Web site? Here are the deciding factors:

- You want to build name recognition for yourself or your company.
- You have information you want to share.
- It's easy to convey the information in a combination of text and graphics.
- The people you want to share it with have easy access to the Web.
- It's more cost-effective to pay $30 a month for online advertising than it would be to print the same information and deliver it into the hands of the same people. (Don't forget to include the setup costs for your Web page—your own time or someone else's.)

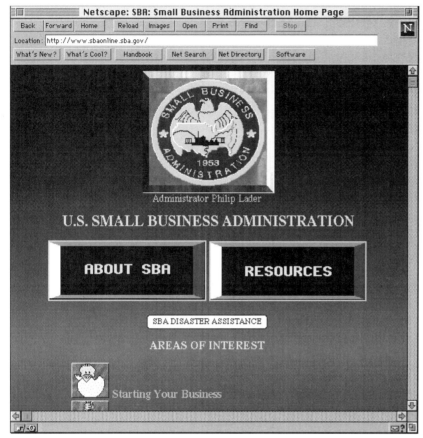

With the World Wide Web, sleek multimedia web pages are a nicer way to get your daily dose of data.

able in Internet starter kits. You can also get them for free at FTP or gopher sites on the Net. For example, you can get tn3270 at:

    http://ftp.uniuie.ac.at/mac/tn3270

or NCSA Telnet at:

    ftp://ftp.ncsa.uiue.edu/telnet/mac.

You also need permission to access the remote computer, of course. This is usually arranged by a system administrator for that computer.

Ready, set, surf...

The Internet is the venue of the moment—with megabytes of mystique and mania but also lots of just plain, down-to-earth good information. You should take advantage of it. Susie Hu, the Delacruzes, and Sam Post all have different networking needs and strategies, so take a look at their solutions. Then, if you're new to network communication, use the steps in this chapter to get you connected. And if you're already on the Internet, you just might find a few tips that will turn you into a real hot-dog.

SUSIE HU, P. I.   THE CASE OF THE LOFTY GOAL

The truth is out there. You just have to have the tools to find it. Of course, knowing where to look is useful, too.

Susie Hu knows where to look.

On the commercial networks, she can get credit reports, inquire about the reputations of businesses and organizations, track down family histories, and even keep up-to-date with home office news.

She can also lurk around newsgroups on every subject from antiques to aberrations, watching who shows up and what they talk about.

The online services come with their own user-friendly client software. For the Internet, Susie needs a Web browser that can also read newsgroups and access FTP sites.

THE TOOLS

AOL software
CompuServe software
Netscape Navigator

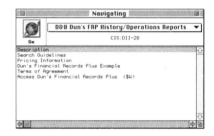

User-friendly client software makes CompuServe easy and economical to use. Susie can buy an online credit report, for example, through Dun and Bradstreet.

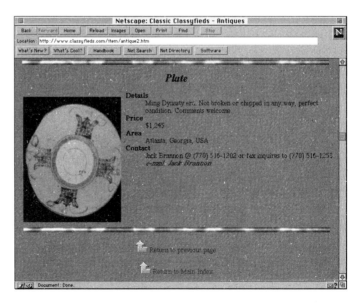

With an Internet account, Susie can use Netscape Navigator to search Web sites—repositories for all kinds of obscure facts on even more obscure topics.

S O L U T I O N S

With four people working in one home, the Delacruzes need a way to share files among their four Macs. They also need to share printers—without having to run from attic to garage or vice versa, with disks in hand, every time they want to print.

The solution? A local area network.

It was an easy solution because they used Farallon connectors that plugged right into their existing phone wiring, so they didn't have to rewire their house.

Once the wires were in place, Dave took on the role of network manager. He used the Mac's built-in file-sharing software to create user profiles on each computer. As new projects come in, he can create project folders that everyone in the group can share. Darcy can put art files in the folders for the others to import into their page-layout documents—but then she grants read-only access, so they can't accidentally alter her work.

Beyond their local area network, the Delacruzes use proprietary software for direct computer-to-computer file exchanges with service bureaus and printers. They use CompuServe for other online communication.

THE TOOLS

System 7
Farallon cables and connectors
CompuServe MacCIM

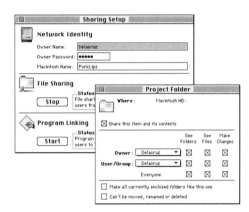

With System 7's built-in file sharing, the Delacruz team can all have access to a project folder, regardless of which computer it's actually on.

Each file has an owner, and the owner can make the file available for viewing or changing or both.

MacCIM is CompuServe's friendly front end to an information service that used to be a little unfriendly to all but the initiated.

S O L U T I O N S

SAM POST CYBERWORK

Sam Post calls his home office his second office. His Web site is his main office.

From his Web site, Sam can advertise his home-plans-on-a-disk and take orders for catalogs and planning kits. Using his Web browser, he can drop in on newsgroups like `misc.consumers.house` and `misc.handicap` to find out what's on the minds of potential customers and to contribute his own expertise—a community service he's happy to offer.

Sam also spends time on CompuServe and America Online because he knows that a lot of people who are intimidated by the vastness of the Internet like the small-town feel of these online services. He wants to know these people, too.

Of course, nobody invests in house plans on the basis of a Web page. That takes a lot of personal consultation. Sam finds that e-mail is a great way to give people individualized attention without being tied to his phone all day. He can also use e-mail to stay in touch with customers after the sale—which provides feedback for future designs.

THE TOOLS

America Online software
CompuServe MacCIM
Netscape Navigator
Anarchy
NewsWatcher
TurboGopher
Claris Emailer

Sam uses Claris Emailer to send messages to contacts and customers on the commercial online services as well as the Internet.

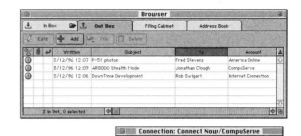

Emailer automatically connects to each network in turn, checks for mail, and puts it in Sam's in-box.

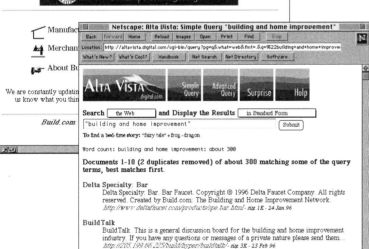

With Navigator, Sam can use many of Internet's several search engines to find Web pages and newsgroups of interest to his trade.

The Alta Vista search engine finds Web pages and newsgroups.

JUMP START: Plugging Into the Network

Ready to surf? Here are the basics you need to get you on the data waves.

STEP 1: GET A MODEM

The first thing you need is a good modem. Modems can be a little tricky. They use communications protocols that make the diplomatic service look like a piece of cake. If everything goes right, you don't need to know those protocols. But if troubles flare up, you're going to find yourself in a communications nowhere land.

You can do several things to avoid these troubles:

Get a fast, Hayes-compatible modem. Fast is 14.4 Kbps, 28.8 Kbps, or 33.6 Kbps. You want a modem for two reasons. First, you may be paying for connect time—the slower the modem, the longer the connect time. Second, you need the bandwidth. Web pages are thick with graphics that take a long time to transmit under the best conditions and are torturous with a modem that's slower than 14.4Kbps. You also need speed for many of the hot new Web features—like real-time audio, for example.

Get a money-back guarantee. Then test your modem with your communications software as soon as you get it home. (Your communications software includes your e-mail software, your Web browser, and other tools for navigating the Internet. Check out your financial software, too, if you plan to pay bills electronically.) Most of this software comes with templates that preconfigure things for your modem. They set all the communications settings for you. You just select the right template for your modem and everything works the first time. If it doesn't work the first time, something is probably wrong with your template. You'll need to contact the modem manufacturer and work out the details. In the end, you may need to get a different modem. That's why you need the money-back guarantee.

Make sure you have a modem cable. Most modems come with a special cable. This cable solves a problem with the serial connector on your Macintosh and the connector on your modem. Both of these connectors use two pins for connecting. Pin 1 sends information. Pin 2 receives information. But they can't communicate with each other if both the modem and the Mac are sending information out from pin 1. The modem cable switches wires so the data sent on pin 1 of the modem goes into pin 2 of the Macintosh . If your modem doesn't come with this kind of cable, you need a *null modem connector* with a serial cable, which you can get from a computer or electronics store.

You plug your modem into the serial port. Once you're plugged in, you have to set up the software to recognize the modem—usually with a Settings command. Then you're ready to go.

If you have an ISDN line, you need a special modem. For details, see "Upsizing" in Chapter 5, "Tangle-Free Telephony."

Tip: People measure the speed of a modem in bits per second—sometimes called baud rate. A 14.4-Kbps modem sends 14.4 kilobits of information per second.

If you're having problems with your modem, see Chapter 11, "Troubleshooting," for some suggestions.

You need to set the type of modem, its speed, and a local telephone access number for all applications that use your modem.

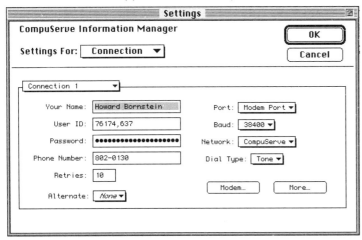

This is the MacCIM Settings window.

When you connect to the Internet or a commercial online service, you usually dial a local phone number. It connects you to a local computer that provides the access to other computers on the network. So you only pay a local telephone charge.

Of course, if you're off in some hamlet in the Himalayas, or even some tucked-away town in the U.S., the nearest local access computer may not be so local. Some Internet service providers have widespread coverage. Others serve only a limited geographical area.

Check the phone access before you sign up with a service. If you travel with your computer, make sure your provider can give you good phone access at all your usual destinations.

WORLDWIDE ACCESS AT LOCAL PHONE RATES

STEP 2: GET AN ACCOUNT

There are two ways to get access to the Internet: commercial online services and Internet service providers.

Commercial services like America Online and CompuServe provide many of the same services as the Internet on their own computers: e-mail, discussion groups, chats, and information resources. (These may have different names on different services.) They also provide gateways to the Internet, with their own browsers. Through this gateway, you can access many but not all Internet services. None of the commercial services support Telnet, and all of them censor newsgroups that they deem inappropriate.

When you join a commercial service, you get an account number, a user name, an e-mail address, and a password. You also get integrated software for all your online activities—from reading and sending mail to surfing the Net.

You usually pay a monthly fee of $10 to $30, for which you get several hours of connect time. If you go over your limit, you pay a per-minute charge.

Signing up is easy. Commercial services will gladly send you their software for free. When you install it, it automatically sets up your account—if your modem is switched on and working. The only thing you need is a major credit card.

Commercial services provide a user-friendly interface to the world of electronic communication.

Internet service providers (ISPs) don't offer their own network services. They offer you access to the Internet from their computers. They may also offer you storage space on their computers—which you need if you want to set up your own Web site with Web pages that others can browse. With ISPs, you usually don't get integrated software. You use software of your own choosing—usually several different applications.

Most ISPs offer both personal and business accounts. **Personal accounts** give you access to the Net but provide limited support for your own Web page—or none at all. **Business accounts** provide more Web page support, more storage space, and more support for traffic to your Web site. They also cost more than personal accounts.

ISPs charge from $20 to $500 per month for their services. You can get a flat fee for unlimited use or choose an hourly rate based on connect time. You can get more or less storage space on the computer. Service providers will also help you set up your Web page for fees that range from nothing to thousands of dollars. If your Web site becomes tremendously popular, they'll raise your monthly fee because each *hit*—each time someone accesses your page—uses computer resources.

When you sign up with an ISP, you get

- an account name
- a password
- the name of your server (the ISP computer where your account is set up)
- the name of the mail server (the ISP computer that handles mail)
- the name of the news server (the ISP computer that handles news-groups)

You need to plug this information into all your communications software. To simplify your life, you can get Peter Lewis's InternetConfig System. This program is a central repository for your Internet account information. You can get ICS software from any standard shareware source. It includes the ICS application and an InternetConfig extension, which you install in your Extensions folder. You use the application to change the settings in the extension. Then when you install a new ICS-compatible communications program, it automatically checks the ICS and plugs in the settings for you.

Commercial online services and ISPs both have advantages and disadvantages. Here's a summary:

ONLINE SERVICES	INTERNET SERVICE PROVIDERS
ADVANTAGES	**ADVANTAGES**
■ One software package does everything.	■ Complete access to all Internet services and newsgroups
■ Easy installation and setup	■ Robust Web page support
■ Easy to use	■ Flexible online storage options
■ Hundreds of access numbers worldwide	
■ Special proprietary services	**DISADVANTAGES**
	■ No integrated software—you have to learn several applications.
DISADVANTAGES	■ Fewer access sites, sometimes limited to a local area
■ Limited online storage and Web page support	■ Setup requires special software and special skills.
■ Restricted access to newsgroups	
■ Not all Internet services are available.	

If you want the simplest way to get started without making a big commitment, start with an online service. Most services have free trial periods, so you can test the waters before you take the plunge.

If you know you need a Web page or if you're just naturally adventuresome, get an ISP from the start. It's not *that* much harder.

ONLINE SERVICE OR ISP—WHICH IS BEST?

PPP is one of two network communications protocols. The other is SLIP. Some service providers may require SLIP instead of PPP—and can usually provide the software.

You also need two special communications tools: MacTCP and ConfigPPP. MacTCP is a control panel that comes with your Mac. ConfigPPP is a control panel that comes with most Internet Starter kits. Or you can get it from `www.jumbo.com/util/mac/cdev/`. Like all control panels, it goes in the Control Panels folder in your System folder.

You have lots of ISPs choose from—and some are better than others. Here's a checklist to evaluate your candidates:

❑ **Complete Internet access**

Some ISPs only provide Telnet access. Make sure you get an ISP that supports all the Internet capabilities—Web sites, FTP sites, newsgroups, and e-mail.

❑ **Local telephone numbers**

If you travel, use a national ISP like NetCom that has nationwide access. If you don't travel, make sure your ISP provides a local phone number for your area.

❑ **Storage and throughput**

If you're going to have a Web page or set up an FTP site, you'll need storage space on the ISP's computer. If you want people to visit your Web site, you want your ISP to have enough throughput power. (If the traffic on their computer is too heavy to handle, people simply won't be able to get to your site.)

❑ **Customer support**

Your ISP should provide phone and e-mail support. The Internet is not plug-and-play. You're likely to encounter problems. Some of these will be problems on your Mac. Some of them will be problems with the provider's computer. You need someone to help you sort out which is which.

❑ **Stability**

Everyone is rushing to get into the ISP business, and some of the entries are a little shaky. Ask for a free trial period—a week or so to test the ISP's computer and commitment to service. It may take a couple of tries to find a service you can count on.

❑ **Price**

Prices range wildly, and the extra services don't always justify the extra cost. Make a list of the services you need and shop around for the best price.

Not sure where to begin looking for ISPs? Ask a friend. Check with local user groups. Check `http://www.thelist.com` for an online list. Read the ads in local computer magazines such as *Computer Currents* or *MicroTimes*. Then call and talk to the company representatives.

BEFORE YOU SIGN UP WITH AN ISP

STEP 3: GET A BROWSER

Your browser is your surfboard. You use it to ride from Web page to Web page—clicking hot links to get you there.

Browsers interpret HTML. But each browser interprets a little differently. That's why hot text may be blue in one browser and green in another. Or why the headlines in different browsers appear in different fonts. Also, some browsers can interpret more of the formatting instructions than others. Some only interpret text, while others can interpret both text and graphics. If you have a browser that only interprets text, you won't get to see all the stunning graphics on the Web.

Some browsers only display Web pages. Some can do other tricks, too—from checking your e-mail to joining the discussion in a newsgroup and downloading software from FTP sites. The trend is toward complete Internet access.

Each commercial online service has its own browser built into its integrated software. If you're a member of a service, you use their browser. No choices.

If you're online with an ISP, you can choose your own browser. Netscape Navigator has become a de facto standard. About three-quarters of all Web users swear by it. Other contenders are NCSA Mosaic and Microsoft's Internet Explorer. While these are all commercial products, you can usually get them for next to nothing. Navigator officially sells for $45, but Netscape offers it free of charge to individuals and students for a 90-day test period. Navigator shows up in lots of Internet starter kits, too. But if you want technical support, you have to pay the bucks.

Once you're up on your browser, you've got several ways to ride it. You can start by typing a Web address if you know it. After that, you just start clicking.

As you can imagine, it's easy to get lost in cyberspace. Bookmarks and history windows are helpful tools for reorienting yourself quickly. You can set a bookmark for any Web page you want to visit again. For example, you might want to set a bookmark for the Apple Web page so you can get to tech support in a hurry when you need to. Or if you're devoted to Photoshop plug-ins, you might need a bookmark for the MetaTools page.

Setting bookmarks is easy. You usually just go to the Web page and choose a bookmark command in your browser. You can organize bookmarks in hierarchies, too, so you can group all your software support sites in one group, all your business leads in another group, and your favorite TV show pages in another.

Bookmarks getting out of hand? See "URL managers" under "Upsizing" in this chapter.

STEP 4: GET YOUR MAIL

Okay, now you're ready to get down to the day-to-day business of business communications. You're ready to get your e-mail—and send some.

The mechanics of e-mail vary from program to program, but the basics are the same. To send mail, you create a new message, give it a subject, address it to one or more people, and send it off. You can usually send it

Click a button to go backward or forward through the pages you've
already looked at.

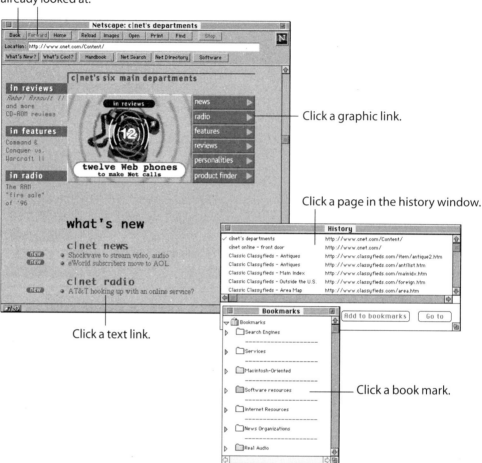

Click a graphic link.

Click a page in the history window.

Click a text link.

Click a book mark.

immediately, if you're connected to the network. Or you can put it in an outbox and mail it later—along with a dozen other messages.

To get mail, you just connect to your service. Sometimes you need a Get
Mail command. Sometimes your messages just show up as soon as you connect—in a list of topics, with the sender's name. You can open the messages
immediately or save them to read later. (Some programs save them to your
disk automatically when you get your mail. Others don't.)

Those are the basics. But you can go further. You can be efficient about it.
Here are some hints:

Set up address books. Most programs have address books where you can
add names and e-mail addresses of all your correspondents. When you want
to address a message, you just open the address book and click the right
address. You can usually select more than one name in the address book to

For more information about
e-mail lists and marketing
strategies, see "Mailing List
Know-How" in Chapter 8,
"The Marketing Plan."

As smart as your browser is, it can't find a Web page if you don't know its address (or have a hot link to it). So you need a search engine—software that can search the contents of all the Web pages on the Net for any keyword you choose.

Search engines abound. They're free. They're available on Web pages. You just go to the Web page, type your keyword, wait a little...er, wait a while...and presto! A long list of Web sites that may be of interest to you. Usually, the lists are arranged so that the first sites in the list are the most likely to have the information you're looking for. Some search engines let you refine your search with multiple keywords, too.

Of course, you need to know where to find the search engines. Here's a good starting list:

Alta Vista	`http://altavista.digital.com/`
Excite	`http://www.excite.com/`
Lycos	`http://www.lycos.com/`
Web Crawler	`http://www.webcrawler/com/`
Yahoo	`http://www.yahoo.com/`

Searching for newsgroups? Try Deja News at `http://www:dejanews.com` You can also use Alta Vista to search for newsgroups.

Search engines work in different ways. So they don't all produce the same results. If you don't find what you're looking for with one, try another.

HOW TO FIND WHAT YOU'RE LOOKING FOR

send the message to several people. You can select all the names, in fact. You may also be able to set up more than one address book—for personal and business contacts, for example, or for special online mailing lists.

Set up groups. Groups are another way to create online mailing lists. You give the group a name and enter all the addresses you want to include in the group. Then you write your message, address it to the group, and everyone in the group gets a copy.

Set up scheduled mail deliveries. With some software, you can schedule automatic sending and receiving. You can put all your messages in your outbox and schedule delivery at the end of the day. Or you can have your mail ready and waiting for you on your desktop when you start work in the morning. Scheduled deliveries are particularly useful if you're paying per-minute charges. The charges are usually less in off-hours (like when you're asleep).

Set up mail rules. Some e-mail software uses mail rules to make more or less intelligent decisions about what to do with your mail on your behalf. Automatic filing is a typical example—you just set up a rule to file all the e-mail messages from your accountant in your Trouble folder. Or you can use rules to automatically forward messages—for example, to forward all messages from certain clients to your assistants who work in home offices of their own. If you go out of town, set up a rule to reply automatically to all your incoming messages, letting your contacts know that you're away and that you'll give them the attention they deserve when you return.

**MANAGING
MULTIPLE
E-MAIL
ACCOUNTS**

If you have several e-mail accounts—for example, if you get e-mail on CompuServe, America Online, and the Internet—you have to check your mail in three places and use three different applications to create and send messages. Not fun.

The solution is a generic e-mail application, like Claris Emailer. This program gives you one-stop mail service. It automatically connects to all your accounts and gathers up all your mail, displaying it in one in-box. It can also send your mail via any network. You just include the network-of-choice in the address.

Emailer also streamlines e-mail management with features like scheduled deliveries, mail rules, address books, and groups. You can use it to set up an e-mail filing cabinet, too, with different folders for different subjects. It will even check the addresses or subjects and automatically file your messages as they come in.

UPSIZING: Now Entering Cyberspace

The Internet is vast, and if you do more than send a little e-mail, you soon find your network expanding. It's inevitable. It's like exploring the universe. Once you start, you can't stop at the moon. Here are some tips as you expand your horizons in cyberspace.

URL management—Or, where did I see that?

You've been around a bit. You use the jargon now. URL. It means *uniform resource locator*—hacker-speak for a way to find something on the Internet. Every Web page has a URL. So do newsgroups, FTP sites, and gopher sites. Even e-mail accounts have URLs.

Your browser's bookmarks use the URLs to take you back to your favorite Web pages. But after a few weeks or months on the Internet, your bookmarks are likely to need bookmarks. When you reach that point, you're ready for a URL manager, like CyberFinder from Aladdin Systems or WebArranger from CE Software.

URL managers integrate the world of the Web into your desktop. CyberFinder, for example, creates folders that look and act like your Finder folders. You can drag things directly from a Web page in your browser to a folder on your desktop—things like the URLs for all the airlines you fly, for support newsgroups for all your major software and hardware, or for your favorite search engines. (Or you can just type Option-G to grab the URL.) When you want to check an airline schedule, you just double-click the icon in your Airlines folder. CyberFinder automatically starts your Web browser and displays the page.

You can embed a URL in a document, too. For example, if you're tracking the price of produce in a spreadsheet, you can include URLs for sites that report current prices of everything from artichokes to zucchini. As you work in your spreadsheet, you can just select the URL and press Option-L to open your Web browser and check the page with today's prices.

Plug-ins—Or, how to get more from the same old browser

Your browser probably supports text and some nice graphics. But the world of information is rapidly becoming three-dimensional, with sound and motion thrown in for real-world verisimilitude. The boundaries between your computer and the computing world of the Internet are also becoming fuzzy. To keep your browser afloat in this world, you need plug-ins.

Plug-ins extend the capability of your browser (provided your browser is built for plug-ins). For example:

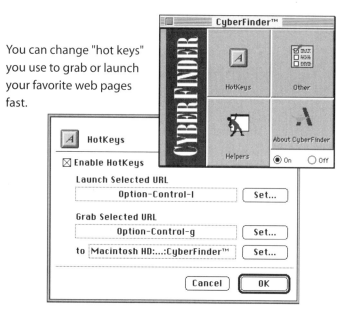

You can change "hot keys" you use to grab or launch your favorite web pages fast.

A QUICK GUIDE TO URLS

Everything on the Internet has a URL—an address with a standard format. All addresses begin by identifying the type of site:

`http:`   **for Web sites (hypertext transfer protocol)**
`ftp:`   **for FTP sites**
`news:`   **for Usenet newsgroups**
`mailto:` **for e-mail accounts**

The type of site is followed by the name of the computer where the site is stored and the path to that site. For example,

`http://www.neosoft.com/sharks/xfiles/xfiles/html/`   means that the site is a Web site located at neosoft.com/sharks/xfiles/html/

`mailto://info/best.com/`   is the URL for an e-mail account for Best.com

You need URLs not only to find things on the Net but also to help others find you. If you're building Web pages, you use URLs every time you create a link to another page, an FTP site, or even an e-mail account. (A link to your own e-mail account is a quick way to get feedback from people who visit your site.)

Real Audio, from the company of the same name, brings you FM-quality monaural sound on the Internet. You can use it to listen to prerecorded sounds on Web pages. Or you can use it open a live feed—so you can listen to the news in one window, *in real time*, while you work in another window. Some Web sites even set up walking tours, with URLs embedded in the audio stream: you go from page to page automatically as the commentator changes subjects. (Real Video is reportedly close at hand.)

ShockWave, from Macromedia, turns your browser into a screening room for Macromedia Director movies. So Web pages can include animations and sequenced slides as objects, and you can click to view them.

Virtus offers a plug-in that you can use to enter 3-D spaces created with Virtus WalkThrough Pro. So you can enter a virtual room on the Web and view it from any perspective.

Java, from Sun Microsystems, runs applets on the Net. Applets are small applications that are automatically loaded from the Net when you use them and purged when you're done.

Plug-ins are popping up everywhere. Result? More multimedia adventures on the Web and more opportunities—and challenges—if you want to reach your market through the Internet.

Want to create your own multimedia message for the Web? See Chapter 9, "The New Information Game."

Local area networks—Or, how to grow your own private network

While Web sites are replicating like rabbits, you may be doing a little growing of your own. A partner or two. An assistant or two. All using computers in your home.

Or maybe you have a couple of computers that you yourself use. One for telephone answering and the other for everything else. Or one for heavy-duty graphics rendering while you run your business from the other.

In any of these cases, a local area network can make it easier to share information and peripherals. With a local area network, you can:

- Connect two or more Macs together to send files or messages directly from one Mac to another.
- Connect all your Macs to the same printer, modem, fax modem or scanner to provide convenient access for all of them. It's cheaper than buying a printer for every Mac in your home.
- Set up file sharing to give everyone on your network access to the same set of files—for example, if everyone needs to add their own data to a spreadsheet or report.

To set up a local area network, you need hardware—cables and connectors—as well as software for file sharing. The simplest way to connect your Macs is with LocalTalk or PhoneNet cables and connectors that you plug into the AppleTalk port. System 7 comes with built-in file sharing that's quite effective for small networks with an occasional need to share files.

To start file sharing, you need to make sure you have the Network Extension in your Extensions folder. (It comes with System 7.) Then you set up each Mac with the Sharing Setup control panel. You use the Users & Groups control panel to create user profiles that determine who can access the files on each computer. Finally, you select the folder you want to share and use the

For a good overview of file sharing via System 7, see *The System 7 Book* by Craig Danuloff.

Sharing command in the Finder's File menu to make it available—for viewing or changing or both. You can share up to 10 folders on any Mac. You can also share an entire volume (which may be your entire hard disk or a partition of it).

For most home offices, this built-in file sharing is more than adequate. However, if you need to share a lot of files often, or if you have significant security issues, you may need to dedicate a Mac as your server—the computer that serves your network. The main problem with file sharing is performance. Your Mac slows down when someone else is accessing your files. A dedicated Mac solves this problem. If you decide to go this route, you'll want Apple's professional networking software, AppleShare, to manage your network.

POWER PLAY: Building Your Own Web Page

So you want to build your own Web page. It's not as hard as you might think—provided you have an Internet account and the right tools. Assembling these tools is your biggest job. Your next-biggest job is designing your Web pages. But once you've got the tools and the content, it doesn't take a rocket scientist to get online. The actual procedure differs slightly for different Internet service providers, but here are the basics:

What you need
- An ISP Internet account
- MacTCP control panel
- ConfigPPP control panel
- InternetConfig System
- A Web browser
- Adobe PageMill
- Dartmouth's Fetch file-transfer software
- Your text and graphics files
- Time: 30 minutes to several days

First, set up your account
Let's say you've already got your account. You found an ISP that offers Web page support with at least a megabyte of space on one of their computers. You've got your user name, password, and the name and number of the ISP's account server, newsgroup server, and e-mail server. Do this:

1. Enter your MacTCP settings.

Open the MacTCP control panel, select PPP, type the Internet address for your server, and click More.

Select PPP if you're using the PPP protocol. ———

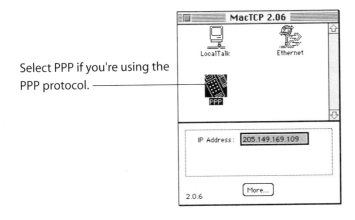

A dialog box opens. Fill in the settings according to the instructions you got from your ISP, and click OK.

```
┌─ Obtain Address: ──┐ ┌──────────── IP Address: ────────────┐
│  ● Manually        │ │ Class:[ C ]  Address: 205.149.169.109│
│  ○ Server          │ │     Subnet Mask: 255.255.255.0       │
│  ○ Dynamically     │ │ [▯▯▯▯▯▯▯▯▯▯▯▯▯▯▯▯▯▯▯▯▯Y▯▯▯▯▯▯]        │
│                    │ │         Net | Subnet | Node          │
│                    │ │  Bits:  24      0       8            │
│                    │ │  Net:  [13473193]       □ Lock       │
│                    │ │  Subnet: [0]            □ Lock       │
┌─Routing Information:┐│  Node:   [109]          □ Lock       │
│ Gateway Address:   ││└─────────────────────────────────────┘
│ [204.156.128.1]    │┌── Domain Name Server Information: ───┐
└────────────────────┘│  Domain        IP Address  Default  │
                       │[best.com    ][204.156.128.1 ] ●  ⇧ │
  ┌────┐  ┌────────┐   │[.           ][204.156.128.1 ] ○    │
  │ OK │  │ Cancel │   │[            ][             ] ○  ⇩ │
  └────┘  └────────┘   └─────────────────────────────────────┘
```

2. Enter your MacPPP settings.

Open the ConfigPPP control panel. Again, use the instructions you get from your ISP to create your logon script, enter basic information about your modem, and perform some sort of witchcraft that will make your Mac talk politely to the server and vice versa. (This will take you through about five dialog boxes.)

Your ISP should give you instructions for choosing these settings.

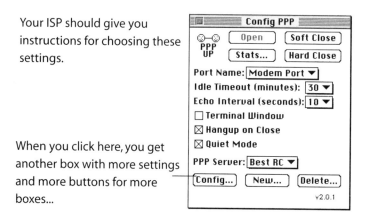

When you click here, you get another box with more settings and more buttons for more boxes...

3. Set up your InternetConfig System.

If you don't have the ICS, you can enter these settings directly in your browser or other communications software. The first time you open the browser, it will try to talk to the network and fail. Then you can use the appropriate settings commands to enter the settings.

4. Open your browser.

If it doesn't work, don't be surprised. Take advantage of your one-week free trial period to check out your ISP's technical support service.

Now create your Web pages

You have lots of decisions to make. How many pages will you have? What will go on each page? Will you use the same graphic header on each page, or change headers from page to page? Will you include buttons? How will you link from page to page?

Before you start, sketch your pages on paper to make sure you know the answers to all those questions. Then, follow these steps:

1. Create the text and graphics you need in your standard word processing and graphics programs.

Don't bother to format your text in your word processor. You'll lose it all when you import to PageMill. You can also create the text directly in PageMill, if you prefer.

Save your graphics in PICT, GIF, or JPEG format. Browsers only read GIF and JPEG. But PageMill automatically converts PICT files to GIF or JPEG. Put all your graphics in one folder. *Name them with simple names with no spaces—you can use the underscore character for spaces.*

(PageMill can convert white backgrounds to transparent backgrounds when you import a graphic—so there's no ugly white square around your graphic.)

2. Start PageMill and choose New Page to create your first Web page.

Each page is a separate file. Type a title for the page. The title appears in the browser window when people visit your web page.

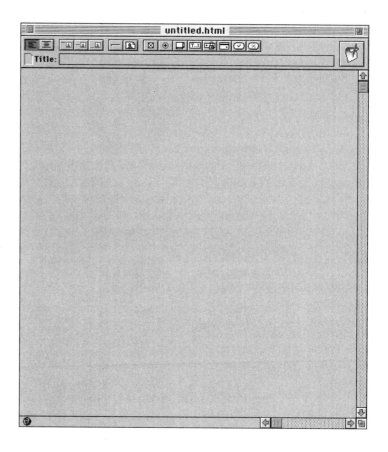

3. Put your text and graphics on the page.

PageMill works like a word processing program. The cursor starts out at the top of the page. You can insert graphics or text at the cursor.

To insert text, you can type directly or copy and paste from your word processor.

To insert graphics, you can copy and paste a graphic, drag and drop a file or image, or use the Insert Image button to select a file name.

Formatting options are *very* limited.

Click here to position text graphics horizontally.

ᴵClick one of these buttons to position a line of text vertically in
relation to a graphic. (You can only have one line of text next to a
ᴵgraphic—PageMill isn't a word-wrap world yet.)

You can use these icons to create response forms on your
web page. See the PageMill documentation for details.

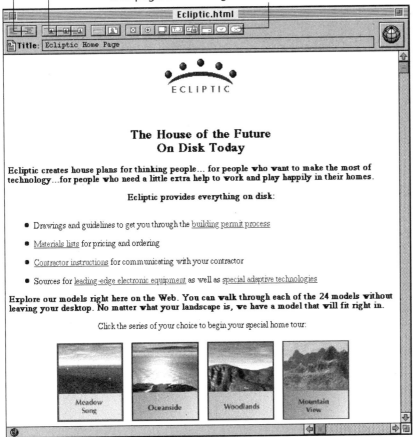

You can also choose Indent Left or Indent Right from the Format menu to
move things five spaces to the left or right.

4. Choose Save As to save the page as a file.

When you save the file, give it a simple name with no spaces. PageMill
automatically adds the extension `.html`.

Repeat steps 3 through 5 for each page. Save all your pages in the same
folder.

5. Create your links.

Go to the page where you want to create a link. Select the text, graphic, or button you want to link. Go to the page you want to link to. Drag the page icon from that page back to the selected text or graphic.

Drag this icon to the selection to create a link.

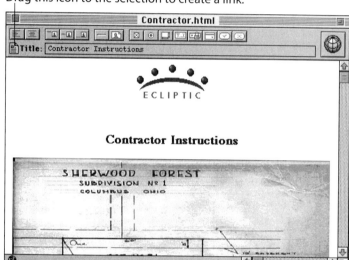

Put your pages on the Web

To put your pages on the Web you need a program called Fetch—not to be confused with Adobe's Fetch graphics database software. Fetch is available with the Apple Internet Connection Kit or from many online sources.

1. Start Fetch.

The Open Connection window appears. Your ISP will provide the information you need for this window.

2. Enter the connection information and click OK.

Fetch connects to your Internet account and opens your online directory—which is like a folder. It will probably be empty.

3. Click the binary button in the Fetch window.
4. Hold down the Option key and choose Put File.

A standard Finder dialog box opens. You can use it to go to the folder where you've saved your Web pages.

5. Select all the pages you want to put on the Web and click Open.
A box asks about the file type.

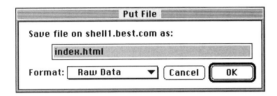

6. Choose Raw Data as the file type and click OK.

The files should now appear in your online directory window.

7. Create an online directory for your graphics.

Choose New Directory from the Directories menu. Give it the same name as the folder where you saved your graphics. Follow steps 4 through 6 to put all your graphics files in the online graphics directory.

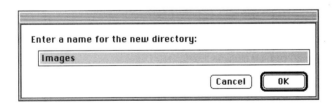

Your Web pages are now on the Internet, but the search engines won't find them if you don't *register* them. You can use Submit It! (available at www.submit-it.com/) to make your pages known to the most important search engines. Follow the instructions that come with it.

ON THE HORIZON: Web Shock

A couple of decades ago, a man named Alvin Toffler wrote a book called *Future Shock*. The main premise of the book was that things were going to change very fast, and the population would be reduced to idiots in the wings of a frightening theater production, watching the show go on without a director. (A slight paraphrase.)

Well, now we have Web Shock. The Web has so changed the world of information technology that even the technologists don't know which direction it's going to turn next. The business folks are even more in a spin. It's quite amazing to sit in the middle of Silicon Valley and hear executives of big computer companies admit that information is the hottest commodity around these days, and they don't know how to make money on the Internet.

Fortunately, you're not a big computer company. You don't have to worry about controlling the channel. You just need to take advantage of it. Of course, you have to stay on your toes to make sure that your marketing strategy can flex with changes in the medium. And you may have the feeling of spinning a bit yourself to keep up with technologies for presenting your company on the Web. For example, are you ready for VRML—the 3-D version of HTML that you'll use to create 3-D walkabout spaces on your Web page?

To keep from spinning too much, we recommend that you keep your investment in the Web and its attendant technologies low for now. If you're already a whiz at graphics and animation, go ahead and play it to the hilt on the Web. If you're not, some simple text pages will get your message across. And don't overlook the power of participation in newsgroups (especially the newsgroups on the commercial online services). They're not as flashy, but they're a great place to build customer confidence.

Of course, if you *like* feeling dizzy...

For more about how the Internet fits into your marketing strategy, see Chapter 8, "The Marketing Plan."

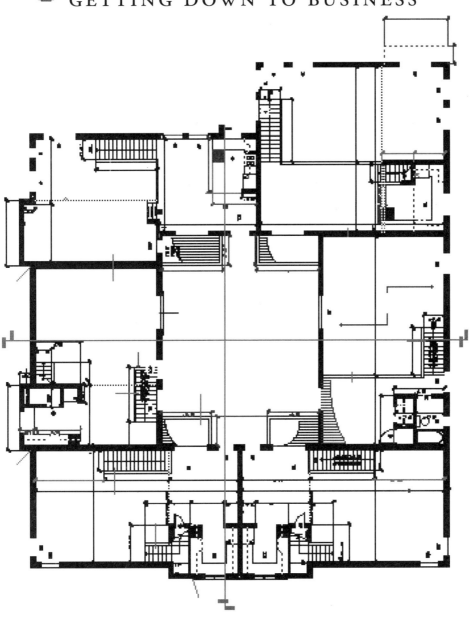

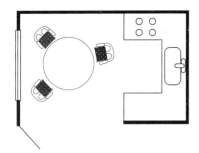

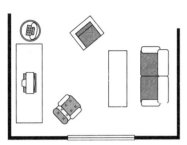

CHAPTER SEVEN

MANAGEMENT BY MAC

How to use your Macintosh to manage your days, your contacts, and your projects

This chapter is about getting organized. But don't panic. It's not about locker inspections or getting locked into schedules that will eat you alive. It's about having the confidence—and information—to relax and enjoy your work.

People have different ways of organizing themselves. Some people work best when every piece of paper is in its slot, every desktop file in its folder. Others lose their edge if they have to divide their attention between getting organized and getting work done. They're driven to produce. They can't afford to spend too much time neatening up. They get stuck, depressed, despairing if they're not moving ahead.

So getting organized may not mean getting everything spiffy and neat. If you're not a neat person, don't waste a lot of time and energy trying to become one. Find good, effective, messy solutions. Here are some of the ways your Macintosh can help.

PIMs are a great starting place when you're ready to get organized. See "Jump Start" in this chapter for details.

Personal information managers

Personal information managers (PIMs) are like pocket organizers on your computer. They include a calendar and address book—and usually much more. You can use them to schedule your days by the minute, if you want. Or you can step back and get a view of the upcoming month, quarter, or year. Just like the fancy pocket organizers, PIMs include lots of fancy forms. But unlike the pocket variety, the computer version links all the pieces together electronically.

The scenario goes something like this: You have to call your biggest distributor at the first of the month to confirm the monthly order. You plug the distributor's name into your desktop calendar. On the first day of the month, you get a reminder at 10 o'clock in the morning to call the distributor. You click the distributor's name on your calendar, and your phonebook opens to the distributor's phone number. You click the telephone icon, and your computer dials your phone. You click another button to take notes as you talk, jotting down the exact order, which is recorded as part of your contact history. You click the document you attached to the distributor's name, which happens to be your newest product price list, so you can quickly update the distributor on prices and new products as you talk. When you hang up, you click a form letter attachment, which is a template for your order confirmation. You fill in the details, you click the fax button, and your computer uses your fax modem to automatically fax the confirmation, with your custom fax cover sheet. That's it. No loose ends. On to the next business of the day.

Of course, you may not want such an intense relationship with your calendar. But if you have lots of people in your business life—or a completely intractable schedule—a PIM can clear the path through your days and your data.

Project-management tools

Project-management tools manage your schedules, too—but with a more analytical flair. These tools are milestone driven. You figure out what the main milestones are. You determine the materials, people, and money you need to get to the milestones. You also show critical dependencies between milestones. Then the program displays all this information in visual form—typically a Gannt chart or flow chart.

When you set up the tasks for a project, you choose a time scale—which may be days, weeks, or months, depending on the length and complexity of the project. This time scale is mapped onto an actual calendar. So if you estimate 15 days for a task, your software can automatically plug the dates into the calendar, skipping weekends and holidays (in case you're faithful about keeping the traditional work week at home).

If you do the same kinds of projects over and over, you can turn one of your project worksheets into a project template—with standard estimates

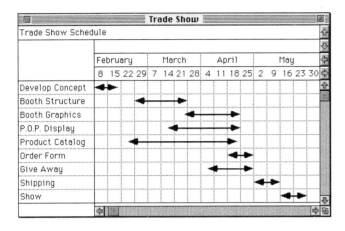

A Gantt chart shows the timeline for a project—with bars for each task or resource. (This is an example from Plan & Track, by Mainstay.)

for task and resources. You just set new starting dates, and it calculates the schedule for you.

Project managers are tools for both planning and tracking. You can estimate deadlines and expenditures and then track the impacts when those estimates change. For example, if a task is delayed, you just plug in a delay symbol, and your program revises the rest of the task deadlines. You can also keep track of both planned and actual expenses and view the differences graphically. This kind of feedback is important—it makes you smarter the next time you start a project.

Outliners

Outliners are like orderly notepads. You can use them for organizing everything from your thoughts to your projects. They're not fancy or complicated. If you don't like to spend a lot of time on organization—or if you just want a quick way to create hierarchical lists—an outliner is a great tool for writing down stuff that you might normally try to keep in your head or scribble on pieces of paper.

The defining feature of an outliner is something called *progressive disclosure*. This is not a legal term. It's a convenience, a way to keep things simple unless they need to get complex. For example, suppose you have a three-part online marketing plan:

Each part of your plan requires different activities and resources. Maybe you just want to focus on classified ads. Then you *disclose* the items under the heading "Classified ads"—without getting tangled up in your web page or mail list strategies.

And if you decide that mail lists are really more important than classified ads, you can just drag the whole hierarchy for "Classified ads" down the page, after "Mail lists."

This is the outliner in
ClarisWorks.

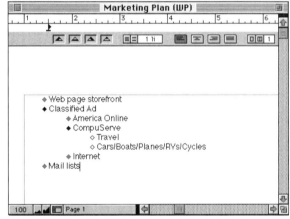

Most word processors and integrated programs come with some kind of built-in outliner. You'll find one in ClarisWorks and Microsoft Word. You'll also find outliners in presentation programs like Persuasion or PowerPoint. These are probably overkill for your basic quick list. But if you're organizing projects with groups of people, you can quickly convert presentation outlines to presentation slides for meetings. If you like to doodle as you think, you may prefer the visual tools of presentation programs to the simple text orientation of the other outliners.

Spreadsheets

Spreadsheets are high-powered tools for financial analysis, right? Yes, but they can also be robust organizational tools—with all the possibilities of a PIM or project manager *and* custom forms that fit your needs precisely.

For example, if you provide fundraising materials for nonprofit organizations, you can set up spreadsheet templates to track the standard stages of your work, much as you would in a project manager:

Want to use your spreadsheets for financial analysis? See "Upsizing" in Chapter 10, "Fast-Track Finances."

Fundraising						
	A	B	C	D	E	F
1						
2						
3						
4		Start Date	End Date	Hours	Materials	Costs
5	Comments					
6	Client Interviews					
7	Concept to client					
8	Client review					
9	First draft to client					
10	Client review					
11	Design to client					
12	Client review					
13	Second draft to client					
14	Client review					
15	Copy edit					
16	Production					
17	Final client review					
18						

Sheet1 / Sheet2 / Sheet3 / Sheet4 / Sheet5 /

You can set up other parts of the spreadsheet for details of tasks, for tracking materials and costs, and even for contact information for suppliers. You can search and sort and export the data to a word processing file to include in reports or to generate invoices and mailing lists. If you have an integrated software package, you can keep To Do lists, project contacts, and your project-management spreadsheet all in the same document, for quick reference.

Spreadsheets don't give you an instant solution like the PIMs do. But if you don't want to make the commitment to maintaining a PIM—or if you like to design your own tools—spreadsheets are probably the most versatile choice.

Databases

PIMs are special-purpose databases. If you have your own purposes, you may need a custom database. And if you need a custom database, you need database software.

Custom databases may be simple designs that you can create as easily as you create a drawing or spreadsheet. Or they may be complex, stand-alone applications with screens and menus that require sophisticated programming skills. For the simple category, you can easily employ the databases that come with integrated applications like ClarisWorks and Microsoft Works. Microsoft's Fox Pro, 4D from Acius, and Omnis 7 are examples of the serious programs you need to build stand-alone applications. In between is the very flexible Claris database program FileMaker 3.0.

You use database programs any time you need to catalog information: text, graphics, sounds, and even video clips. But simple databases are also a good way just to manage lists—for example, anything you need to alphabetize or sort by numerical order or recall by date. They're also the ultimate aid for complex research tasks. You can use them to gather data on everything from industry trends to market competitors to hot job leads, all on the com-

Want to dig into databases? See "Upsizing" in this chapter.

puter equivalent of 3 x 5 cards. Of course, on your computer, you can search your "card file" in about a half second to find all the cards that contain a particular keyword.

Don't take databases lightly, though. All but the simplest custom databases demand a considerable commitment of time and skill. It's not a ten-minute job.

WHAT KIND OF DATABASE— FLAT-FILE OR RELATIONAL?

When you're shopping for databases, the first questions is this: Do you need a relational database or will a flat-file database do the job? Here's how to decide:

■ Do you know all the possible fields you'll need in each database record? If you don't, a relational database works better. For example, if you have repeat customers and you keep track of all your customer transactions, you have no way of predicting how many transactions each customer will have. So you can't set a predetermined number of fields to record the transactions.

■ Do you need to use the same information in several different places? If you do, a relational database will spare you from keeping duplicate information in different databases.

With relational databases, you can link records from different database files. You can set up one file with all your customer names and addresses and another file with customer transactions. Then when you add a transaction for a customer, you simply add a pointer from a name in the customer database to a transaction in the transactions database.

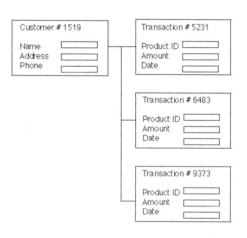

Personal digital assistants

Personal digital assistants (PDAs) are hardware. They're handheld computers. Some are built like PIMs—they track calendar events, sound alarms, remind you when to call someone back, and keep track of your phone lists and some simple notes. Others, like Apple's Newton Message Pad, are much more versatile. You can sketch ideas in them, use them to get your e-mail from your hotel room, or share information with your desktop Mac.

The Newton version is particularly useful if you're on the road a lot and need to jot down information that you want to work with on your Macintosh when you get home. Say you're an independent sales rep in just about any industry. You're probably making calls all day long. But when you get home, you need to record orders and names and special interests in your customer database on your Mac, and then send out order confirmations, invoices, and promotional materials for future sales. Or maybe you're a contractor who needs to gather measurements and other specs in the field and then go back to your office and plug them into your estimating spreadsheets. Or maybe—well—you see what we mean.

PRODUCT FOCUS

Computer companies have been working on handwriting recognition for a long time. Even though this input method is much slower than typing, the consensus is that millions of people who don't use computers would use PDAs if they could just scribble on them. The promise is great, but handwriting recognition is not quite there yet. While the recognition software in the Newton continues to improve, there are still enough mistakes—and it is still slow enough—to frustrate many users. However, it's likely that this technology will improve sufficiently in the next few years to be of use to almost everyone.

CAN YOU REALLY SCRIBBLE?

A question of aim

Everyone wants to get organized. Life is messy. PIMs and PDAs might help. But they shouldn't run your life. If you're spending all your time creating Gannt charts for CD-ROM projects, but what you really want to do is learn how to paint some of those incredible electronic scenes to illustrate the text, getting your Gannts more organized is not going to get you closer to your goal.

Here's something to watch out for: "If I could just get organized, I could . . . ." This is a dead giveaway that you're on the wrong track. What is it you want to plug into that space after "I could"? Whatever it is, just start doing it now. Doing it will get you organized to do it. Of course, if you're addicted to your PIM, it *could* help. Here are some tips:

- Block out regular times in your calendar for the things you really want to do—even if they're not the big money-makers right now. Treat them as seriously as any other calendar item. Don't set them aside to catch up on your organization.
- Scan your contacts list for people who could help you grow in the direction you want to grow. Schedule a lunch with them. Schedule these lunches once a week. If you don't have the right people on your list, find them and add them to your list. It's tremendously helpful to have the support of like-minded people.

Nothing ever happens on the first call. Andy Fine knows this.

That's why he needs a fast, efficient way to track his contacts and remind himself when he needs to call again. He needs to know where to start in the morning—without spending the first hour of every day refreshing his memory about what happened the day before.

He needs a sophisticated contact manager.

He also needs a fast, efficient way to sift through the dozens of résumés he receives each week. His brother suggested a simple Mac solution: a scanner with OCR software to scan the résumés into text files, plus HyperCard to set up a simple database with quick Find features.

HyperCard is a good solution because it can search through all the text on a card—without having to move the data into individual fields, as in most traditional databases.

HyperCard comes with a simple built-in Find feature, but a little plain-English programming adds more useful search options.

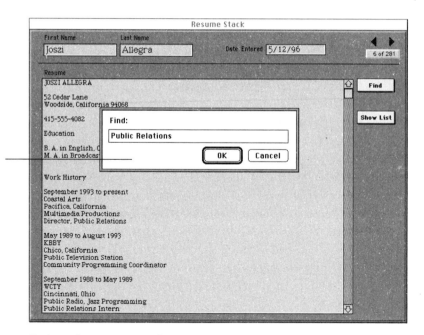

Each card contains a single résumé. When Andy finds one that meets his needs, he gets the original paper copy from his file cabinet and faxes it to his corporate client.

THE TOOLS

ACT!
OmniPage Professional
Visioneer PaperPort VX
HyperCard

Andy uses ACT! to keep a record of all his contacts. When he ends a phone call, he makes a note of when to call back or send a fax or meet for lunch.

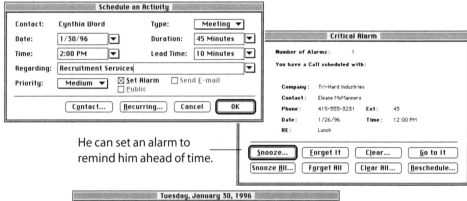

He can set an alarm to remind him ahead of time.

Everything he schedules shows up on his task list—a daily plan, ready for him each morning.

(He can also get the week's list, the month's list, or the complete list.)

Susie Hu tracks people down. Sometimes finding out how to contact them is as important as actually talking to them.

Of course, when she does talk to them, she's taking notes like crazy. Notes that she may well want to share with her clients in weekly or monthly reports.

She also needs a quick way to get back to any little detail in those notes—some little fragment of a conversation that's niggling at her, something that may be the missing puzzle piece.

So she needs a contact manager with lots of room for notes and the ability to search for words or phrases in those notes. She needs to be able to format fields in the contact manager just the way she wants them so she can copy them directly into her reports without reformatting.

And she needs to be able to group these records by job. She doesn't want Nora C's network of friends and acquaintances digitally mingling with her own.

Claris FileMaker Pro gives her the database flexibility she needs, and a few other tools fill in the missing pieces.

Susie keeps things simple and quick with the Cal shareware calendar by Mosaic Codes.

The ClarisWorks diamond outline format works great as a To Do list.
(ClarisWorks also has the traditional Harvard and legal outline formats.)

S O L U T I O N S

THE TOOLS

ClarisWorks
FileMaker Pro
PhoneDisk CD-ROM
Cal shareware calendar

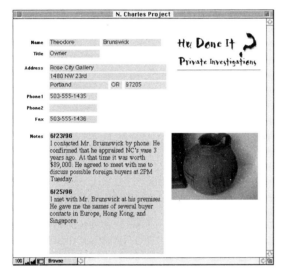

Susie uses a FileMaker Pro database she custom built to track her contacts and keep notes for each session with a person.

She can format the fields with the fonts and sizes she uses in her reports.

The PhoneDisk PowerFinder provides a fast way for Susie to find addresses for anyone with a listed telephone number—or to find a phone number for any address.

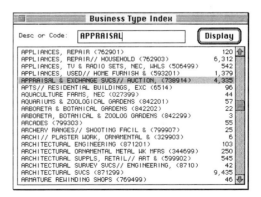

Weddings are organizational nightmares. That's why Ellen Gant is in business. And that's why she needs organizational tools that keep track of every thread, with no loose ends.

A full-fledged project-management program might appear to be the right choice for Ellen, but it's not her choice. She doesn't like the engineering approach with flow charts and diagrams. She prefers to focus on her two primary needs: contact management and materials planning.

Her contacts are primarily wedding suppliers. She works closely with them on a well-defined schedule. So she needs strong links between her contact files and her To Do list.

For materials planning, she needs spreadsheet power. Plug in the number of guests and calculate food and beverage costs, rental costs for tableware, costs for centerpieces.

You get the picture.

THE TOOLS

Claris Organizer
ClarisWorks

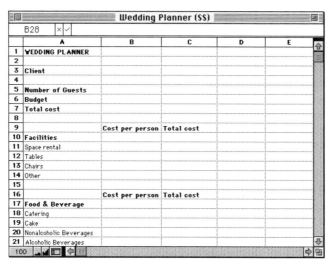

Ellen uses a custom ClarisWorks spreadsheet to plan and estimate all the material details of each wedding.

S O L U T I O N S

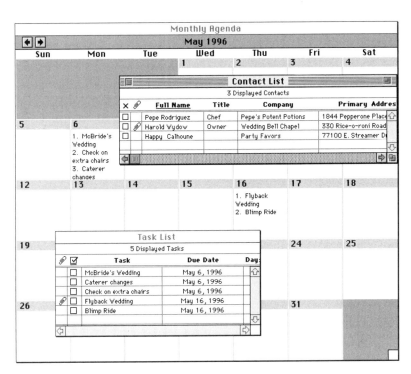

With Claris Organizer, Ellen can attach task lists and contact lists to a wedding date, with automatic entries in a daily, weekly, or monthly calendar to keep her on track day-by-day.

■ Take advantage of online chats. Invite people who share your interests to meet at regularly scheduled times. Once you get a crowd, invite an expert or celebrity in your area of interest. Lots of accomplished people are willing and eager to share their knowledge with a group of inquiring people. (Of course, for online chats, your celebrity has to be computer literate, too.)

■ Plan ahead. Sometimes it's easier to commit to a big new undertaking 3, 6, or 12 months from now. For example, if you don't have time for an electronic arts workshop right now, find one that's coming up in 6 months and schedule it. Actually put it in your calendar so you don't schedule other things in that time space. Then schedule another one 3 months later. The things you put on your schedule a year from now are the things you're going to be doing. It's that simple.

So now you have a reason to read the rest of this chapter, whether you just want to do your current work with more ease or you want to ease into a more satisfying work day. Check out the solutions for Andy Fine, Susie Hu, and company. Try on a PIM. Delve into databases, if you want. And then take a spin on a CD-ROM phone book to see what new business it can net you.

JUMP START:
Setting Up Your Personal Information Manager

You've got a collection of business cards, hand-scribbled notes in your phone log, an out-of-date Rolodex, and a pocket organizer with a smattering of business and personal contacts jotted in its pages. You've got sticky notes with To Do lists hanging off the bottom of your monitor like fringe on a surrey that's getting you nowhere fast. You've got e-messages to e-mail if only you could find that last message that has the right address.

Here's how to get a little order in your office.

STEP 1: CHOOSE A PIM

The first question is, Which PIM is right for you? This is a little like the question of which closet-organizing system is best for you. It depends on what you're organizing, how you work, and whether you like wood, acrylic or enamel-coated wire baskets.

By definition, PIMs give you a phone book and a calendar, with some links between them. Beyond that, they have features and functions that may or may not be useful. Here are some test questions for your PIM-to-be:

How much do you need to customize it? All PIMs come with pre-designed phone book entries. Most have standard fields for name address, phone number, e-mail address, and perhaps an alternate address. Some give you a couple of alternate layouts. How well do these layouts fit your needs? Can you use the PIM right out of the box, or do you have tweak it to suit your information?

How much *can* you customize it? Say, for example, that you like to assign a customer number to each of your customers—and you want to keep it in your contact list. Most PIMs have some user-defined fields just for this purpose. Some have a few. Some have lots more. With some, like Symantec's ACT!, you can design your phone log from scratch if you want to. Some PIMs have customizable calendars, too. With Datebook Pro, from Now Software, you can even create you own icons for tracking events like trade shows and conferences or due dates for your ads—or design special banners to mark significant dates.

How well does it support your workstyle? Some PIMs offer more work-specific support than others. For example, ACT! is a very sophisticated contact manager designed to support the work of people who have lots of contacts every day and often have to call them back several times—as sales people often do. Claris Organizer has many of the same capabilities, but is more event-oriented. So is Datebook Pro.

How versatile is it? ACT!, for example, has a built in word processor with dozens of templates that you can choose to use or not. If you don't have extraordinary text requirements—or if you create most of your text in a page layout application—ACT! is almost like an integrated works program with an emphasis on contact management, but support for most other activities (except graphics).

Does it support special data requirements? Maybe you need to include graphics in your phone book. Maybe you represent baby models and need photos of all your babies in your contact manager. Or maybe you represent bed-and-breakfast inns and like to keep pictures of the inns with their contact information to remind you what they have to offer. Can your PIM handle such requests?.

How are all the parts linked? All PIMs have some links among their various parts—but the ease-of-use and methods of making links vary. Some have drag-and-drop links. In Datebook Pro, if you type a name as an calendar item and that name is in your TouchBase phonebook, the phone number automatically appears when you click the item in the calendar—whether TouchBase is running or not. (If it's running, you get more complete information).

How does it print information? If you're accustomed to using one of the standard pocket organizers like DayRunner or DayTimer, you'll probably want to print your calendar pages in the familiar format and slip them into your trusted binder. Many PIMs have these formats built into their print options—but some do a better job of printing them than others. (By the way, be sure to print both your calendar and contacts regularly—in case your power goes out and you can't get to your computer files for three consecutive business days. It happens sometimes.)

STEP 2: SET UP YOUR PHONE BOOK

Think before you type. It's tempting to just start plugging all those names and addresses into the tidy forms in your PIM. Don't do it. Stop and do a little planning first.

Here's what you're going to be doing with your phone book: You're going to be searching it. You're going to be sorting it to create sublists. These searches and sorts can be easy, hard, or impossible—depending on some decisions you make up front. For example:

How many contact files do you need? With many PIMs, you can create groups of contacts—such as Personal and Business, or Customers and Suppliers. If your PIM supports these groups, you may be happy with a single contact file. If not, you probably want to create separate files for major categories of contacts, particularly if you have lots of contacts. Even if your PIM can create groups within a single file, you may want more than one file if you have lots of contacts in one group, or if you keep significantly different information for different groups. (All contact forms in a file must have the same fields.)

What groups do you need? You usually create groups by searching the contents of a particular field—such as Company or Title. For example, if you want to create a group of all your marketing contacts, you search for "marketing" in the Title field. Then you create a group for all the contacts that you find. Or you might create groups by company, if you have lots of contacts in the same company. If you sell insurance, you might want to group your clients by the type of insurance they have. You need to plan these groups before you set up your contacts because the fields you define and the terms you use in those fields will limit your ability to search—and create groups—later on.

What fields do you need? Fields are the blanks you enter information into. You need fields for all the types of searches you want to do—by name, by city, by state, by title, by date of last contact, by product purchased, services offered, fields of expertise, or any other way that you might want to contact someone. You may also need standard lists of terms to fill in those fields—standard titles, standard services, standard fields of expertise, for example. All PIMs come with both standard fields and some you can define yourself. (Claris Organizer makes it easy to create and use such terms—with pop-up menus for both standard fields and custom fields that you create.)

So, before you start to enter data in your PIM, follow these steps:

1. Create multiple contact files—such as business and personal files—if necessary.

2. Define your custom fields and create lists of standard terms (either as pop-up menus or as a list in the PIM's list manager).

3. Create groups that you know you'll want to use on a regular basis.

Now you can enter your data.

Most PIMs have alarms. You can set them when you set up an activity or you can set a free-standing alarm—maybe to remind you to look out the window and relax your eyes for three minutes. Sometimes PIM alarms have snooze buttons, so you can ignore the alarm the first couple of times if you're not ready to respond.

Most alarms have both sounds and visual cues. You can set them to go off at a particular time of day—or when you first start your computer. (If you leave your computer on most of the time, the former work better. The type that sound when you start your computer aren't very helpful.)

If you don't use a PIM, you have other alarming options:

- Use the Alarm Clock utility that comes with System 7 to set a simple sound alarm at a particular time. (It uses your current system beep.)
- Use the Now Utilities AlarmsClock to set alarms—including messages that appear in the menu bar at the time you set or when you start your computer.
- Use QuicKeys to do something at a set time—display a To Do list or a dialog box with reminder text, check your e-mail, or play a sound recording, for example.

(In our two-person home office, one of us is a prankster who likes to set strange alarms on the other's computer. Sound bites from Star Trek are a favorite: *Captain, I think the crew is de-evolving!*)

SETTING ALARMS

STEP 3: SET UP YOUR CALENDAR

Compared to setting up your phone book, setting up your calendar is a snap—especially if you've already set up your phone book. You don't *have* to do anything ahead of time. You can just start using it, plugging in activities of the various kinds your PIM supports.

Of course, if you want to be really organized about it, you can do some or all of the following:

Schedule all your recurring events. Recurring events might be anything from monthly professional meetings to weekly online chats to birthdays of your clients, if you know them. (Sending birthday cards to clients is a good way to say thanks for their business, and a good way to keep them thinking about you if they or their friends need your services again.) Most PIMs have a special feature that automatically schedules recurring events. You just set up the first occurrence and specify how frequently it will occur in the future.

Schedule time off. This one is *real* important. When you work for yourself, it's easy to let work drift into evenings and weekends and holidays. And that's OK. Flexible working time is one of the benefits of working at home. But in your enthusiasm—or sometimes out of despair—it's easy to give up your time off to make deadlines and income targets or to accommodate a new client. And you *need* time off. So pick a day of the week, or two half days, to be yours alone. (Weekdays can be really great if you like to get out on your day off—none of the weekend crowds!) If you have family and friends who long to see you for more than a hug in the hallway, schedule some time for them, too. Scheduling personal time on your calendar really does help.

Create activity templates. When you schedule an activity in a PIM, you do more than type a couple of keywords in a time slot. You usually define the activity by indicating who's involved (often someone from your phone book), how long the activity will take, when it will start and end, and what supporting documents (attachments) you need. You might also set an alarm. With some PIMs, such as Datebook Pro, you can create templates for these activities. For example, suppose you're a financial planner and you have a standard plan for your first meeting with prospective clients. You always allow two hours. You always use several standard documents to create a portfolio for the client. And you always call the client the day before to confirm the appointment. So this is what you do with Datebook Pro: you set up a custom item with attachments for all the documents you need and an alarm to remind you to make the confirmation call. When the alarm goes off, you click the client's name in the item to make the call. Then you print the attached documents and the directions to your client's home, which you have in your TouchBase contact form. You're ready to go—two days ahead of time.

UPSIZING: Developing Database Dexterity

Need to track customer transactions or inventory levels? Check out the accounting packages in Chapter 10 before you start building a custom database.

OK. You've got your contacts and calendar in order, but what about the rest of the digital data scattered about willy-nilly in the hinterland of your hard disk? Or worse, what about all that stuff layered in paper towers on your desk. Is there any hope for all of that?

Sure. There are databases. Databases are like tidy workshelves with boxes for nails and screws or staples of all different sizes, shapes, and colors. They're the electronic equivalent of Rubbermaid's closet and garage organizers. And they're easier to set up and use than you might think—provided you know how the pieces fit together. Here's a summary to get you started:

Fields—A box for each detail

In databases, you organize details in fields. The details may be things like customer names, product numbers, pictures, photographs, QuickTime movie clips, or sounds. They may be calculations that use details from several other fields (like cells in a spreadsheet), or they may be pointers to the contents of one or more other fields. You specify the kind of field when you create it.

In general, you only want one detail in each field. So if you have to enter a city and state, it's often better to put them in two different fields. Then you can search and sort by either cities or states later. You can also include formulas and functions in fields—to perform calculations on the values in other fields. For example, if you're tracking customer transactions, you might want a field to calculate the total value of all the products in a single transaction.

As with PIMs, an all-important first step is to think through all the types of details you want to keep in your database—and the ways you'll sort and search them—before you begin defining fields.

Records—The actual data

Records contain your actual details, organized according to the fields you've defined. For example, if you're creating a parts catalog, each record contains all the information for one part—its name, number, cost, sales prices, and reorder information, for example.

While records look like documents when you work with them on your desktop, they're not. They're actually entries in a table that's hidden from view when you're using the database. In order to work with records, you need to display them in some format or layout. Database programs have standard formats for displaying a record, but you can actually create your own—or several different formats.

You can create some layouts that include all the fields and some that show only a few of the fields. For example, if you want to simplify data entry for an assistant who only needs to enter change-of-address information in your subscriber list, you can set up a special change-of-address format that doesn't include any information about subscription start and end dates or the price paid for the subscription.

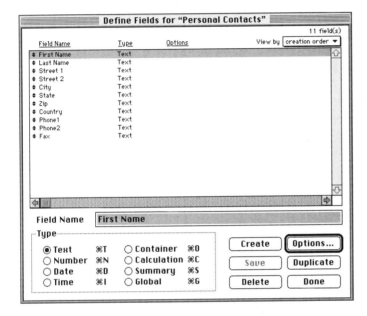

In FileMaker Pro, you define all the fields you need in a dialog box—you just give them a name and choose the type.

The fields you define appear automatically in the layout you've currently selected. FileMaker comes with three standard layouts, but you can also create your own.

Reports—Different ways to use your data

Reports are different ways to view your data—and print it. You create different reports for different purposes. For example, if you have a client database, you may create one report to compare sales volume per client and another to print mailing labels for a promotional mailing.

You can create reports to display individual records, a set of records that you've found and sorted, or summaries of records. If you want to show a report of sales by product, you can create a report that lists the individual products and their sales volume. Then you might include an overall summary of sales as well as summaries of sales by categories—if you want to compare direct sales to distributor sales, for example.

Database reports, like other Macintosh documents, can be formatted with the usual Macintosh flair—using typefaces, styles, colors, borders, and graphics. So you can actually use a database to compose a catalog, a business report, or some other presentation based on the information in your database.

PRODUCT FOCUS

HYPERCARD AS A DATABASE

HyperCard is a delightfully flexible multimedia authoring environment. But because it uses the simple metaphor of a card file, it can also serve as a handy organizational tool, taking the place of both custom databases and PIMs.

The feature that makes HyperCard so useful as a database tool is that it has a super-fast Find command—and you don't have to organize cards into fields to use this command. You can store free-form information on cards and quickly retrieve it by searching on a keyword. Our Andy Fine solution takes advantage of this flexibility by using OCR software to scan the contents of an entire résumé—unformatted—onto each card in Andy's stack. Andy can then search for keywords to find job candidates who meet his needs. It's a lot simpler than typing all the details of a candidate's history into fields in a contact database.

Setting up such a HyperCard stack requires no programming skills at all. But if you have some programming skills, you can go several steps further, creating buttons for special-purpose searches and sorts.

A basic HyperCard player comes standard on all new Macs. You also get some pre-designed organizational stacks, including a calendar and phone book. You can get the authoring software from Claris.

Queries—Sifting through the data

Queries are what you do when you want to get information from your database. Most databases have tools for two main kinds of queries: searching and sorting.

Searching finds all the records that match certain criteria that you set—for example, all customers who bought over $500 worth of merchandise, or all customers who live in California, or all customers who bought over $500 worth of merchandise *and* live in California.

Sorting organizes a collection of records that you've selected by fields you specify. By sorting, you can list all your customers alphabetically by the Last Name field. Or you can sort them numerically by the Zip Code field—which is handy if you want to take advantage of postage discounts for pre-sorted mailings.

Sorting and searching capabilities are built into all database programs. Some have more capabilities than others. Some of the more exotic searches you might be interested in are the ability to find all records that *don't* meet two criteria—or either of two criteria.

The sophisticated database programs like Fox Pro, 4D, and Omnis 7 actually produce stand-alone applications with their own custom screens, buttons, and menus. Users of these custom applications don't need the big, expensive database program to use the database. You may want such an application if:

■ You have several field representatives who need to track the same data in the same format, and you don't want to pay the price for a full-blown package like FileMaker 3.0 (about $200) for each representative. You own the stand-alone applications you create with Fox Pro, 4D, and Omnis 7, and you can distribute them as you see fit.

■ You need a kiosk-style data entry program for people to use in public places—for example, a video store online catalog. You want it to be simple in the extreme, with no generic database menus lurking anywhere to confuse any computer-naive customer.

■ You need to build custom databases for other people as part of your consulting business. More and more people are looking for computer-based information instead of print-based information, so more and more consultants may be building databases in the future.

Of course, developing such a database is a major undertaking that requires considerable time and programming skills. Unless database development is your trade, you're probably better off hiring a consultant if you need such a database.

DO YOU NEED A CUSTOM APPLICATION?

Scripts—Automating database tasks

In some database applications, you can use scripts to automate database operations that you do frequently, such as finding records and printing reports for them in the proper format. You can create buttons as part of a record's screen layout to perform these operations—or to find the next record that meets certain criteria.

Scripts will not only save you time. They're also particularly useful if you're hiring part-time assistants to do your data entry. If you use scripts to simplify the data entry process, your assistants need less experience, less training, and they'll work faster—saving you money. (They'll probably also be happier. No one likes to do unnecessary repetitive work.)

POWER PLAY: Instant Customer Contact Lists

It's easy to create a custom contact list or mailing list using a CD-ROM–based phone directory and a PIM-like TouchBase Pro. With minimal effort, you'll have an accurate, current listing of targeted businesses in any area of the country.

What you need
- PhoneDisc PowerFinder CD-ROM phone directory
- TouchBase Pro
- Time: 5 minutes

Start with a business category
PhoneDisc PowerFinder comes with a Business Type Index that list hundreds of business categories.

1. Open the PhoneDisk database you want to use and choose Business Type from the Index menu.

PhoneDisk databases are organized by regions on separate CD-ROM disks.

2. Type the category description or a Standard Industrial Classification (SIC) numeric code for the industry.

The index scrolls to the category or code you've specified.

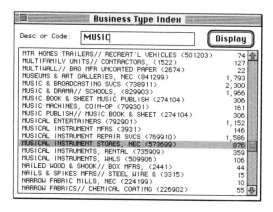

3. Click Display to see the phone directory list.

The directory displays all the businesses in that category on the CD-ROM you're using. PhoneDisc divides the USA into five regions, so your list will most likely cover several states.

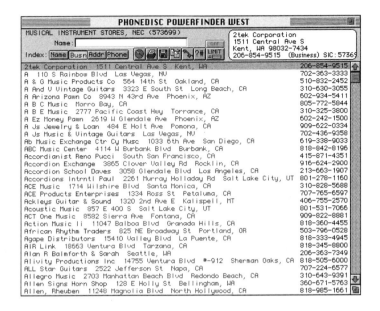

Focus in on your target

You may want a tighter focus, of course. PhoneDisk includes the tools you need to limit the list to a specific state or subcategory in the PhoneDisc directory program.

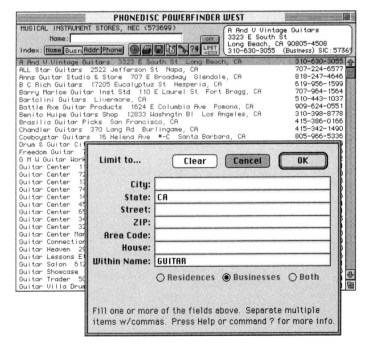

These entries limit your search to California stores with *guitar* in their name.

1. Click the Limit button and type some limits in the dialog box.
2. Click OK to display the new list.

Export to your PIM

Once you've got the list you want, you need to save it as an export file in a format your PIM can read.

   1. Choose Export Listings from the File menu.

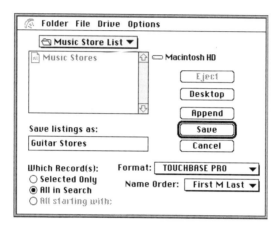

   2. Give your list a name in the directory dialog box and choose TOUCHBASE PRO from the Format popup menu.

   That's all you need to do with PhoneDisc PowerFinder until you decide to create a new list.

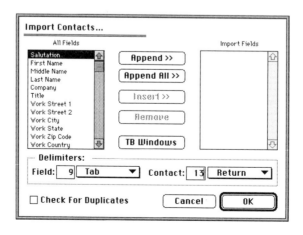

Enter the new contacts in your PIM

Now you need to create a contact file with contact records for each of the contacts in your list. Big job? Nope. Just two quick steps:

1. Open TouchBase Pro and select New Contact File from the File menu.

2. Click the Append All >> button, click OK, and then select your exported directory file.

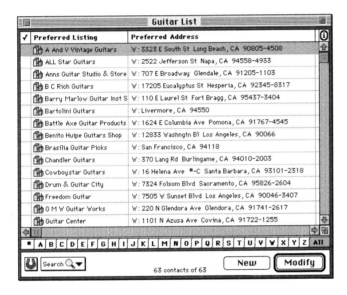

TouchBase Pro reads the list into your new contacts file.

That's all there is to it. Now you can use the TouchBase features to search and sort the list and create mailing labels. With just a few mouse-clicks, you've got a customized mailing list ready to go.

ON THE HORIZON: The Intelligent Home Office

While you're trying to get your office organized, a lot of visionaries and engineers are trying to get your home organized—electronically. The intelligent home, as envisioned, is a hybrid of cable TV, programmable appliances, and a "Star Trek"-style communications computer. It's a heat-sensing system that follows warm bodies around the house asking if they're a bit too warm, would they like the temperature a little lower, an iced tea with or without lemon? It's a system that knows what time you get up, what time you take your shower and how hot, and which radio station you like to listen to while you eat your Rice Krispies.

As a home office worker, you're likely to get first crack at testing out some of these new intelligent home technologies. The first products won't seem so exotic. You probably won't even notice it happening. Maybe you'll start with an innocent little infrared keyboard. Then it will just make sense to use your TV cable as your data communications line. And you'll find it's a lot faster to use your provider's database engine than your own to search your online contacts file—it will even automatically switch to a nationwide directory if it can't find the name you're looking for in your file. Pretty soon, you're carrying a smaller, lighter, brighter Newton around in your pocket, beaming it at your cable box to massage your handwritten notes and create a three-dimensional model of your project on your large-screen TV. Feeling tired? Take a nap. The screen in your bedroom will gently wake you with your favorite midafternoon music and remind you about the people you promised to call back between 3 and 5.

Hmm . . . this is starting to sound an awful lot like a sci-fi story that one of us wrote a few years back. Don't worry. It turned out fine.

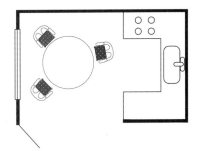

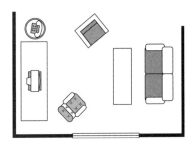

CHAPTER EIGHT

THE MARKETING PLAN

Using your Mac tools to build

relationships that build your market

L ay down your guns. Marketing is not warfare. Marketing is a cooperative relationship between you and your customers. It works best when
that relationship is based on mutual understanding and respect.

We started a mail order business a few years ago with a self-published
book for a niche market. We didn't expect it to make a lot of money. It did.
But that wasn't the best part. The best part was all the phone calls and letters
from people who were really grateful for the book. Our post office box wasn't
just overflowing with checks. It was overflowing with fan mail too.

Marketing directors in big corporations probably don't get that kind of
mail. Fortunately, as a small-business owner, you can build closer relationships with your customers—relationships that make you both happy. That's
what good marketing is all about. And here are the basic tools:

Direct marketing—From your house to theirs

You want to reach them directly, these people who will become your customers and clients. Let's say you already know them. You've done your

market research. You know who they are, what they like and don't like. You know what they need and what they can afford to spend for it. And you've got it. You just need to let *them* know how to get it.

This is when direct marketing works best. The traditional tools of direct marketing are mailings, telephone calls, and door-to-door solicitation. The new guy on the block is Internet e-mail. All of them work best when used with discrimination—that is, with lists that focus your time, effort, and materials on the most likely customers.

"Working best" means getting a response rate of 1 to 2 percent. Yup! That's the most you should hope for. If you send out 5000 postcards advertising your bird feeder to a well-chosen list of people known to be birdwatchers who regularly buy bird seed by mail, you can expect to get 50 to 100 orders. (You might get 4 to 6 percent—200 to 300 orders—if you're very well targeted.) Here's the key question: Will those orders pay for the cost of the mailing, your time, and the bird feeders themselves—and still give you a profit?

That is the kind of calculation you have to make every time you consider a direct marketing campaign. Of course, on the Internet, the costs of mailing are going to be small. But to do them effectively, you need to invest time—sometimes weeks of time—finding the right mailing list, building an online reputation, and watching for just the right moment to make your pitch. You don't want your message to be gobbled up by junk-mail filters. You don't want to do a scatter attack, called *spamming* on the Net. You don't want to harass potential customers with daily advertisements. You want to behave like—well—sort of like an online buddy. After all, this is as close as many of your customer relationships are going to get.

Whichever medium you use, make your message stand out. You want quick recognition—of your company, your product, or the problem it solves. Use words and images that appeal to your would-be customers. Use your own skills when you can, but get professional help if you need it.

Need tips on how to make the most of your medium? See Chapter 9, "The New Information Game."

Word of mouth—For building on your reputation

If you a have a few customers—and those customers have a few friends—pretty soon, you've got more customers. This is word-of-mouth marketing, and it's actually one of the most effective methods of increasing your customer base. People like to have what their friends have. They like to get it from people their friends recommend.

Word-of-mouth marketing happens naturally all by itself. You don't have to do anything except provide a good product and good service. But you can help it along. You can send thank-you notes to customers—by mail or e-mail—and ask them to tell their friends about you. You can offer promotions for friends.

Give your customers a 10 percent off coupon for their next purchase and one for a friend, too. Or offer a two-for-one price. These offers are well worth the discount, particularly if your business is a repeat business such as a catering or shopping service or subscriptions to a niche-market newsletter.

You can buy phone and mailing lists from lots of sources. Just look in the yellow pages under Mailing Lists. If you're in a large metropolitan area, you'll probably find at least a dozen national companies advertising mailing list services. But better sources for targeted mailings are trade and specialty magazines that sell their subscriber lists.

On the Internet, mailing lists are a little different. They're ongoing discussions. If you join a mailing list, you send one message to the list, and everyone gets your message delivered as e-mail. You also get all the messages from everyone on the list. These lists are usually moderated—the moderator can decide to block any messages that aren't appropriate. And most moderators don't look kindly on blatant advertising messages.

Joining a few appropriate mailing lists can be a great way to build a reputation for you and your products on the Net. If you're a valuable contributor to the list, no one will mind if you briefly mention your company, products, or services from time to time.

Here are some places to look on the Web for lists of lists:

```
http://www.liszt.com
http://www.tile.net/lists/
http://www.mhpcc.edu/training/vitecbids/SurfInternet/
maillist.summary.html
```

Some Internet lists are open and some aren't. Anyone can join an open list. But if the list isn't open, you have to apply to become a member. The moderator decides whether to accept you or not.

MAILING LIST KNOW-HOW

Make good use of referrals, too. Give your customers brochures or business cards to pass on to their friends. If appropriate, ask them for names and addresses of friends who would also be interested. If a customer writes you a letter of praise, ask if you can use it in your marketing materials. Find out a little bit about the person—something you can include when you quote them in your next brochure or catalog. Something like: *Dr. Jansen retired from her veterinary practice four years ago, but she still knows a great doggy toy when it squeaks.* Ask your contented online customers to pass the word along to friends on the Net. They'll probably do this on their own anyway, but don't be shy about asking if they're enthusiastic. They may belong to some lists or groups that you've overlooked. Or if they have Web pages of their own, ask them to build in a link to your Web page, so their friends can find you.

In addition to customers, cultivate word-of-mouth referrals from friends and colleagues in your field. In many service businesses, there's more demand for services than there are providers, and your fellow service providers can be a great source of referrals. When you're too busy for a job, be sure to recommend one or two colleagues—and call or send a note to let them know you did. If your friends send referrals your way, send them a thank-you note, too. If business is slow, don't hesitate to send your business card or brochure to some of your colleagues, asking them to pass it along if they know someone who needs your services. In the small-business world, everyone has slow periods, and friends are usually happy to help out when they can.

Public relations—For referrals with clout

Public relations is like word-of-mouth marketing. It's a way to get someone else—an expert authority—to say something nice about your product or service. In public, of course. And for free.

When you're planning your public relations strategy, look for people who have the right audience. These may be

- Product review editors in specialty magazines and journals, or anyone else who is likely to write about your product in print.
- Radio or TV hosts who might have a particular interest in your product or service.
- Teachers of adult evening classes—a cooking teacher, for example, if you have a cookbook to sell.
- Local business establishments—a pet store for example, if you run a pet-care service.

For step-by-step guidance in creating a press release, see "Power Play" in this chapter.

Find as many of these authorities as possible and send them information about your product. Send them a personal letter explaining why you think they might be interested in your product. Send a press release that describes your product exactly the way you would like it see it in print or on the air. Often product review editors clip paragraphs from press releases and use them verbatim—it's like putting words into their mouths.

If you can, send review copies of your product, too. The real product is always more convincing than a description of it. If your product is not too expensive and your market is large, you can afford to give a few away to get a lot of future sales. If your product is too expensive to give away, you can offer to send one as a loan or at a special review price.

Advertising—For coverage when and where you want it

Public relations and word-of-mouth marketing have two big benefits: they're free, and they carry more authority than anything you yourself will say about your product or service. But you're not in control of PR and word-of-mouth messages. You can't count on them.

You can count on advertising. Advertising is media coverage that you pay for. You control the content. You control where it appears (which magazines, for example) and when it appears. Almost. When you buy advertising, you can sometimes request a particular location in a newspaper or magazine or a particular time slot on the radio. But unless you're buying a prime space—such as the inside front cover or a page opposite a feature article—the location is at the editor's discretion. And editors have even been known to bump small ads to the next issue when space is a problem.

To buy advertising space, you work directly with an advertising representative at the magazine, newspaper, or radio station. These reps are sales people who know their magazine and subscribers well. They can help you choose your space and sometimes even help you plan your ad (particularly in small newspapers or the yellow pages.) Some publications have in-house staff that can design and create your ads for you. Or they can refer you to an agency who can.

Should you do it yourself? It depends on the publication and type of ad. If you're buying a **classified ad**, sure, go ahead and do it yourself. Ask the advertising rep for advice if you're not sure you're communicating the most important details. If you're buying a **display ad**—which is bigger, prettier, and much more expensive than a classified ad—think seriously about getting professional help. Advertising writing is an art, and even experienced writers can make a mess of it. Graphics help, too. If you don't have these skills well honed, use a professional. If you're buying radio or TV time, definitely use a professional.

Distribution channels—For expanding your market reach

You can sell your products directly to the public. Or you can sell through retailers. When you sell directly, you make more money per product. When you sell through retailers, you get the benefit of the retailer's advertising, reputation, and existing customer base. You also have less bookkeeping because you sell in bulk to a few distributors rather than to hundreds or thousands of individuals.

As with advertising, look for distributors who target your audience. Unless you have a product with very broad appeal—as well as a huge manufacturing capacity—don't start with K mart. For example, if you produce decorative mats for art and photographs, start with local frame shops. If you produce a special antenna for shortwave radios, look in shortwave magazines for the ads of distributors of radio equipment.

Contact the distributor and ask for their wholesaler information. Some distributors have formal guidelines for submitting products for consideration. Whether they have formal guidelines or not, most distributors will want a sample product, a product description, and a cost sheet. This sheet details the cost per unit at different sales volumes, as well as shipping charges and payment requirements.

After you send these, follow up in a week or two—unless your distributor specifically discourages phone calls. You may have to call several times before

Web pages are an entirely new way to advertise—see "Power Play" in Chapter 6, "Weighing In on the Web."

*S*ome advice from the experts: The best months for advertising are January, February, September, October, and November.

you get an answer. These folks have tons of products to review. Don't be discouraged if the first distributor you try isn't interested. Look for others. Look for smaller, more targeted distributors. There are plenty out there, and some are likely to be interested in your offering.

It's all in the plan

You want to build your business? *Everything starts here,* with your marketing plan. You need market forecasts to build financial forecasts—how can you predict income without an accurate picture of your customer base? You need these forecasts to make manufacturing commitments and pricing decisions,

---

Here are some guidelines for making the most of your advertising campaign:

■ Get the audience statistics for several publications and/or radio and TV stations. These statistics include not only the total number of subscribers, but often other marketing information—such as income group, age, education, and areas of interest—as well. You're not just looking for the largest audience you can find. You're looking for the consumers who are most likely to buy your product. Biggest isn't necessarily best.

■ Get rate cards for all the publications and stations you're considering. Compare the rates with the audience statistics. Figure out the cost per likely customer.

■ Ask the advertising rep to send you a six-month or annual editorial schedule. You may want to schedule your ad to coincide with an editorial feature. For example, if you sell veterinary software, you may want to include your ad in the issue of the veterinary journal that features software solutions.

■ Ask the advertising rep about special advertising sections that might be appropriate for your product. For example, many small papers have home improvement, gardening, pet, or seasonal advertising pages. A small ad on one of these pages is more visible than a small ad randomly placed.

■ Get an advertising schedule and plan your advertising strategy for an entire year. Publications often have long lead times—you may have to submit your request for space five months before it will run, and the actual ad three months before it will run. Yearly planning will also give you better control of your advertising budget.

■ Set alarms on your Macintosh calendar to remind you when it's time to place or renew an ad, so you don't miss the deadlines. (See Chapter 7 for details.)

■ Ask if you can have an agency discount on the cost of the ad. Many publications have a discounted rate for advertising agencies. Usually ad representatives will be happy to give you this discount if you're producing your own advertising.

■ Build a relationship with your advertising reps. Often they can let you know when special advertising opportunities arise.

■ Take advantage of small, very targeted publications. For example, many specialty products have devoted user groups with their own newsletters. Often you can buy a lot of space in these publications for little money—and also support the user groups.

STREET SMART

**TIPS FOR
BUYING
ADVERTISING**

too. You can't do it like a patchwork quilt, piecing things together month by month. You need to think a year ahead, and you need to think continuously.

This chapter walks you through the planning process. If you need some ideas, take a look at the way Andy Fine, Sam Post, and Ellen Gant are using their Macs to market themselves. Then make sure you know the basic steps from market research to tracking results. If you've already got a customer base, check the "Upsizing" section for ideas of how to use your Mac to take advantage of it. And then get hands-on help with building your publicity campaign—via press releases—in this chapter's "Power Play." Buena suerte!

As an independent agent in the world of executive search and recruiting, Andy Fine has marketing challenges—to say the least.

The field is crowded and competitive and not always well regarded. Andy needs a way to distinguish himself.

He needs to demonstrate that he's a professional who's a bit ahead of the rest. Who can offer a bit more than others. Who understands the needs of his clients per-haps even better than they do.

He needs to keep his name in front of his clients all the time.

His solution? A monthly newsletter with tips for hiring, interviewing, and evaluating new employees in a constantly changing job market.

THE TOOLS

Act!
Adobe HomePublisher
WordPerfect Clip Art for the Office

Andy keeps a few graphics, clipped from WordPerfect's Clip Art for the Office CD, in the workboard for his newsletter.

 S O L U T I O N S

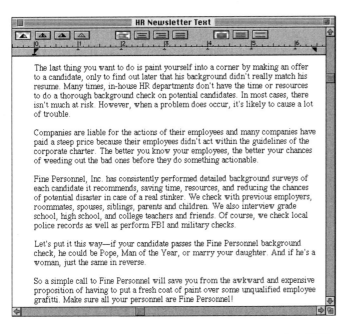

Andy can use the simple word processor in ACT! to create his newletter text. He can also use ACT! to create his mailing labels from his contact list when he's ready to mail.

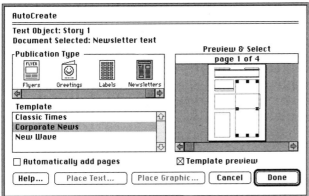

With the AutoCreate option, Home Publisher walks Andy through the process of creating his montly newsletter—step-by-step—using a predesigned template.

Sam Post has developed an aggressive online marketing program. His Web site serves as an online catalog with pages for each of his home designs, plus valuable information for anyone who needs or wants to be on the cutting of edge of electronic home technologies. With his own Web site, he can easily provide information about each design at no charge—and take orders for more detailed background kits if customers want to investigate one or two designs in more detail before buying. (The price of the kit is applied to the purchase of final plans.)

Sam knows, however, that he can't wait for people to discover his web page. So he actively shops for customers, using mailing lists, newsgroups, and classified ads to target people with special needs as well as people who just want the latest conveniences or energy-efficient home designs. He takes the time to join the lists and groups, and shares his expertise generously. Many of his customers have become good friends—online, on the phone, and sometimes even in person.

For now, Sam's not pursuing the more traditional advertising media. The online market he's reaching includes his most likely customers because they're not technology-shy. In fact, they're technology-smart, and that's good for him. But he does make sure he gets press coverage in magazines and newspapers whenever he can—with an active public relations campaign that includes not only press releases, but also talks to special needs groups that can benefit from his specialized knowledge.

THE TOOLS

Adobe PageMill
Virtus Walkthrough Pro
Netscape Navigator

With Adobe PageMill, Sam can create his web pages without inserting html codes. He can use Virtus Walkthrough Pro to create 3-D models of his homes online. Anyone with a VRML player can view these models.

Sam regularly searches for lists of mailing lists that may be of interest in his work. Both mailing lists and newsgroups are a good source of information about the customers he's trying to reach—and by participating actively, he builds his reputation as someone with good products and good "netiquette."

Ellen Gant's main marketing tool started out as a planning tool.

She needed a quick way to help her clients zero in on the features they wanted for their weddings. Leafing through heavy albums with glossy photographs of cakes, flowers, dresses, table settings, and all the rest was just too cumbersome.

She wanted them on her Mac, like a slide show. Once she realized she could do that, she took the whole idea a step further. She turned it into a promotional piece to show prospective clients what she could deliver—complete with video clips from her best weddings.

While her multimedia presentation is now the centerpiece of her marketing strategy, Ellen doesn't ignore other opportunities. For example, all her suppliers have a stack of her cards—which are actually wedding invitations, engraved with a brief summary of her services.

(Her StyleWriter wasn't quite up to this task—with embossing and gold ink—so she just had them done by a traditional stationer, who gave her a great price. After all, she refers all her clients to him.)

With Adobe Persuasion, Ellen can take her clients down different paths—clicking a video clip to set the mood and then clicking topics to display options for everything from facilities to food.

Persuasion uses an outline format to organize slides.

THE TOOLS

Adobe Premiere
Adobe Persuasion
Macromedia SoundEdit 16
Apple Color OneScanner

S O L U T I O N S

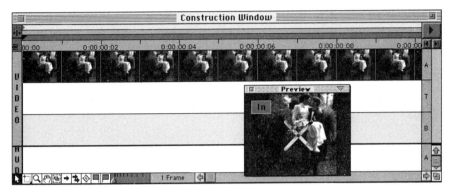

Ellen uses Adobe Premiere to select and edit clips from wedding videos—showing the fun of it all, but also zooming in on details like the bride's bouquet or a table centerpiece to highlight the choices a bride can make.

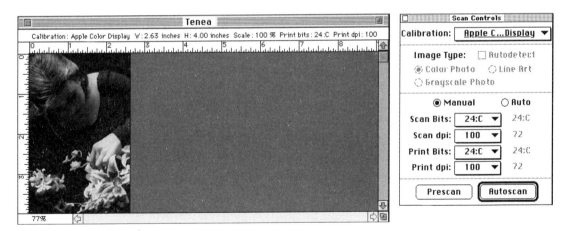

She uses the Apple Scanner to scan photography—and crop and size them to fit in the slide presentation.

JUMP START: Putting the Plan in Place

So you're convinced. A marketing plan is essential—not only to reach your potential customers effectively but to make sure that you can actually make money in the market. Here are the steps to do it:

STEP 1: DO YOUR RESEARCH

Market research is how you find out about your customers. This is what you need to know:

Who are they? Define your market in a simple phrase. For example, if you happen to sell leather cases for a PRO-43 handheld scanner, your market is *the people who own a Pro-43 scanner*. Depending on your product or service, you may also need to know things like the age, gender, geographic location, income level, occupation, and family size of your potential customers. Details about their life-style and working style may also be important. Get as much information as you can. It will not only help you evaluate market potential—it will also tell you how to target your marketing messages.

How many of them are there? This is the starting point for all your calculations of income and growth. It's your total potential customers. It may be a single number, or several numbers for different market segments. It may be a number that will grow in the future, or it may be a fixed number that offers no growth potential once you've reached a certain percentage. You need to know this.

What do they want? You need to know as precisely as possible what your customers want from the product or service you're offering—as well as when they want it and how they'll use it. Always design your product or service to meet a clearly perceived need. Watch out for situations where you see a need, but your customers don't. The cost and time to educate them can consume all your resources before you have a chance to make any profit.

How do you reach them? You need to be able to talk to these guys one way or another. You could reach just about anybody in the world with a mass media campaign, but chances are you won't be able to afford that. So what other channels link you to these people? Professional and community organizations? Workplace contacts? Libraries? Niche media?

Who else is reaching them? Competition will eat into your market share. If the market is large, it may not matter. Competition can even help—someone else's advertising dollars keep your customers thinking about products or services like yours. Lots of companies even succeed entirely on me-too sales. But when you're calculating your market potential, you've got to give something to the competition. Take the time to figure out how much.

Not sure where to get information about your market? Sources are everywhere:

■ First, read everything you can: newspapers, magazines, business journals. Scan the ads as well as the articles for tips about possible markets.

■ Go to the library and get help from the reference desk.

■ If you live in a university town, check to see if the university has a business school, with its own business library. You may have to pay a fee to use it, but its librarians will be specialists in the kind of information you're looking for.

■ Check out the growing number of commercial libraries that offer memberships for a fee—and have more targeted information than you'll find in your local public library.

■ You can always turn to the government documents libraries. These are federally supported libraries that keep copies of all public government documents, including census data and Department of Commerce trade studies that may be useful to your search. Your public librarian can point you to the nearest government repository.

■ Do online information searches for information. Online information and retrieval services can provide very targeted market information for a fee. Try these. Some people who offer these services are:

Dun & Bradstreet Information Services `http://www.dbisna.com`
Reuters Information Services `http://reutersnm.com`

■ Conduct surveys and focus groups. Surveys get you fast, quantifiable answers to specific questions. They're traditionally done by mail or by phone. Focus groups give you the details, the impressions, the emotional side of the story. They're traditionally done in person. However, you can set up response forms on your Web page to collect typical survey information: names, e-mail addresses, and basic profile data. You can also set up chats for focus groups. In both cases, be clear and honest about your intentions. You don't have to give away your product secrets, but don't pretend to be something you're not. (By the way, designing surveys and focus groups is a science. You may want to consult an expert.)

■ Contact others in your business. Retailers in your product area are often happy to talk about who's interested in what, how well a similar product is selling, and what people like and don't like about the products that are out there. Just walk into a store and strike up a conversation with a salesperson. You can learn a lot in a five-minute chat if your salesperson is knowledgeable.

■ Talk to the professional associations—the local artichoke growers' association, for example, if you're manufacturing artichoke bowls.

■ Compare notes with manufacturers in related but not competing markets. For example, if you want to publish a book about a popular software game, the game publisher may be happy to tell you how many games have been sold.

■ Do product beta testing. Find good candidates to test your product before you offer it to the public—online enthusiasts or media people or just friends and colleagues who know the product market. They can give you valuable feedback on your product and even become product promoters for you.

WHERE TO GET MARKET FACTS AND FIGURES

STEP 2: DESIGN YOUR MARKETING PROGRAMS

Your plan should be based on a general overall strategy—such as marketing your guitar album to the new wave of university students interested in the folk music revival. Once you've defined this basic strategy, you can figure out the best ways to reach your target audience.

For example, you might start by comparing the cost and projected returns on three different approaches: online marketing, college newspaper ads, and campus arts-and-crafts fairs.

Once you're chosen one or more of those approaches, figure out the actual components of the marketing program. For example, if you decide to pursue direct online marketing, you might:

- Design a new Web page every month, featuring a new clip from the album as well as historical folk music notes of general interest.
- Participate in a folk music newsgroup.
- Distribute a special discount offer message via a mailing list to people who buy two copies of your album, one for themselves and one for a friend.

Design these components in detail and then check the costs of your plan again to make sure they fit your budget and offer the kind of payoff you need to make a profit.

Some general strategic advice: Focus on niche markets. Niche markets are small, well-defined markets with unique needs. They're the best starting place for small businesses—especially important if you're offering a new technology that isn't widely accepted. Even though the markets for the product may ultimately be large, you need a focused marketing strategy to bridge the gap between early adopters of your technology and those who will wait until you've proven yourself.

STEP 3: CREATE YOUR MEDIA

For help in getting your point across in any medium, see Chapter 9, "The New Information Game."

Marketing almost always means media—from simple résumés and corporate brochures to slide presentations and online Web pages. With some writing and graphics skills, you can use your Macintosh to produce these media. And even if you don't have these skills, a professional consultant can provide you with Mac templates for easy updating as you add products or services to your list.

The starting place for developing all of your marketing materials, regardless of the medium, is your corporate identity. And the starting place for your corporate identity is your company name. You may want to use your own name, but a company name has advantages: if you expand, a company name is a better umbrella for several colleagues, and if you sell your company, you don't have to sell your own name with it. Also, a company name can tell the public more about the company than a personal name—and give it some style.

You can get software help for all the stages of your market planning with software like Market Builder from JIAN and Marketing Plan Pro from Palo Alto Software.

Market Builder is a series of templates for developing all parts of your marketing plan. These are not just empty documents with a few headings and styles built in. The word processing templates come with text already in place—you simply fill in the details for your own products to create a complete plan. The templates include advertising schedules, market analyses, a marketing communication plan, a sales plan, a trade show checklist, and 20 top questions to help you refine your marketing message. If you're not an accomplished writer, these templates could be a godsend.

Market Builder's spreadsheets help you prepare everything from break-even analyses and sales forecasts to charts for helping you develop comparative ratings for advertising and public relations agencies that you may decide to work with.

Marketing Plan Pro takes a slightly different approach, starting with a planning pyramid. You develop one or two main strategies. Then you develop tactics for each of those strategies. Then you develop programs for each tactic—with budgets, target market, product focus, and sales forecasts. You can convert all these elements of your plan into a document, merging spreadsheets, tables, and text that you've created for each program element. Marketing Plan Pro also has some simple tools for tracking the results of your marketing programs to see if they're working.

GETTING SOFTWARE HELP WITH YOUR MARKETING PLAN

The second element of your corporate identity is your logo. A logo may be as simple as a standard typeface for your company name on your letterhead and report covers. Or it may include graphics and color. Individual products in your product line may also have their own logos. With logos, simpler is usually better. They don't have to *illustrate* your company. They just have to be pleasing and distinctive.

Corporate identity goes beyond your name and logo. It's a look and feel. Are your materials funky and fun or sleek and sophisticated? Are they techno-chic or romantically feminine? What makes them uniquely you?

You can simulate a classic watermark on pages that you print. The watermark can be your company logo or name—or even a message like "Confidential"—all printed in a pale tone behind your main message.

If you know PostScript, you can write a little program to create your watermark. Check your word processor's features, too. With Microsoft Word 6.0, for example, you can put a watermark in a document's header or footer, positioning it to appear anywhere on the page. It can be either a graphic or text.

If your word processor can't handle the task, check out Watermarker by Working Software. It adds a few options to your print dialog box, so you can watermark any document you print with custom text or graphics that you create. Watermarker also comes with lots of little dingbats that you can enlarge to any size you like and use as watermarks.

WATERMARK YOUR PAGES

The extra deep indent in all your paragraphs? The barely perceptible watermark on all your pages?

Start your corporate identity program with your stationery and business cards, but make sure it's flexible to enough to fit all your company communications—including product packaging. Be consistent. Consistency builds your visual reputation. It makes you look reliable. And start with something good. Lots of small companies that grow to large companies end up regretting an identity that's tied to an unfortunate corporate ID that the company can't afford to change now that it's widely recognized.

DO YOU NEED A PROFESSIONAL DESIGNER?

A good professional designer can start you off on the right foot with your corporate ID. Even if you have a good sense of type and graphics, a professional is likely to add a little something extra—extra distinctiveness, extra style, extra versatility.

Some design firms specialize in corporate ID. It's the only thing they do, and they're good at it. But they tend to charge a lot. Many of them won't take a project for less than $3000. For your home office business, this may be a bit steep. Fortunately, there are lots of designers around, and you should be able to get the basic elements—logo, letterhead, envelopes, and business cards—for $500 to $1000.

Look for a designer who works with the Macintosh. Make sure your designer gives you template files so you can tweak your letterhead if your phone number changes, or use your logo on other materials, such as stick-on labels for packaging. If you can afford color, ask for both color and black-and-white treatments. If you're going to be producing a lot of your marketing materials on your black-and-white laser printer, you want to make sure your logo looks as great without color as with it. Also, be sure to get written type specifications for your design so you can reproduce it if something nasty happens to your templates.

STEP 4: TRACK YOUR RESULTS

One of the most difficult tasks for solo workers is recognizing when something is working and when it's not. When you work alone, no one is there to reflect on your mistakes with you. It's easy to explain away disappointments or throw yourself at the same strategy with more vigor, when what you really need is a new strategy. That's why tracking your actual market performance against your projections is important.

If you don't do anything else, track these two things:

Projected vs. actual marketing expenses If your marketing expenses are too high, your profit margins will be lower, even though you're selling projected volumes.

Projected vs. actual sales If your sales are too low, you'll have to dig into your profits to meet your expenses.

Track each program—your Web page, your direct mail postcards, your discount offer—separately. If you're selling by mail, you can track the effectiveness of ads in different publications by adding a code to your mailing address. For example, if your post office box is 1234 and you're running an ad in *Sunset Magazine*, you can list your address as P. O. Box 1234-SM. (The post office will ignore your code.)

Every dollar you spend on marketing eats into your profits, so you need to know precisely what's working and what isn't. If all your programs are failing, go back to Step 1. Check what you know about your market and reconsider your overall strategy.

UPSIZING: Making Your Market Grow

First you establish your market. Then you build on it. You can use your Mac to help you out here—to set up some systems that will help you get a higher return on your efforts, streamline your marketing programs, and create a basis for growth. Here are some ideas.

Customer databases

For general database guidelines, see "Upsizing" in Chapter 7, "Management by Mac."

A good customer database is worth its weight in megabytes. Your past customers are people who know you, who have an interest in your product and a willingness to spend money on it. So make good use of their names and addresses. Set up a customer database and use it to

- Get more customers—with your "friends" promotions.
- Promote new products—with direct mail campaigns.
- Sell accessories for your product or service—with announcements that you include when you ship the original product.
- Find out more about your customers—with return mail cards for product registration, warranty, or general feedback.

Some business accounting products, such as MYOB and QuickBooks, include customer database modules that help you keep track of customers as you fill orders. You can also use contact managers such as TouchBase Pro or Claris Organizer to track your customers and create special purpose mailing lists. Or you can design a custom database to track all the details you want. What you want will probably be some combination of these:

Contact information: Names, addresses, phone numbers, fax phone numbers, and e-mail addresses.

Product purchasing history: Which products they purchased and when—as well as personal information such as style, color, and size preferences, or responses from registration and feedback cards.

Payment information: Method of payment and miscellaneous information from checks, such as a driver's license number or a different address on the check, just in case you have payment problems. (In our five years of mail order business, we've had less than five bad checks—and we don't hold checks to clear before we send out products. Your market may be different, of course, but don't start out expecting the worst.)

Personal contacts: Any letters, phone conversations, e-mail messages, or other personal contact you've had with the customer. (You can cut and paste the e-mail message directly into your database.)

When you set up your database, be sure to consider how you'll want to use the information. If you want to do mass mailing, make sure you have a separate field for the zip code—you'll need to sort by zip code. If you want to target a segment of your customers, make sure you have fields for those segments. Or use a HyperCard stack to create unstructured cards that you can search word for word, as we mentioned in Chapter 7.

Public relations lists

Let your Mac help you manage your public relations campaigns with finesse. Start by creating a public relations list—a database of editors and other media people who can help you promote your products and services. Here are some ways to build your list:

- Check the editorial masthead of magazines, newspapers, and journals that might run your announcements. Look specifically for new-product editors or other editors who are most likely to be interested in your press releases. If you don't find a specific editor, target the managing editor (not the executive editor). The masthead should include the address and phone number of the editorial offices. If you suspect that your editor has a different address, call and ask. You can also call and ask for general guidelines for submitting press releases.

- Read these same publications to identify regular columnists who might put in a good word for you. You can address mail to these columnists in care of the magazine, but you might also be able to get their addresses from the editorial offices. A lot of columnists include contact information in their columns—often e-mail addresses. Even if they don't, do a quick search on the Internet to see if you can find them.

- Consult one of the many directories of publications that list editorial staff for both print and broadcast media. These directories are usually available in the reference section of your public library. They are particularly useful when you don't already know the publications you need to target—or if you want to target a large number of publications but don't particularly want to buy them all or stand at the magazine rack of your local bookseller scribbling names and addresses in your Newton.

- Check the directories of professional organizations that you'll also find in the reference section of your library. Many of these organizations have newsletters that are always looking for news that's of interest to their members. If the directory doesn't list an editor's name, just address your press releases to Editor and the name of the newsletter at the organization's headquarters. Or call to ask for the name.

Once you have your lists, use them carefully. You can take a broadcast approach, but you'll probably get the best coverage if you take the time to build personal relationships with the editors and columnists. Always include a personal cover letter, and always, always, call or send a thank-you note if they give you coverage. Send seasonal greeting cards with personal notes about upcoming products or new directions you're heading.

If you're not getting coverage, call them up and ask if they think your product is inappropriate for their audience. (It might be. This is good information to have.) Find out what their particular interests are so you can write a good cover letter with your next press release—one that will catch their attention. And keep your lists up-to-date. People change positions frequently in this business.

MARKETING TO THE MARKETEERS

> Big companies have big sales forces—sometimes hundreds or even thousands. Almost all these big companies have incentive plans and rewards to encourage better performance. Often the incentives are products or services. This is a market.
>
> Companies with big marketing budgets also use products as incentives for the public. For example, they may give away bags, books, CDs, and various trinkets by the thousands at trade shows. This, too, is a market.
>
> If you have a product that you think is an appropriate reward for good performance on the job or for distribution at marketing events, put together a list of marketing managers at large organizations. You can usually get their names, addresses, and phone numbers simply by calling the company. Send them a letter, a price list, and a free sample. (Marketing people love free samples.) You may even want to donate a sample for sales award programs. Just make sure the envious coworkers of the lucky winner know how to get in touch with you.

Joint marketing

Another way to grow your market is to make some marketing allies and develop joint marketing programs. A good marketing ally is someone who wants to reach the same market segment as you do, but is not a direct competitor. For example, if you sell a line of professional massage oils, someone who manufactures massage tables is a likely ally. If you do fine-art photographs of historic homes, someone who manages historic tours might be a good ally.

The difference between a distributor and an ally is that a distributor buys your product at a discount, sells it with a markup, and pays for any marketing; an ally pools resources with you to get more value for your marketing dollars. You get more impact, you benefit from each other's reputation, and you may reach a wider audience. Consider these possibilities:

Develop a joint advertising campaign. Large advertising spaces are expensive. But they obviously have greater impact than small spaces. So you can develop integrated ads that sell both your products. For example, the historic homes campaign might lead with a line like, "Two Ways to See Monticello"—and go on to show your fine photography and describe your ally's tour program.

Distribute each other's marketing materials with your products. For example, if you're selling massage oils, your ally can include your brochures or even small samples with each massage table shipped. And you can include your ally's brochures with every direct-mail order of massage oil that you ship.

Do joint promotions. Product discounts can be an incentive for people to buy both your product and your ally's product. The message goes something like this: Take a tour and get 10 percent off the fine-art photograph. In some cases, you negotiate to split the cost of the discount. In other cases, the added sales you get from the joint promotion may be well worth the discount you offer.

As with customers and the media, the key here is to develop relationships. Even though you're working alone at home, you don't have to go it alone all the time. Take advantage of every business encounter to build cooperative relationships and explore the possibilities for mutual support. Many of the people you meet will be small-business owners like yourself. Help each other out. It feels good, and it's good for your business.

POWER PLAY: Getting Publicity with a Press Release

The media is always looking for news, and you can be the news if you can get their attention with a good press release. A good press release follows a standard format and carries a clear message. The format may vary slightly, depending on the type of announcement you're making. But if you're announcing a new product or service, these guidelines should help get you in print.

What you need
- Word processor
- Your logo art
- Time: 1 to 3 hours

First, create a banner
All press releases carry a standard banner that gives editors key information they're looking for.

1. Open a new document in your word processor

If you have a standard stationery template, you may want to start with that.

2. Copy and paste your logo at the top of the page and type your company name and address if it's not part of your logo.

If you don't have a design grid established for your company, align your logo to the left or center it. If you don't have a logo, just type your company name and address in bold type.

3. Type your contact information.

You need to include your name or the name of someone who can answer questions about your product and company. You also need to give a phone number and a fax number. You should provide this information in this format:

FOR IMMEDIATE RELEASE
Contact: Your name
Phone: Your phone (with area code)
Fax: Your fax number

If your logo is aligned left, position the contact information at the right side of page.
If your logo is centered, center the contact information beneath it.

Add a headline

The purpose of the headline is to summarize the main message of your press release in a short phrase.

1. Compose a simple headline and type it just below the banner.

Type it in upper- and lowercase, bold, 12-point type. Don't do any special formatting. You just want a simple, straightforward headline that gets the main message across.

2. Center the head.

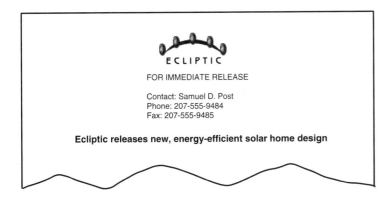

Write the introductory paragraph

Your introductory paragraph should summarize your message again—this time with a few more details.

1. Type the dateline.

The dateline includes your city and state and the date that you expect to mail the press release. If you're announcing an event that will happen somewhere other than your city, use that location instead of your own. Type the dateline like this:

Mars Hill, ID (July 1, 1996) —

2. Type a brief paragraph that expands the headline and summarizes the most important facts.

This is a *very* brief paragraph—one to three sentences. Its purpose is to tell what's new and why it's important. You might be announcing a new product, a new service, a new discount, an important new addition to your staff, a new location, or a charitable contribution to your community.

If appropriate, be sure to identify what your company is known for. For example:

Ecliptic, known for its best-selling kit home designs, announces its new SuperSolar line, designed to cut energy costs by 30 to 50 percent without cutting quality or convenience—and without increasing home construction costs. The new line is particularly timely, as energy costs are forecast to rise significantly this year.

BUILD YOUR PR SKILL WITH PUBLICITY BUILDER

If you want more help getting your press releases in shape, take a look at JIAN's Publicity Builder. It's a template-and-worksheet package for building your entire public relations campaign.

Publicity Builder's worksheets help you set PR goals, define the features and benefits of your products, position both your product and your company, and follow up on press contacts.

Its templates step you through press releases of all kinds—from product and personnel announcements to charity and sports announcements. It also includes templates for pitch letters, thank-you letters, and even nondisclosure agreements. The manual includes dozens of actual press releases from well-known companies—so you can see what the competition is doing!

Fill in the details

The rest of your press release fills in the details you want the public to know—any special features, as well as who would benefit and why. It may also include endorsements if you have them.

1. Provide a more detailed description of the new product or service.

Explain how the product or service produces the benefits you claim for it in the headline. This is a good place to talk about prices if you want to include this information. If you're announcing a new partner or location, explain how the change will benefit the company, its customers, and the community.

2. Provide a more detailed description of why the product or service is important.

If possible, draw on an outside authority to validate the importance of your product or service. For example, quote existing research or newspaper articles or public figures. Be careful not to make it sound as if these authorities are endorsing your product—unless they are.

3. List the features and benefits of the product or service.

A bulleted list is a good way to highlight the features you want the press—and the public—to focus on. Keep the items short and simple. Make sure the benefit of each feature is clear. It may be clear to you but not to the public.

4. Summarize by telling the reader clearly who will benefit and where the public can get the product, or get more information.

In most cases, keep this information brief enough to fit on a single page. The shorter your press release is, the more likely it is to go into print unedited—which means you get to have your say.

Don't forget attachments: photos of products or people, product spec sheets, review samples, and anything else that will help the press evaluate your offering.

ON THE HORIZON: Information Sells

While the world is atwitter with possibilities for cashing in on the Internet, the real trend that will shape marketing in the future is one that's already solidly in place—and growing steadily. It's the use of information to sell products. More and more, marketing goes hand in hand with *informing*. You give people healthcare information to sell them healthcare products. You give them gardening information to sell them gardening tools. You give them home remodeling tips to sell saws and drills and lumber.

Of course, in the short term, the World Wide Web is going to be the venue for exploring and expanding this concept. The most successful Web pages will be those that provide something extra—not just product descriptions, but information that people can use whether they buy your product or not. Information will draw visitors to your Web site—which is what you need. The more traffic, the more product exposure.

Look for innovations in online stores, too. Apple currently has the technology to display 3-D objects in 3-D spaces: it's called QuickTime VR. With it, your online store can be a virtual store where your customers walk in and virtually handle the merchandise, examining it from all sides. A whole new industry will probably spring up around 3-D virtual merchandising. (It's a job you could do from home, by the way.)

As digital cable provides wider bandwidth in homes and offices, *narrow-casting* will become a key strategy for targeting your high-return market segments. Entire channels will be devoted to people with narrow interests—who will be looking for both information and products. As the wall that separates information and marketing is chiseled away, customers will volunteer their information about themselves, making it easier to develop ongoing relationships with the kind of customers you want. Which is sort of where we started this chapter.

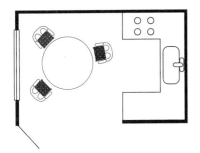

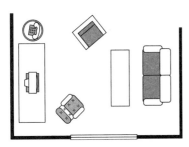

CHAPTER NINE

THE NEW INFORMATION
GAME

How to present yourself and your

information in the new information

universe

Information isn't what it used to be. It used to be words on a page, organized all neat and tidy in outline form, the way they taught you in
school. Now it's graphics and photographs and video clips and hyptertext
links that send you flying from one end of the information universe to
another in a second.

In this universe, people don't read. They swallow up information in bite-
sized pieces that they can digest on the run. They're not interested in long,
well-developed treatises where the ideas flow logically from start to finish.
They're attracted to shapes and sounds.

The Mac has the best tools in the world for creating shapes and sounds
that attract. All you need is a strategy for finding the right shapes and sounds
for your information—which is what we want to give you in this chapter.

The key to this strategy is to work with *types of information*. Then organize your thoughts in *modules* rather than beginning-to-end outlines. Work with *presentations* rather than documents, presenting different types of information in different types of modules so your audience can quickly recognize the information by its shape. Here are some basic information types and some suggestions for how to shape them.

STREET SMART

THE NEW INFORMATION UNIVERSE

For decades, electronic media like television and radio have been reshaping information. For the vast majority of information needs, these media are just too expensive. But the Macintosh now offers tools to produce the kind of information you've seen on the mass media. And the World Wide Web offers the opportunity to use them effectively.

The two big differences in this new world of communication are hypertext and multimedia. Hypertext gives you the ability to jump from place to place in an information space. As a user, you click to quickly follow a thread of information without taking time for all the stuff that's not what you're looking for. As a producer, you provide links between related topics.

Multimedia gives you the ability to present your information in text, graphics, sound, animation, and full-motion video. As a user, you can click one of a dozen graphic icons on your computer screen and see a video of a procedure for connecting a ceiling lamp to the wires hanging out of your ceiling. As a producer, you need to decide whether a video is the best way to explain how to connect a ceiling lamp—and then you produce the video, of course.

Hooks—For getting attention

Hooks capture your audience. They tug at heart strings and purse strings. They tell people something they want to know—or lure them into something they've never imagined. Examples of hooks are newspaper headlines, the photograph you can't stop looking at, the flashing neon sign, the part of a song you just can't get out of your head.

Hooks are starting places. They orient. They tend to be bold—in appearance, content, or both. But this doesn't mean that they have to be in bold type. You can make a small, fine word bold by placing it alone on a blank page or screen or slide. A pastel image can lure a tired audience with its peacefulness.

A hook can be as simple as a single word in a bold heading. Or it can portray an image that goes right to the heart of your customers' concerns. Here are two options for the same hook.

Bloom.

*Some flowers get old before they have
a chance to bloom.*

Notice that this hook could lead in lots of different directions. It could sell a product that helps keep flowers fresh in the vase. It could lead to gardening advice. It could warn of the dangers of teen pregnancy.

Graphics make great hooks because they say so much so fast. But always include at least a little text. The text can link the graphic to your company, your product, or the rest of the information that you're presenting. By using both text and graphics, you appeal to the intellect and the emotions at the same time, and your message comes across more strongly.

If you're working in a multimedia environment, such as a slide presentation or Web page, you can include sound with your hooks. Here, its function is to get attention, not to explain. Music and isolated sounds—like frogs croaking, engines starting, or doors closing—work best. If you have to click to get the sound, it doesn't work as a hook.

A video clip can work as a hook if it's short, simple, and compelling. But if it takes very long to get to the punch line, the hook effect is lost. The video then needs its own hook. Unless you're very skilled with animation or video, don't rely on video hooks.

Everything needs at least one hook—from letters to slide shows to ads, brochures, newsletter articles, and even technical manuals. If your presentation is long, you may need several hooks. You may even need levels of hooks—primary hooks and secondary hooks. Don't get too many levels, though. Three is probably the max. And keep in mind that the hook may be more than a single headline or image. It may be an image and a short paragraph that puts the image in context. Or it may be a title and subtitle, or a topic head and summary of the topic.

Facts—For defining and describing

Facts are descriptions of things. They're the features of your product. They're the list of services you offer. They're price lists, rate charts, sales figures, and production costs. They're parts of a machine, a building, a city, an ecosystem. Sometimes they're related to other facts. Sometimes they're not.

Facts work best in lists, charts, graphs, tables, and diagrams. These formats give your audience a quick way to scan the details without having to dig into paragraphs of text. Here are some guidelines:

Lists Use brief, straightforward text. If possible, include a graphic element for each item in the list. This element may be as simple as a bullet but can communicate a lot more if you choose one that illustrates the point you're making. It can be an actual illustration of a product or an abstract icon that stands for a service you have to offer. For example, if you provide your service internationally, you might use a globe icon with a sentence or two about your international experience. If you're working in a hypertext environment, these graphics might be hot—jumping to other topics that give more details. Don't be fooled into thinking that lists are just straight columns of text, either. Elements in a list can be arranged in circles, zigzags, or other patterns to add visual interest.

Charts and graphs Use charts when you want to compare things visually—especially things you can measure. It's a lot easier for most people to look at a bunch of bars that show how your product beats the competition in speed, safety, and cost than to read text comparing all those numbers. One glance, and they've got the message.

Tables Use tables when you have to compare things that you can't necessarily measure—or just to list the same kind of information for several different products or services. Maybe you sell walking tours—five of them. They each have different starting points, durations, physical fitness requirements, and prices. This is good table information. Don't leave graphics out of tables, either. Use pictures as well as column or row headings to identify the things in your table. Or use shading and color to highlight cells in the table—for example, to spotlight a feature of your premier tour. In a multimedia environment, you may even want to include video clips in the table. Click a tour, get a preview of some of the scenes.

Tip: Not enough bit space for all those graphics? Use a product like Macromedia's Fontographer to turn small graphics that you use frequently into "font characters." You use them just like letters of the alphabet, and they take up a lot less storage space.

Diagrams Use these when you need to identify and define parts of something. The something may be a physical object like a car or a toaster or scuba gear. Or it may be something abstract, like the structure of an organization or the flow of a production process. Diagrams show the relationships among parts of the whole, with connecting lines and text labels to spell things out.

Instructions—For telling people what to do

Sometimes you have to tell people how to do something. Most people like to learn by watching someone else do it—or better yet, by having someone else do it for them. But direct observation isn't always practical. It might seem that the next best thing is video. And sometimes it is. But if you're up in the attic trying to wire your security system by flashlight, you're not going to want to climb back down the ladder and go find the place in the video that explains which color wire attaches to which terminal of the siren.

Videos are good for gaining an overview of the steps and the confidence to start them. Printed step-by-step instructions, with clear graphics, are better for the details. If a computer can be at the scene, instructions can be viewed on the screen, with hot links to a short video sequence, if appropriate.

Whichever media you choose, here are some basic guidelines for giving instructions:

■ Organize the instructions into a few steps (less than seven if you can). You can divide complex procedures into parts to limit the number of steps in each part.

■ Number steps that have to be done in order. In a hypertext environment, make it clear how to get back to a previous step, just in case your student lands at step 5 first. Or fix it so your students can't land at step 5 first.

■ Don't number anything that isn't an instruction. For example, if a jack-in-the-box pops out of the box when you turn the handle, don't say:

1. Turn the handle.
2. The jack pops out.

■ Don't describe things that are obvious. When you nail two boards together, they stick together. You don't have to say, "Now your boards are stuck together."

■ Use illustrations to make things obvious. Then you don't have to write more words, and your students don't have to read more words.

■ Don't mix instructions with other kinds of information, like facts or stories. But make it clear where people can get this information if they need it.

HOW TO GIVE INSTRUCTIONS

Stories—For making sense

Stories are the glue of life. They make things make sense. They provide a context for understanding facts and instructions. They build concepts, provide a map of the world you're defining, lead your audience to conclusions you choose.

Stories can be true or fictitious. They can be romantic or technical. For some kinds of information products, the story is the main event. For others, it's the background that makes the rest of your presentation make sense. For example, if you're an educational consultant, your report might be an account of how a learning program was set up in your community, with separate sidebars that feature the list of benefits of the program and a summary of the steps for setting up the program. Or it might be a detailed set of procedures for setting up the learning program with several stories presented as case studies in sidebars throughout the text. In a multimedia environment, the case studies could be clickable videos instead of sidebars.

You can tell stories in any medium—text, cartoon graphics, animation, video, song. But remember that audiences have to pause to read or watch or listen to a story. They have to stop doing what they're doing for a while. So you need a strong hook for the story—and you need a good story. In today's market, it's better to keep your stories short.

Take-home points—For summarizing and reminding

Take-home points are the messages you want your audience to remember. They can be a call to action: *Call 800-555-4040 now!* Or they can be a few key facts. If the hook promises your audience what they're looking for, the take-home point should deliver on that promise.

You can deliver your take-home points at the end of a short presentation or throughout a long presentation. You can put the take-home points at the beginning of your presentation—together with your hook—as an executive summary for people who may not get past the first page or screen. Then you can repeat the points throughout your presentation and summarize them again at the end. Repetition is useful.

Take-home points are a lot like hooks and can use the same media treatment as hooks—bold text, graphics, sound, or a very short, very compelling video clip. You can label them with tags like *Don't forget,* or *Key to success,* or use a graphic icon to point to them. You can put them in a box in the middle of a page and let the text flow around them. In a multimedia environment, you can display them automatically when the user finishes a module. Your goal is to make sure your audience gets them—without even trying.

Putting it all together

You've got all the pieces—hooks, facts, instructions, stories, and take-home points. Each type has its own distinctive media treatment, but they all need to work together. Here are some guidelines:

Create a visual hierarchy. Some things should stand out more than others. Usually hooks should stand out the most, followed by take-home points. The rest is up to you. Use size, boldness, color, isolation, and position to make some types of information stand out more than others.

Always treat the same type of information the same way. Consistency is important. You're teaching your audience a visual body language. You don't have to be boring, of course. If you choose a bold color text treatment for your hooks, you can use a different color for each hook. If you use a graphic icon with your hook, you can change the graphic slightly for each hook. If you have take-home points to go with all your hooks, you could use the same icons, but make them smaller. Make the text smaller, too.

Use strong access points. Today's audience doesn't usually read from start to finish, so you need to provide clear access points to different parts of your information product. In traditional books, headings are the main points of access. In newspapers and magazines, the headlines, photographs, captions, sidebars, and pull quotes are all points of access. In a multimedia world, clickable icons and buttons are points of access. Use access points judiciously, though. Clutter defeats your purpose.

These are general guidelines. As you work with them, you'll find variations that work and don't work. The important thing is to start with a simple framework. Don't worry about constraints. Constraints provoke creativity. The combination of consistency and creativity will make your presentation both accessible and alive.

Her professional mystique notwithstanding, Susie Hu is essentially an information worker.

She sells an information gathering process that may or may not lead to the results the client wants. Because she can't guarantee her results, she needs to document her process in clear, professional reports.

She needs to make a lot of diverse data make sense. She needs to make it accessible. She needs to make it seem worth the money.

She also needs to minimize rewriting and reformatting.

Her strategy is to use a simple report template that she herself created. Into this template she copies the notes from her contact records, as well as photographic exhibits that she has captured and stored with her digital camera. She also includes an expense report, created from a ClarisWorks spreadsheet. An executive summary at the beginning is the only new writing required.

TOOLS

ClarisWorks
Claris FileMaker

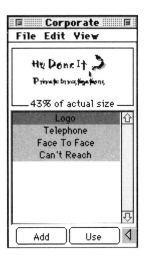

Susie keeps these icons in the Library window for quick access as she works—she just drags the icon from the Library window to her document.

 S O L U T I O N S

257

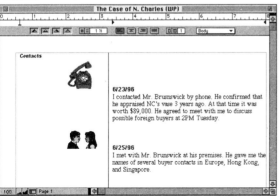

Susie starts with a ClarisWorks text document—a report template that she created and uses for all her reports.

Then she copies the notes from her FileMaker contact database into the Contacts section of her report.

A report may contain many pages of these notes. To make them more accessible and mark the beginning of a new contact, Susie uses clip art icons to indicate a phone contact, a face-to-face meeting, or "unable to reach."

Dave and Darcy Delacruz produce all kinds of information products. They do high-volume and high-quality work, so they use high-end tools and processes that make the most of those tools. Here's how they set up their projects.

Each product begins with a page layout document. They start by creating master pages, using a page design that they create themselves or one that the client supplies. Then they build all the styles into the document. If the document is long, they create several documents—for chapters, sections, or parts.

Next, they assemble the components. They work with text in a word processor where they can make sure all the styles are properly applied. They keep all their project graphics in Fetch databases. From there, they can easily import them directly into a document or onto a pasteboard where they're readily accessible.

This careful prep work makes it a snap to actually build pages—and it reduces mistakes that could mean starting over from scratch.

THE ESSENTIAL TOOLS

Adobe PageMaker
Adobe Photoshop
Microsoft Word
Adobe Fetch

The Fetch database catalogs graphics for easy retrieval during page layout.

S   O   L   U   T   I   O   N   S

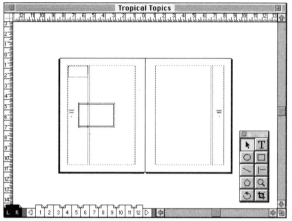

Master pages define the elements that recur on each page of the document. The Delacruz team can define several different master pages for the same document to accommodate pages with special treatments.

Styles are the key to fast formatting. PageMaker reads the Word style names and interprets them according to the PageMaker design, so it's easy to change design elements at any time.

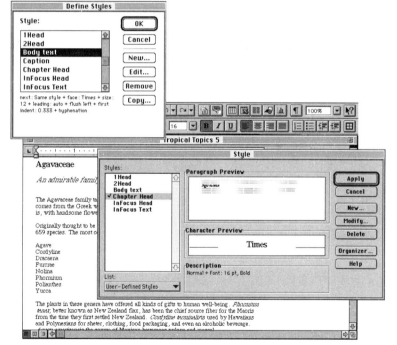

JUMP START:
Setting Up the Information Assembly Line

Think of your Mac as an information assembly line. You create all the pieces and then assemble them. Here's how to set it up:

STEP 1: CHOOSE YOUR MEDIA

You have two basic choices: the printed page or the small screen.

The printed page includes everything from letters and newsletters to brochures and books. This medium works well when

- Your audience doesn't have easy access to computers.
- Your audience needs the information when they're away from their computers.
- Your audience prefers printed information.
- You want an image of permanence.
- Your message is a long text narrative.
- The information doesn't change often.
- You need to reach specific people.

The small screen includes everything from Web pages and electronic kiosks to CD-ROM magazines and books. Choose this medium if

- You have large volumes of encyclopedia-style information.
- You have lots of graphics.
- You want to include video or audio in your message.
- Your audience is computer-literate and has access to computers.
- You want to tailor information to lots of different audiences without producing several different products.
- You need to update information frequently.
- Your audience will actively seek the information you're providing.
- You want your audience to be able to interact with your information product, perhaps adding to it or responding to questionnaires.

Once you make this basic choice, you have lots of other options, as the tables on the following pages show.

TABLE 9.1   THE PRINTED PAGE

THE CHOICES	THE THINGS TO THINK ABOUT
REPRODUCTION METHOD *Desktop printing* You print directly from your Macintosh. *Electrostatic copier* You print a master on your desktop printer or an image setter and then make copies on a copy machine. *Offset Printing* You print a master on your desktop printer or an image setter or save it on a disk. Then a commercial printer prints the copies on a press.	**Number of copies** Use your desktop printer for less than 100 pages. Use electrostatic copying for 100 to 1000 pages total. Use commercial offset printing for more than 1000 pages. (This is a general rule of thumb. Check actual printing costs in your area to confirm. **Color** Use your desktop printer or electrostatic color copier for quick color highlights. Use commercial printing if you need high-quality color. **Paper** Use your desktop printer or electrostatic copier for standard-size, letter-weight paper or lightweight cover stock. Otherwise use a commercial printer. (Your desktop printer may be able to handle other sizes and weights, but they're hard to handle and may reduce the life of your printer.) **Quality** Your desktop printer can produce better quality print than many low-end commercial offset printing presses. But if you want really high-quality, you need high-quality offset (or other commercial printing processes such as rotogravure).
NUMBER OF PAGES	**Your information** How much do you have? Can you condense it? Do you want a lot of white space—to make your pages look open and easy? **Your audience** How much do they want? Is more really more? Or will less get your point across better? **Your budget** The number of pages is the single most important factor in determining the cost of printed products—the more pages, the higher the cost.
PAGE SIZE	**Packaging** How will you deliver the product? Will you need a special envelope to mail it? Does it need to fit in a notebook or folder? Does it go in a package with other products? How big are they? How big is the package? **Usability** Is it easy to handle? Does the information fit on the page? Do you have room for graphics and other special elements on the page, perhaps in wide margins? **Standards** Paper comes in standard sizes. Whether you're using your own desktop printer or a commercial printer, you save money—and trees—when you use a standard paper size.

(continued)

TABLE 9.1   THE PRINTED PAGE (continued)

THE CHOICES	THE THINGS TO THINK ABOUT
COLOR	**Cost** If you're using a commercial printing process, each color requires an extra pass through the press (or a larger, more expensive press with multiple printing stations). It also requires extra setup costs on the press and extra work on your computer. If you're printing on a desktop printer or color copier, you pay extra for color toner, too. **Quality** Color adds a quality look. It also adds real meaning when you need to highlight parts of an illustration—for example, to call out a particular part of an engine, map, or chart. Often you can get the color effects you need with only one or two extra colors, not full color.
PHOTOGRAPHS	**Your message** Do you need literal illustrations? Do you need to show real people, real places, real life? Photographs lend reality to your message. **Quality** The quality of photographs depends on the resolution (dots per inch) of the printing process. Both desktop and commercial printing offer a range of resolutions. Get samples before you decide. **Cost** Photographs can cost extra because they require extra preparation. You can save some of these costs if you use special tools like scanners and Adobe Photoshop to prepare them yourself. But you need special skills.

TABLE 9.2   THE SMALL SCREEN

THE CHOICES	THE THINGS TO THINK ABOUT
DISTRIBUTION METHOD Floppy disks CD-ROMs Web pages	**Size of presentation** Floppy disks hold up to 1.4 megabytes. (Look for superdensity floppies to hold 120 megabytes soon.) CD-ROMs hold up to 600 megabytes. The capacity of Web pages depends on your arrangement with your service provider. Typical storage spaces for business sites are 20 to 50 megabytes. **Accessibility** All computer owners can use floppy disks. CD-ROMs and Web pages require special hardware CD-ROM drives and modems respectively. Does your audience have these? **Cost** It costs about 50 to 75 cents to duplicate a floppy disk.

(continued)

TABLE 9.2   THE SMALL SCREEN (continued)

THE CHOICES	THE THINGS TO THINK ABOUT
	A CD-ROM mastering system costs about $1500, but you can pay someone else to master your CD-ROM for about $100. Individual copies are about $1.00 each. You pay a one-time setup charge to establish your Web site—plus the cost to develop and maintain your web site. Your users pay connect time to access your Web page, depending on their network service.
PLATFORM Mac Mac & Windows Platform independent	**Target Audience** There are many more Windows users than Mac users (sigh). If you're producing a commercial product, you'll vastly increase your audience if you offer both Mac and Windows versions. If you want to be truly platform independent, you need to use a standard like HTML—which can be translated to almost any operating environment. It has limitations, of course. **Display choices** Take into account the variety of monitor displays available to your audience. They range from small portable screens to large graphics-display screens. Consider also color capabilities, resolution, and installed fonts. Do you want to work with the lowest common denominator, or do you want to set your own minimum standard and exclude some users? **Development and testing time** It takes longer to develop and test a product for multiple platforms than for a single platform.
AUTHORING ENVIRONMENT High-end multimedia tools HyperCard & look-alikes Slide presentation software	**Cross-platform compatibility** Does your authoring environment produce products that can run on all the platforms you're supporting? While you can play Macromedia Director movies on either a Mac or Windows machines, you can't play the play-only versions (called projectors) on both platforms. HyperCard currently works only on the Macintosh. Oracle Media Objects, a HyperCard look-alike, works on both platforms. **Run-time software** Most tools provide a player that plays your presentations without the software you use to develop them. Check to make sure that this player is easily available to your audience or that you can easily supply it if it's not. (A HyperCard player comes with all Apple machines, for example.) **Interactivity** Most tools provide ways for users to interact with your presentation—by choosing different paths through the information, by searching for information, and sometimes even by contributing to the information. Slide shows are at the low end. A lot of interactivity requires sophisticated programming. **Animation** All tools support QuickTime video movies. But if you want to create your own animated illustrations, you need the high-end tools. Slide presentations have very simple slide transitions that can simulate minimal animation. **Ease of use** If you don't have a lot of programming skills and don't want to acquire them, stick to slide presentation software. High-end multimedia software is complex to learn. HyperCard is somewhere in between.

THE SPECIAL CASE OF SLIDE PRESENTATIONS

If you're looking for a quick entry point into multimedia presentations, take a look at slide presentation software like Persuasion and PowerPoint. These tools offer a great middle ground between traditional print and high-end multimedia productions. You can print them on paper or on slides for overhead projection. But you can also view them on-screen—either your small screen or a big projection screen. You can incorporate them into online displays where they can run unattended, automatically sequencing through a series of slides.

These programs handle graphics like champs, but can also do a fine job of presenting text—especially if you want to make your points...well...point by point. They use outlines as their foundation, so you can organize your points before you start building your slides. You can include video clips for a real multimedia effect when you're using the small screen, but not give up the flexibility of slide-by-slide presentations when you only have an overhead projector. Of course, you can also turn your presentation into regular 35mm slides, too.

If you want to give graphics the primary place in your presentations but don't feel ready to take on the multimedia authoring environments, slide presentation software is your best bet.

STEP 2: CHOOSE YOUR TOOLS

You need two kinds of tools for building your information products: **specialized tools** for building components and **platform tools** for putting them together.

Specialized tools include word processors, as well as graphics, video, and audio applications. They may also include database and spreadsheet applications. These tools give you depth of control and the ability to craft individual pieces of information down to the finest detail.

Platform tools include page layout software for printed materials and multimedia authoring environments for small-screen presentations. A Web page authoring program like Adobe PageMill is a platform program, too. Slide presentation applications like Adobe Persuasion and Microsoft Power-Point can cross media lines and serve as a great platform for building either printed or small-screen presentations—with some limitations.

Platform tools give you breadth of control. They have some of the same features as the specialty tools—such as text-formatting commands and drawing tools—but they're not as efficient for composing components, and they don't offer as many options.

Sometimes you may not need this efficiency. For example, if you're creating a short brochure with just a little text, you can skip the word processor and compose in your page layout application. Of course, the opposite may be true. You may not need the breadth of the platform tools. For example, if you're creating a simple text report, with few graphics, you can just use a robust word processing application or integrated software package. Or if your information product is a single diagram with a paragraph or two of text, all you need is a good draw program. Even Adobe Premiere—a video editing package—can be a platform, if video is the primary medium.

STEP 3: SET UP YOUR GRID

An outline organizes information logically. *A grid organizes information visually.* It tells you what kind of information goes where—and how it looks.

You usually set up your grid in your platform application, often with *masters.* These masters define the elements that repeat on every page, slide, or screen:

- Borders
- Running heads
- Page numbers
- Standard graphic elements, such as your company logo or decorative art
- Standard text elements, such as your company name or confidentiality notices

Master pages may also define columns, text blocks, graphic blocks, and other elements that you use to position things that occur on some pages and not others. They help you plan the placement of information from page to page, screen to screen.

Many platform applications come with some sample masters that you can use right out of the box. They're a good starting place if you don't have much experience with information design. As you gain experience, you can tweak these masters or even design your own grids to fit your information—and give your products a unique look.

For more about these templates, see "Upsizing" below.

A master page from Adobe PageMaker

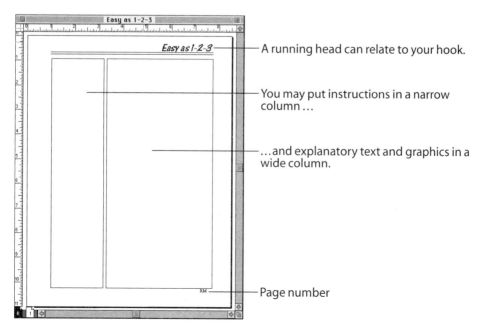

— A running head can relate to your hook.

— You may put instructions in a narrow column ...

— ...and explanatory text and graphics in a wide column.

— Page number

A master slide from Adobe Persuasion

The slide head may be your hook.

The take-home point might go here.

The facts—graphics or text—may go here.

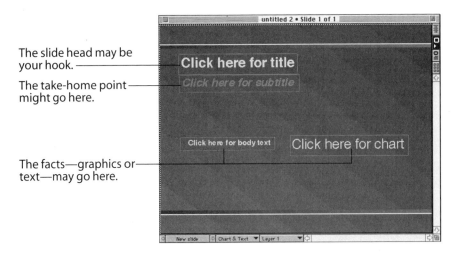

Macromedia Director doesn't use masters, but you can use a background image on the stage...

...and then place cast members on the background to animate them.

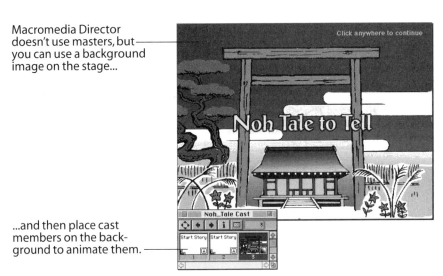

STEP 4: SKETCH YOUR PRESENTATION

This is where you assign content to the presentation. Using your grid, sketch the information into the proper blocks on the grid. Don't worry about getting everything just right. Put a rough heading and a few quick thoughts in a text block. Draw a square or circle to represent large graphics.

You can actually create every page, slide, or frame of your document this way. Or you can print lots of thumbnails of the masters and then sketch the information in pencil on the thumbnails. (*Thumbnails* are tiny representations of the page or screen—usually printed about 8 or 16 to a sheet of paper.) In some multimedia authoring environments, you can print story-boards—the sequence of frames in your presentation. Storyboards are tradi-tional planning tools for video, film, and animation.

For long presentations with lots of text and graphics that you'll develop in a special-purpose application, it may be better to work in pencil. Otherwise, you'll have to take out a lot of placeholder material before you import your real content.

Slide and multimedia software often make it easy to switch back and forth between this kind of visual planning and standard outlines. Slide pre-sentation programs like Persuasion and PowerPoint have links between the grid areas of your slide and a standard outline, so you can sketch visually and then refine in outline mode, or vice versa. Multimedia environments like Macromedia Director have different windows for ordering the various files and animation effects that make up your presentation and for playing them. As already mentioned, you can also print storyboards that show the content of each frame.

Here are some tips to help you put your presentation together with as few hassles as possible:

TIP 1: Organize all the pieces in one folder (or folders within a folder if you're composing a long, complex presentation). Some applications don't actually import your component documents—they just point to the file. If all the pieces are in one folder, you won't have any trouble moving your presentation from one machine to another.

TIP 2: Use a high-capacity removable drive like a SyQuest removable cartridge or an optical disk drive to store backup copies of your data. Graphics and video files can be huge—too huge to fit on a single floppy. Also, If your project folder is large (see TIP 1), you won't be able to fit it all on one floppy disk.

TIP 3: Divide long presentations into parts. It's easier and faster to work in shorter files, and most applications have features for working with more than one file. For example, page layout programs can create tables of contents and indexes across file boundaries. You can also string several slide files together to produce one presentation.

TIP 4: Set up libraries of elements that you can draw on. See "Upsizing" below for the kinds of things you can put in your libraries.

TIP 5: For standard boilerplate information that you need to use over and over again, consider setting up a database with records that you can use to create custom documents for custom audiences as you need them. For example, if you do financial consulting and have descriptions of lots of different insurance plans, investment plans, and other financial strategies, you might set up a database with each of these plans in a different record. Then you can quickly import the individual plans you need to build a complete custom program for each client.

PUTTING IT TOGETHER FAST

STEP 5: FILL IN THE PIECES

The first four steps are all planning steps. But by the time you've finished them, you're almost through. You just have to fill in the information. You use your special-purpose tools to create these pieces. Then you place them on your platform—the page, the slide, the screen.

You may have to adjust your plan as you develop the details. Some text may require more space than you allowed. Or you may not be able to get the photograph you wanted. But even if you move things around or substitute one graphic for another, the basic framework will be sound if you've followed Steps 1 through 4.

UPSIZING: Expanding Your Repertoire

Okay, so you've got the basics down. Now you want to streamline, expand, work faster, and produce more variety with higher quality. You've got lots of possibilities. Here are a few.

Templates & style sheets

Style sheets and templates are basic tools for fast work and good looks.

Style sheets are a set of formats—things like font, size, style, and indentation—that you apply to a paragraph or selected text, depending on your application. You can and should set up standard styles for your documents. For example, you can always use the same style for the types of information we talked about in the introduction to this chapter—hooks, facts, instructions, stories, and take-home points. Or in traditional documents, you can set up standard styles for chapter heads, first-level heads, second-level heads, footnotes, and other traditional outline elements.

You set up styles in different ways in different applications. But the typical steps go something like this:

1. Format the text in the style you want.
2. Select it.
3. Use a Define Styles command to name the style.
4. Save or add the style to a style list or palette.

In most applications, you can also copy a set of styles from one file to another, so you can use the same styles in several presentations. For example, you can set up a report style sheet, a brochure style sheet, and a catalog style sheet. Some applications export the styles to a separate file. In Microsoft Word, you just choose the Define Styles command in a new document and open the document with the styles you want to use. The styles are automatically added to the new document.

You may also be able to copy styles from application to application. Macintosh applications that can read other Mac files usually retain most of the formatting when you copy or import. For example, if you import a word processing document into a PageMaker file, you can click Retain Format to import the styles with the text. Note, however, that if you have already defined styles with the same name in the PageMaker document, the PageMaker style overrides the imported style.

Templates are documents that have some styles as well as design or text elements already in them. A template can be as simple as the last copy of your résumé. You just save a copy of it and make changes to fit your current needs. Or it can be a special document that you or your designer sets up for a special purpose. Again, you make a copy and add your new material to the copy.

Tip: When you're moving formatted text and graphics between applications, use Rich Text Format to save as much of the formatting and graphics as possible. You can usually choose the Rich Text Format when you save a file or import it.

Styles can save you time in several ways:

■ You don't have to use multiple commands for font, size, style, and other text attributes each time you format the text. Once you create the style, you just use one command to apply all the text formatting at once.

■ You can create a new presentation with the same styles as an old presentation. You get consistency—which reinforces your company image—and you don't waste time reinventing the wheel every time you have a new report, newsletter, or Web page.

■ You can quickly redesign a entire presentation—or a part that isn't working—simply by redefining the styles. You don't have to go through and reformat the whole presentation. Everything changes automatically to match the new styles.

Some applications also supply special templates that automatically create a new duplicate copy when you open them—as in ClarisWorks. Templates not only speed up the process of formatting your presentation—they often help you structure your content as well.

Printing from your desktop printer? You can get a design boost from predesigned papers—stationery with borders and banners and color just waiting for a bit of text and graphics to complete the story. You can get coordinated envelopes, letter stationery, tri-fold brochure stationery, business cards, mailing labels, and more.

In some cases, you can get templates to go with the stationery you choose. ClarisWorks includes PaperDirect templates in its Small Business Solutions Pack. In addition, Paper Direct sells dozens of paper designs with corresponding templates for Microsoft Word, Adobe PageMaker, and QuarkXPress. (You can call 1-800-A-PAPERS to get the catalog.)

The main advantage of predesigned papers is color. You can incorporate two, three, or more colors into your presentation without paying for the extra color press runs at a commercial printer. (As color laser printers become more affordable, this advantage will fade.)

The main disadvantage is that your materials are not unique. Other people are using the same design as you are. For your market, it may not matter. The color advantage may be more important than originality. Unless you're in a very design-savvy environment, it's probably not a problem.

Set up templates for all your standard documents and presentations: product specifications, catalogs, quarterly reports, your Web page, letters, invoices, service contracts, and project estimates. If you do it more than once, do it with a template. You may have to invest a couple of hours to learn all the secrets of styles and templates in your applications. But you'll save weeks of work every year.

Digital input

In today's information market, you need graphics, and lots of them. If you're not a graphic artist—or even if you are—digitizers are a fast way to get great graphics. Digitizers turn nondigital information—like faces and buildings and cars and abstract images—into digital information your screen can display and your computer can manipulate. There are several different types of digitizers.

Digital cameras look and work a lot like regular film cameras, but they record the images electronically in memory instead of on film. You can transfer these images via a cable and special software to your Mac. Then you can use the images in documents—and even fine-tune them or wildly distort them with photo processing applications like Adobe Photoshop.

You may not need to invest in a digital camera. Unless you have a photographic flair, you'll probably want to hire a professional to photograph your products. And even if you have some photographic skills, you may be frustrated by the lack of resolution—and the lack of control—in the current crop of affordable digital cameras. You're a candidate for a digital camera if no-frills photographs can help you communicate your message. Typical users are real estate agents, architects, insurance adjusters, and appraisers.

Digital cameras are starting to replace traditional film cameras in many areas. High-end digital cameras can duplicate the quality you get with film cameras, but these studio-quality digital cameras cost in the tens of thousands of dollars. So what do you do on a home office budget? Check out the new breed of low-cost, consumer-quality digital cameras like the Casio QV-10 and the Apple QuickTake 150.

The QuickTake 150 acts like a traditional camera—except that you store the images electronically rather than on film. You aim through a clear viewfinder, and your control information appears on an LCD screen. The QuickTake also has a built-in flash. When you're ready to view your images, you hook the QT150 to your Mac via a serial cable and send the images to the computer. There you can view them—and even change them—with Apple's PhotoFlash software.

The very compact Casio QV-10 has a more modern electronic camera architecture. You use the color LCD display on its back to compose your images instead of focusing through a viewfinder. You can also use this LCD screen to view the images you've already taken without hooking up to a computer. If you don't like the results, you can shoot them again right then and there.   (continued)

THE CASIO QV-10 AND THE APPLE QUICK-TAKE 150: A CLOSEUP VIEW

(continued)

Which kind of digital camera is the right one for you? It depends on what you need. One of the most important things to look for is resolution, which determines how big and sharp you can make your image. The resolution in digital cameras is measured in pixels. The Apple QuickTake 150 can take color pictures with a resolution of 640 x 480 pixels. The Casio QV-10 can shoot color, too, but only 320 x 240 pixels' worth. That's one-quarter the resolution of the QuickTake. However, the QuickTake camera can take only 16 high-quality images (or 32 in standard quality). With its lower resolution, the QV-10 can take 96 pictures.

Of course, these specs will be out of date before you can say "Smile." Look for digital cameras to take off as the resolution goes up, the features expand, and the price comes down.

QuickTake 150 image

THE CASIO QV-10 AND THE APPLE QUICKTAKE 150: A CLOSE-UP VIEW

Casio QV-10 image

Scanners scan flat surfaces, much like a copy machine, and turn them into files on disk. A scanner is the perfect tool when you need to use photographs, sketches, paintings, or some other form of flat art in your documents. You can also scan text pages, but if you want to be able to edit that text or search it in a database, you need *OCR* software. OCR stands for optical character recognition. If the text isn't clear, the results can be poor indeed. You can scan text without OCR software, but it turns into a single image that's not editable as text—which may be just fine if all you want to do is use a newspaper clipping as an illustration, for example.

Scanners come in several models: flatbed, handheld, and a paper-feed style that works like your fax machine. The flatbed and paper-feed models produce more reliable results than the handheld models—they use a mechanical drive instead of your arm.

If you're not interested in honing your graphic arts skills, however, scanning might not be for you. It can be a mighty art, especially if color is involved. If you don't do a lot of graphic arts work, it may be best to get your scanning done by a service bureau. Look in the Yellow Pages under Computer Graphics or Reprographics.

Clip art and stock media

Another way to get quality graphics if you're not an artist or photographer is to buy them. Today you can buy just about any kind of graphics you want,

Flatbed scanners take up a lot of desk space and have traditionally been aimed at artists and graphic designers. Unless this is your field, you may wonder if a scanner can do your home office any good. Well, take a look at the PaperPort Vx by Visioneer. It's one of the most innovative pieces of hardware to come around in a long time—a compact scanner, designed to sit right under your monitor.

The PaperPort lives up to its name: it's a direct way to get paper-based information into your computer with the least amount of effort. You simply slip a piece of paper between its rollers and it draws the paper in automatically. Your scanned document appears on-screen on the PaperPort desktop, where PaperPort automatically straightens and trims the edges. Then you can organize, alter, and annotate your scanned documents. You can also search for documents using your annotations as search words. (Your annotations may also include graphics, by the way.)

PaperPorts has desktop links to your other application programs. You set up the window with icons for your main applications—your word processor, your photo processor, your paint program, your database program.

PRODUCT FOCUS

PAPERPORT VX: A DIFFERENT TAKE ON SCANNING

(continued)

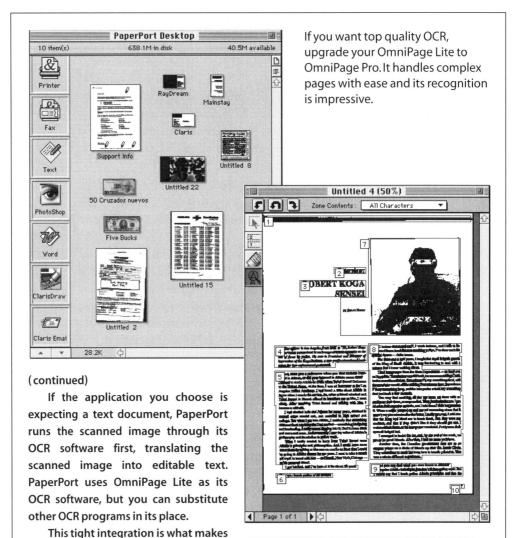

If you want top quality OCR, upgrade your OmniPage Lite to OmniPage Pro. It handles complex pages with ease and its recognition is impressive.

(continued)

If the application you choose is expecting a text document, PaperPort runs the scanned image through its OCR software first, translating the scanned image into editable text. PaperPort uses OmniPage Lite as its OCR software, but you can substitute other OCR programs in its place.

This tight integration is what makes PaperPort stand out among scanners. It's so seamless, you can easily convert any information you have on paper into computer-readable format for filing in folders on your computer or to send via e-mail. If you don't need to keep the originals, you can store much of your paperwork electronically. You can then print scanned documents, making your PaperPort—plus—Laser printer into a copy machine.

PAPERPORT VX: A DIFFERENT TAKE ON SCANNING

PaperPort scans in black and white, with up to 256 shades of gray, at a resolution of up to 400 dots per inch.

from simple clip art drawings and icons to stock photos, stock video, and stock audio.

You can buy graphics two ways: royalty-free and under license. The clip art CDs you buy from software catalogs fall in the first category. You buy them outright. You can use their art anywhere you want, as often as you want. And so can anyone else who buys the CD.

In the second category are the stock media. These may be photographs, original art, video clips, or sound recordings that a stock house owns. You license the right to use one of these for a particular purpose and for a particular period of time. The price may be a royalty on copies you sell, or it may be a fixed fee. And it varies depending on the potential of your product—if you have a hot product, you may pay more than your neighbor down the street who's using stock images for a nonprofit fundraising brochure.

You have to be a little careful with stock media. Usually, you get an exclusive. No one else can use your photo or clip for a specified period, maybe five years. But you don't actually own it. You may give up the rights after five years or 500,000 copies. It all depends on the deal you negotiate. You may also have to publish appropriate credits and meet other copyright obligations. Also, be sure that your dealer has the authority to license the image. You don't want to publish and then find out your dealer didn't have any rights to license to you or anyone else.

Once you start to build your library of clip art and stock media, you need a way to store it—and then to retrieve it. Some clip art CDs come with their

WHERE TO FIND STOCK MEDIA

> There are hundreds of stock media houses. The simplest way to find one is on the World Wide Web. Here are a couple of addresses to get you started:
>
> `http://www.plannetonline.com`
> `http://indexstock.com`
>
> For a great discussion of stock media and long listings of sources, see "The Interactivity Guide to Stock Media," beginning in the November/December 1995 issue of *Interactivity*, a multimedia magazine. (Its Internet e-mail address is `interactivity@mfi.com`.)

own built-in cataloging software, but many don't. Some have a few primitive categories and then just a list of titles that may be more or less descriptive. As your library grows, you may well want to invest in general-purpose cataloging software, like Adobe Fetch.

With Fetch, you can catalog drawings, photographs, video clips, and sounds, with information about the size and format of each image, as well as comments such as where you've used the image before. Then you can search this text, display a thumbnail, and even preview a video or audio clip. It's well worth the money—about $100—to have fingertip access to a large library of graphics.

Special effects

It's a 3-D world out there, with extravagant extrusions, sassy shadows, and tempting textures. You don't have to be an accomplished graphic artist to get these special effects. You just need the right tools.

Start with special effects software. These are special-purpose packages that help you do everything from creating special textures to turning 2-D pictures into images with 3-D depth.

For example, you can use programs like Adobe TextureMaker and Specular's TextureScape to design unlimited textures, which are great for backdrops for multimedia presentations or web pages. You can also give text and graphics depth with Adobe Dimensions or AddDepth from Ray Dream Design. These packages cost about $50 to $200.

If you really want to add spice to your images, go for the complete 3-D packages, like Specular Infini-D, Macromedia's Extreme 3D, or Ray Dream Designer 4. These packages produce photo-realistic 3-D models that will blow away any flat art you've been using. For multimedia presentation, turn these models into movies using the companion animation programs—Ray Dream Animator and LogoMotion from Specular. Ray Dream's 3-D program and animator also come in one package called Ray Dream Studio, which also has hundreds of pre-built 3-D models you can use. Specular, too, provides a CD with hundreds of its own 3-D models.

You can easily model 3-D text or objects with Infini-D.

If you want to invest more time and money, get Adobe Photoshop. It's one of the most versatile graphics applications you can buy. You'll use it for everything from touching up photos to creating elaborate layered graphics—blending several photographs, or textures with photographs, or text with art that you've scanned or clipped from your clip-art CD.

Once you've mastered all of Photoshop's capabilities you can get dozens of plug-in extensions and filters to create additional special effects with lighting, shape, color, and texture. You can even animate your Photoshop graphics. A popular plug-in package, and one of our personal favorites, is Kai's Power Tools, from MetaTools. In fact, we drool over all of MetaTools products: Convolver, Vector Effects, and especially KPT Bryce.

You can find lots of plug-in packages by checking your software catalog or local retailer or by wandering around the Web, searching the keywords: *Photoshop, Plug-in,* or *special effects.*

Beware in the world of special effects, however. They can swallow you up—hook, line, and profits. You may find yourself pressing the preview button until 4 a.m. Unless you're a graphics professional, set up a special effects schedule—short sessions during the slow part of your day or week to explore the possibilities. And set a timer to remind you when to return to the world of ordinary effects.

Audio and video

If you've always imagined yourself as a Hollywood movie director, here's your chance. The Macintosh has powerful audio-video technology built into its operating system. It's called QuickTime. Just like text and graphics, Quick-Time movies are objects that you can put into documents of all sorts—including everything from databases to slide shows to Web pages.

To work with existing video clips—for example, the clips you get from a stock media house—you need a video editor like Adobe Premiere. With it, not only can you select the sequences you want and edit out bad frames, you can also sync sound and apply special effects.

To create your own video clips, you need a video digitizer. If you have an AV model Mac, you have a video digitizer built in. If you don't have an AV model, you'll need to get a special board. Then you can plug your VCR or video camera directly into the video port. You can capture TV and movie sequences—careful, these are copyrighted—or create your own.

You can also create animated transitions between still frames. For animation, you don't need a video digitizer. You can start with simple line drawings, photographs, or complex illustrations. But you need software to build the transitions, which is what programs like Macromedia Director and Ray Dream Animator do.

Want sound to go with your video? Apple provides lots of sound samples as part of the QuickTime package. You can create your own, too, if you have a sound digitizer like an electronic keyboard and a MIDI input device. To edit these sounds, you need a sound editor. Try Macromedia's SoundEdit 16 for sophisticated sound work. (If your Mac came with a microphone, you can make and save short recordings with the Sound item in the Apple Menu Items folder.)

QuickTime makes it easy to put your audio and video together because it creates time-based presentations. This means that it automatically skips video frames, if necessary, to keep in time with the sound track. QuickTime also makes it easy to move your finished product from platform to platform—it's machine independent.

Now, back to the real world. The Mac's audio and video technologies are empowering and provocative. But you need more than the technology. Even with all the Mac support, audio-video is hard to do well. It takes time to learn the tools—and lots of time and planning for each project. There are practical considerations, too. Sound and video files are big—really big. Even if you're producing your own CDs, they'll eat up your information space faster than a hungry bear in spring.

If you want to get into the world of digital video quickly and cheaply, check out the Quick-Cam by Connectix. QuickCam gets you into the game for about a hundred bucks. It's a gray-scale camera the size of a pool ball. It just plugs right into your serial port—no need for a video board—and the software that comes with it lets you grab still frames or make movies at up to 15 frames per second.

You can use the QuickCam to grab stills for brochures, catalogs, and presentations. You can save these images in PICT, TIFF, or JPEG format—the desktop computer graphics standards. The QuickCam images use 16 shades of gray, which is enough for basic quality images of people or objects.

Of course, QuickCam does video, too. You can use the QuickMovie software that comes with QuickCam to save QuickTime movies directly from the camera onto your hard drive. Don't expect to be producing MTV hits with this system, though. The largest image you can capture is only 320 x 240 pixels, and at that size, you'll probably only be capturing about four frames per second.

So what does a home office person like you do with camera like this? You create simple instructional videos and video narrations for your products and services. You put a short video letter or announcement on a floppy and mail it to a client for a more personal touch. You build a video-conferencing system between your basement office and your partner's attic office. And if you absolutely must have color, you can get the Color QuickCam for an extra hundred bucks. It acts just like its gray-scale brother but in 24-bit color.

**DIGITAL
VIDEO WORLD:
QUICK ACCESS**

POWER PLAY:
Keeping Your Corporate ID In Style

Big companies spend big dollars to create style manuals that keep their corporate ID intact. They have guidelines for everything from preferred corporate spellings to rules for when, where, and how to use the corporate logo.

You can shortcut the process—and speed up all your production projects—by turning your Mac into your style guardian. This example uses ClarisWorks, but most of your desktop tools will have what you need to save you time and guarantee a consistent look when you're producing information products. Here are the basic guidelines for organizing your desktop for good, consistent corporate style.

What you need

- Your publishing tools
- Your logo
- Any standard company art
- Time: Ongoing

Set up your graphics library

Most publishing products now have libraries that you can set up and access directly as you work. One of the first libraries you should create is your corporate graphics library. It should include your company logo, any product or service logos you have, and other standard elements that you use in your publications, including icons and standard product illustrations.

1. Create a library for your corporate graphics.

For example, in a ClarisWorks document, choose Library > New from the File menu. Then Choose Save As from the File menu in the new library window and give it a name such as Corporate.

2. Copy your graphics from their original documents and paste them in your library window.

In ClarisWorks, choose Paste from the Edit menu to paste the graphic into the library window. You can name each graphic as you add it. You can also view your icons by name with the By Name command in the View menu.

If you work with more than one publishing tool, create a library for each one. Then you'll always have your graphics available at your fingertips.

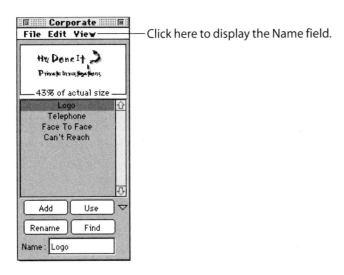

Click here to display the Name field.

Create your corporate word list

Every business has certain words associated with it. Some of your business words may be unique to you. Maybe you have products and services that you've named. Maybe you have special words that you use in a special way or with a special spelling to highlight your uniqueness. You have preferences, too, about ways to spell words: maybe you like *catalog* better than *catalogue*. Or you like *online* better than *on-line*.

You can set up your spell-checker to recognize these unique spellings. Then when you use your spell-checker—as you always should—it doesn't think you're misspelling your company name just because it's not in Webster's Standard Dictionary. And it *does* alert you when you've deviated from your standard preferences.

1. Create a word list in a text file.

Type each word on a separate line with the capitalization you prefer. Go through your existing company materials—brochures, stationery, letters, business plans—to identify your special words. Be sure to include your name and street or city names from your address. In ClarisWorks, save the list as a text file. (Choose Text from the format pop-up list in the Save As dialog box.)

2. Create your custom dictionary.

In ClarisWorks, choose Writing Tools > Select Dictionaries from the Edit menu. Select User Dictionary from the drop down menu and then click New to create a new user dictionary. Type the name of the dictionary and click Save.

3. Import the word list into your custom dictionary.

In ClarisWorks, choose Writing Tools > User Dictionary from the Edit menu. Click Text File and then click Import. Select your word list and click Open. ClarisWorks imports your word list, but it doesn't import any words that are already in the main dictionary.

You can add to your dictionary simply by typing in the Edit User Dictionary window. Then you can periodically export your user dictionary to save your updated word list as a text file. You may want to give this list to consultants who are helping you develop marketing or other corporate materials. You may also want to create a second version of the list with special notes about the words—for example, whether you always want them to appear in all caps, or if you only want to use them as adjectives, not nouns.

Set up your templates

You probably have several standard types of documents—from letters to invoices to product brochures, spreadsheets, and even Web pages. While the contents of these documents change, you probably want to use the same format each time, both for consistency of image and for ease of production.

Take the time to set up templates for each of your standard corporate documents.

1. Open a document and save it as stationery.

If you already have a document that's formatted the way you want it, open it. If not, just open a new document. In either case, save it as stationery. In ClarisWorks, choose Save As from the File menu, give the template a name, click the Stationery button, and then click Save.

2. Create the styles you need for this type of document.

If you're using an existing document that's been created with styles, you can skip this step. You've already got your styles.

If not, start by analyzing your document. What elements does it include: A title? A chapter title? A couple of levels of heads? Special quotes from endorsers? Checklists? Make a list of all the different elements in your document and give them simple, easy-to-remember names.

Then create the styles. For example, in ClarisWorks, choose Show Style from the View menu and then click New to create a new style. Choose the type of style (usually Paragraph for text documents), give the style a name, and click OK. Now choose the style choices you want for the new style from the Font, Size, and Style menus. You can also select ruler settings; these appear in the Edit Style window. Click Done when you're finished.

Tip: If you work with a designer, ask him or her to give you a template with the styles already defined—plus a written set of specs for the styles. You can ask the designer to set up master pages, too.

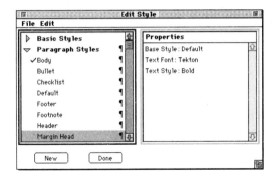

3. Set up your master pages if appropriate.

If you're working with a tool that uses master pages, set them up, too. Include all the elements that occur on standard pages throughout your document. ClarisWorks doesn't use master pages.

4. Include any actual text and graphics that will always be part of the document.

For example, if you always include your logo on the title page of your reports, put it in place. If you always include a company profile as the last page of your document, put it in place. If you always use the same headings throughout the document, type them and apply the appropriate style.

5. Save your changes to the document, and create a backup copy on a floppy disk.

Follow these steps for all your standard documents. Then when you have to create a brochure or report or even just write a letter, a lot of your work is already done. And all of your documents look as if they came off the same assembly line—which is just what you want for a strong corporate identity.

ON THE HORIZON: The Real World of Games

Remember those pictures we showed in you Chapter 3? The vales of *Myst*? The vaults of *Marathon*? The world of computer games has grown side by side with the world of business software, but don't be surprised if sometime soon, the two worlds begin to collide—or at least merge into one online culture.

Games are a way to move around in a 3-D information space. In the past, the information has been limited: small, mouthy head eats things that can be counted so points can be given. The worlds of *Myst* and *Marathon* are much more information-rich, however. Sure, they're addictive to play. But what you care about is how they organize information in 3-D spaces. Why? Because in the online information worlds of the future, people are going to learn by interacting with objects. They're going to experience information rather than think about it. Game technology may well become the backbone of future information systems, and the ability to build a game-like structure will be as important to communicating as the ability to create an outline.

Imagine your business plan as a game. Imagine you're the financial investor who needs to test your product, your market assumptions, your financial wherewithal. Imagine that you do that by proceeding through levels in a 3-D space where each level takes you into new objectives, new market realities, and new financial opportunities and constraints. Imagine how compellingly you could make your case by playing out the scenarios in worlds that model real-world activities.

Of course, if you're having trouble imagining all that, it's probably because you haven't gotten to the chapter on finances and business planning yet. That's what's next.

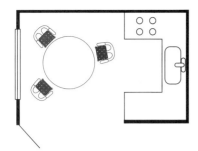

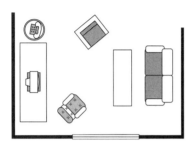

CHAPTER TEN

FAST-TRACK FINANCES
*How to streamline financial
operations and make better
financial decisions*

Money drives people crazy. But it doesn't have to. It's really not the life source, the means of survival, the key to happiness. Money is like air. You breathe it in, and you breathe it out. There's lots of it out there, and your job is just to keep track of what's coming in and what's going out. That's all. That's what money is about—breathing in, breathing out.

So how do you do it? You keep records. And you analyze the records. Your Mac can help you do both simply and correctly. You just need to know a few of the basics.

Legal requirements

You're required by law to keep certain records—your income, your deductible business expenses, and the amounts you pay employees or contractors. These must be reported accurately to the federal government and to some state governments. Depending on your location, you may also be required to keep records of sales tax you collect for products and/or services. The purpose of this record keeping is—obviously—to ensure that you pay the appropriate taxes.

For complete information about all of the tax records you're required to keep on file, see the "Tax Guide for Small Businesses," available from the Internal Revenue Service. You can find it online at: http://www.irs.ustreas.gov/prod/bus_info/tax_kit.html.

In addition to tax records, you may need to call on your financial records in case of legal actions, including civil and criminal suits, as well as more felicitous business contracts such as partnership agreements, incorporation, or sale of your company. To serve you in these situations, your records must use accepted accounting practices. These practices fill volumes of books that certified public accountants study in order to be certified. Fortunately, you can buy a lot of this knowledge, predigested, in accounting packages for your Macintosh. You can also buy the services of an accountant to check your books from time to time to make sure they'll withstand the scrutiny of the law.

Professional requirements

Your financial books are part of your professional conduct of business. They ensure that you can accurately bill your customers and pay your suppliers in a timely manner. You use them to generate invoices, track payments, and remind customers when they've fallen behind. If you sell products, you use them to track inventory, to order new products or materials when needed, and to ensure that you always have the products you need to satisfy your customer's demands.

Your books help you with pricing products and services, too. They help you estimate jobs so that you make money on them. They help you track project costs as they accrue—so you can make midcourse adjustments if necessary.

Different types of businesses have different requirements for this kind of record keeping, so there are lots of different acceptable accounting systems. You've seen these at your stationers in the form of journals with names like *Dome Simplified Monthly Bookkeeping Record* or Ideal System's *Merchants Bookkeeping and Tax Record* or *Business Service Bookkeeping and Tax Record*. With your Macintosh, the acceptable practices are built into the software, and in some cases the software itself helps you figure out which practices are appropriate to your type of business.

Practical requirements

Your books should make it easy for you to handle money day to day—paying bills and depositing receipts.

On a daily basis, you need to know how much cash you have on hand, your current bank balance, and your current day's receipts.

On a weekly basis, you should check how much people owe you and how much you owe others.

On a monthly basis, you should check your total assets and liabilities as well as your monthly income.

In addition to these basic money-management tasks, your records should also make it easy for you to get more money when you need it—in the form of loans, investments, or leases, for example.

Most important, your books let you know what you have and what you need. This is the real secret to financial success. Financial success isn't an open-ended journey to an ever-growing net worth. Financial success is having what you need to live a life that makes you happy.

Macintosh financial software can do a lot for you. You might even think it can take the place of an accountant. It can—but not all the time.

Setting up books for any but the simplest business requires planning and an understanding of business bookkeeping. The Macintosh accounting packages do a good job of simplifying things. QuickBooks 3.0 comes with an excellent Business Guide to help you plan your bookkeeping system. Best!Ware's MYOB comes with a video to get you started. Both QuickBooks and MYOB start you out with an extensive interview process that helps you figure out what kinds of accounts to set up and what kinds of records to keep. But even so, you're going to spend some time learning and planning. You may be able to reduce that time by getting help from an accountant.

You should also have an accountant check your books from time to time, just to make sure you're tracking things the way you should. If you ever face the IRS or a lawsuit, you'll be happy to have an accountant who knows you and your books.

DO YOU NEED AN ACCOUNTANT?

The Mac solutions

The world of Macintosh software offers solutions for all these record-keeping problems—and more. It has accounting packages for streamlining your record keeping, creating budgets, and tracking your financial status. It has tax preparation programs for converting the data in your accounting system to impeccable tax forms. It has spreadsheets for analyzing data to tell you how your business is doing. And it has planning software that helps you put together a business plan you can bank on.

This chapter shows you how to put these solutions to work for your business—starting with an overview of financial terminology and a quick look at how some of our sample businesses are approaching the world of finance. Then we'll walk you through the process of setting up your accounts to get the reports you need to manage your business–and then analyze them. Turn to the "PowerPlay" section for step-by-step help in setting up your own business plan.

ACCOUNTS   These are categories of things you need to keep track of: assets, liabilities, income, and expenses, for example. One of the big decisions you have to make when you set up your business and your books is how many accounts you want to keep track of. See "Where to Start."

ACCOUNTS PAYABLE (AP)   These are moneys you owe—usually by a certain date. See also "Liabilities."

ACCOUNTS RECEIVABLE (AR)   These are invoices you've sent to your customers—also due by a certain date. See also "Assets."

BOOKS   These are records of your accounts. On the Mac, they're not actually books at all. They're files. But no one talks about balancing your files. It just doesn't have the right ring to it.

CHART OF ACCOUNTS   This is a summary of several accounts (see above) that you use to track the flow of your money. Different kinds of companies need to track different accounts. Your bookkeeping software will help you figure out which accounts to include in your chart.

ASSETS   This is what you own or will own when everybody pays you what they owe you. Assets may be liquid, which means you can spend them whenever you want. Or they may be fixed, which means you can't get them from your local ATM machine. Fixed assets include things like your Macintosh, your company car, your inventory, and all those customer checks sitting on the piano waiting to be deposited.

LIABILITIES   This is what you owe—bills, loans, payroll obligations, unpaid taxes.

EQUITY   This is assets minus liabilities, sometimes referred to as the net worth of your company.

BALANCE SHEET   This is a listing of your assets, liabilities, and equity on any given date.

SINGLE-ENTRY ACCOUNTING   This is the simple method of bookkeeping. It's the kind of accounting you do with your checkbook. You keep a daily list of income and expenses. At the end of each month, you prepare a monthly summary of income and expenses. At the end of the year, you do an annual summary. This is your income statement, also known as a profit or loss statement.

DOUBLE-ENTRY ACCOUNTING   This is a form of torture developed by someone in the late Middle Ages. Someone can probably tell you why it's better than single-entry accounting, but we didn't find anyone who could (including bookkeeper friends and relatives). The important

MONEY-SPEAK:
THE TERMS OF
PROFESSIONAL
BOOKKEEPING

things to remember are that debits equal credits, that everything gets posted in at least two places, and that it all works out in the income statement and balance sheet. The other important thing to remember is that the business accounting packages do it all for you. If you need more help than that, see your accountant.

(continued)

CASH BASIS With this method of accounting, you include only money that you've actually received as income and bills that you've actually paid as expenses. You don't include amounts you owe or amounts you've billed but haven't yet received.

ACCRUAL BASIS This is the alternative to cash basis accounting. You record income at the time of sale and expenses at the time you receive the bill.

POSTING A fancy word for entering dollars and cents in the appropriate column of the appropriate form.

AGING Everything ages, but you may be particularly interested in the aging of your accounts payable and accounts receivable. Aging reports show what's overdue.

MONEY-SPEAK: THE TERMS OF PROFESSIONAL BOOKKEEPING (continued)

Andy Fine gets paid by the placement. The checks are large and frequent enough to reassure him that his business is growing. But they're not so frequent that he needs a high-end business accounting package to track them.

His expenses are minimal, too. With a credit card devoted solely to business expenses, he can easily keep track of office expenses, business entertainment, and other tax deductibles.

A personal accounting package works just fine.

THE TOOL

Intuit's Quicken

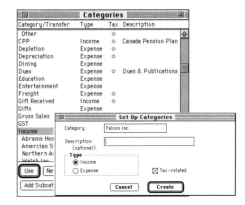

He tracks his income sources in his categories list–creating a new income category for each client.

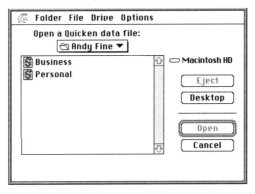

Andy uses separate files for his business and personal accounts.

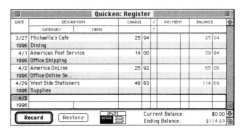

Andy uses a separate credit card and checking account for all his business expenses. He can quickly itemize his credit card expenses with an electronic statement from his Quicken credit card.

Susie Hu works on a retainer. She needs to track her expenses and time against the retainer. The accounting is simple, as long as she can quickly and easily enter the data.

Susie uses ClarisWorks for all of this. She uses a custom spreadsheet, one for each account, to track her hours and expenses.

She uses a custom database document to prepare an expense statement. (This is the document she imports into her reports. See Chapter 9.)

Because Susie keeps all her documents—contacts database, expense spreadsheet, statements, and reports—in one folder, it's easy to keep up with the data entry as she works.

In addition, Susie uses ClarisWorks' built-in accounting templates for writing both her business and personal checks, for assigning expenses to categories, and for balancing her books.

THE TOOL
ClarisWorks

ClarisWorks comes with checks, desposit slips, and spreadsheets set up to track them. Susie customized the check design to go with her marketing materials.

Susie uses a ClarisWorks spreadsheet to track her expenses against her retainer fees.

Sam Post has a product line with lots of products shipping to lots of customers. Like most people who sell products, he has to keep track of how much stock he has, how much he has invested in that stock, and when he has to reorder. In his case, restocking means making disks and slipping them into preprinted shipping envelopes that also double as start-up guides. In fact, once he pays for the time he invests in design work, the main product cost is the packaging.

When he gets orders, Sam needs to track them by product, so he can evaluate how each product is contributing to his business. Most of his customers are not repeat customers—people just don't build a new house that often—but it's important to him to keep in touch with his customers. He likes to know what they like and don't like when they're building. So a customer database with contact information is important to him, too.

Best!Ware's MYOB provides all these capabilities with an easy-to-navigate interface.

THE TOOL

Best!Ware's MYOB

One of the first things Sam did when he set up his MYOB system was create the inventory list—assigning an item number, name, and cost to each product.

S O L U T I O N S

MYOB has robust contact-management capabilities. When Sam gets an order, the first thing he does is enter the customer information in the card entry file. (He can also use the contact-management module to track his business with vendors or to stay in touch with professional colleagues.)

Then he creates an invoice. MYOB automatically enters the customer information from the contact card and the product information from the inventory list. It updates the inventory status, too.

The contact log has plenty of space for recording notes about Sam's conversations with customers before and after they buy.

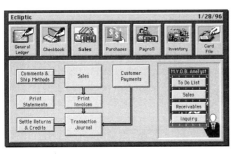

MYOB's interface makes it easy to move quickly among parts of the accounting package—and shows how everything's connected.

Like many service providers, Ellen Gant manages her clients' money–collecting a lump sum from them to pay for lots of different supplies and services.

So she needs a way to track payables and receivables. She also needs a way to track reimbursable expenses and bill them to her clients.

Ellen has a reseller's license that allows her to purchase goods without paying sales tax. But that means she has to track sales tax on taxable items.

With such a variety of accounting requirements, Ellen needs more than the simple accounting spreadsheets that come with her ClarisWorks package. She could design her own, but accounting is not where she wants to put her creative energies. So she uses an off-the-shelf small-business accounting package.

THE TOOL

Intuit's QuickBooks

Ellen has an account set up for each of her clients. When she gets a bill from one of her suppliers, she records it in her accounts payable–with information about the client to be billed.

S O L U T I O N S

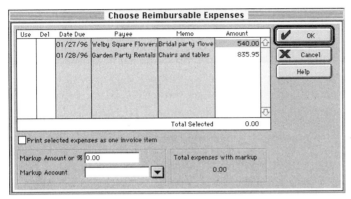

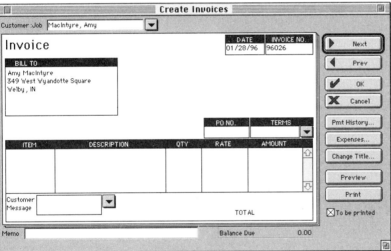

When Ellen is ready to bill her clients, she creates an invoice. QuickBooks automatically supplies the address information and shows the list of reimbursable expenses for each client's account.

JUMP START: Getting Your Accounts in Order

If you're just starting your business, take advantage of the moment to do it right. It's so simple in the beginning.

If your business is already steaming along and you're converting your books to files, you need a little bit of faith. At first, everything will seem to take too long because you already know how to do things pretty efficiently by hand. But it really is much easier on your Mac. Make a commitment. Choose a month when business is a little slow, if you can. And wait for the new routines to settle in.

STEP 1: SET UP YOUR BUSINESS ACCOUNTS

The first principle of good clean bookkeeping is: Keep your personal and business accounts separate. Deposit business receipts in your business account and pay business expenses from your business account. Pay yourself a salary from your business account but don't pay personal expenses from your business account. That's the basic good advice, and here's what you need to do it:

A business checking account Set up a separate bank account for your business. If you're operating under a fictitious business name, open the account in that name. You'll need the documentation you got when you filed your fictitious name. If you're using your own name, you can simply open a second account in that name. Some banks offer special services as part of their business account packages, such as free money orders and traveler's checks, but they often require a high minimum balance. Your bank officer should be able to tell you which kind of account makes the most sense for you.

A business credit card account Keep your business and personal expenses separate whenever you can. Use your business credit card to pay for gas, travel, business meals, office supplies, business seminars—anything you plan to deduct from your taxes. If you can, get a card that offers electronic statements, either via modem or disk. Then you can simply read the transactions into your expense account rather than entering them by hand. Quicken offers a Visa credit card with this service. It's not the lowest interest rate around, but if you pay your bills off in full each month, you don't have to worry about that. You can always transfer a balance to a card with a lower interest rate if you need to.

An electronic payment service Many banks now offer electronic payment services as part of a home banking package. In addition, Quicken offers its own electronic payment service called CheckFree. With these services, you can write checks from your computer and send them via modem to a bank or payment center. The payment center then transfers the

For more information on fictitious business names, see Step 1 under "Jump Start" in Chapter 1.

appropriate—amounts directly from your bank account to pay your bills—
or writes the checks, if necessary. And you don't have to spend extra time
entering the checks in your register.

Your goal is to make your computer the center of your financial life. You
want to minimize paperwork. You want to minimize the time you spend
entering the same information in more than one place. You want to make all
your information available on your computer because that's where you can
gain the power of analysis—which is how you're going to start making
smarter financial decisions and grow your business.

**DO YOU
REALLY NEED
A SEPARATE
ACCOUNT?**

A separate account is not a legal requirement. It's an easy, definitive way to establish your
business income and expenses for reporting your taxes. But you may not need a separate
account if your expenses are few and well defined, if your income is from just a few sources
and tends to come in large chunks, and if you keep impeccable records. For example, can
you keep track of how much postage you spent on business mail versus how much you
spent on letters to your kid at college? Do you want to keep track of those kinds of details?

If you're a little casual about record keeping or have any gray areas in your business
expenses, or if you just want to keep your bookkeeping as simple as possible, you're better
off with separate business and personal accounts.

**GETTING
THE RIGHT
INSURANCE**

As soon as you start using your home Mac for business, you need to insure it. Most homeowner's policies do not cover computers used for business purposes. Some companies
won't even issue you homeowner's or renter's insurance if you have a work-at-home computer on the premises.

Fortunately, there's Safeware. Safeware is a company that specializes in insuring computer hardware. You can get up to $5,000 worth of coverage for about $70 a year, or $30,000
for $300 a year—with lots of choices in between. Safeware offers maintenance insurance,
too. You can set up your policy on the phone. Just call 1-800-800-1492.

In addition to computer insurance, you may also need several other kinds of insurance:
Liability insurance protects you if your products or services cause harm to anyone. The
cost depends on your products and services. For example, health professionals have very
high liability insurance costs. If you write educational software, your liability coverage is
probably pretty basic.
Workers' compensation is a state-run insurance program to cover your employees for loss
of income in case of job-related accidents or illnesses. The laws for workers' compensation
insurance differ from state to state, but in many states you're required to make payments if
you have employees. In many states, you're not eligible if you're a sole proprietor.
Disability insurance protects you or key employees in case of long-term illness or disability.
This is the insurance you need if you're working alone without employees and don't

(continued)

qualify for worker's compensation. Private disability insurance is expensive, but if your business can't go on without you, you can gain considerable peace of mind from the investment.
Health insurance protects you and your employees from high medical bills. The premiums for personal policies are painful. You may be able to lower them a little by joining a professional organization, club, co-op, or credit union that offers a group policy. For a fee, you can also get a personalized report of best-bet policies for you from Wilkinson Benefit Consultants at 1-800-296-3030.
Property insurance protects business property other than your computers in case of fire, flood, vandalism, or theft.
Business interruption insurance in case of disasters such as earthquakes, floods, or hurricanes that shut your business down for more than a few days.
Credit insurance protects you in case you can't meet your obligations on loans and credit cards.

For all of these, you need to weigh the costs of the insurance against the risks. Insurance is a gambling game. If you're comfortable taking risks, you can save money by keeping insurance coverage to a minimum. If you're not, you can still reduce your costs by using high deductibles—as high as you can afford—and by checking your policies carefully to make sure you're not duplicating coverage or paying for coverage that you don't really need.

An insurance agent or financial planner can help you sort out your insurance needs and find the packages that work best for you. An agent that specializes in one particular type of insurance may know more about the field and offer better policies. You can also work directly with a commissioned employee of an insurance company. Employees won't be able to offer you a range of policies from different companies, but may be able to give you lower premiums because their own commissions tend to be lower than those of independent agents. If you want to spend a lot of time on research, you can probably get better coverage at lower cost by working directly with several insurance companies or agents. But if you would rather spend that time earning income, a single agent or financial planner is a whole lot simpler.

GETTING THE RIGHT INSURANCE
(continued)

STEP 2: SET UP YOUR BOOKS

Personal computers won the hearts of corporate America with their financial spreadsheets. You can use a spreadsheet to track your financial records, too. But it's a lot easier to use the custom bookkeeping packages that are available for the Macintosh. These will do everything from writing your checks to winning you investors. You just have to choose the right package for you. You have three basic choices:

Personal accounting software. For many small businesses, a personal accounting package like Quicken is all you need. You can keep track of your business accounts in separate files or in separate accounts in the same file as your personal accounts. (Separate files provide better analysis of your company's financial health—as opposed to your personal financial health.) If your expenses are minimal, if your income is from a few regular sources, and if you don't need to track a lot of project expenses, a personal accounting package will work just fine.

Entry-level accounting software. These are the basic small-business accounting packages—products like QuickBooks and MYOB. They walk you through the process of setting up your accounts for double-entry book-keeping. They also provide special-purpose modules for things like payroll management, product pricing, job estimating, invoicing, and order and inventory tracking. If you need any of these services, or if you want to do sophisticated business analysis, you need this kind of software.

Midrange accounting software. Think of these as high-volume, mutiple-user packages. They're appropriate for businesses with several workstations that need to access your financial database at the same time. For example, if you have a phone order business with three or four people entering order information at the same time, these systems can handle the job. Or if you just have a very high-volume business with lots of data entries, they may be more efficient than the entry-level packages. Examples include Components from Satori Software and Mac P&L from State of the Art.

Whichever software you choose, you're going to have to do at least three things:

Set up your accounts. In personal accounting systems, accounts are your bank accounts, credit card accounts, and investment accounts. In profess-ional accounting systems, accounts are a standard grouping of records, such as assets, liabilities, equity, income, cost of sales, expenses, and so forth. Applications like MYOB and QuickBooks interview you when you first set up your books and create these accounts for you automatically. Your accounts are linked. When you enter information in one account, other accounts are updated automatically, as appropriate.

Enter vendor or merchant information. Vendors are the people who sell you goods and services. You set up lists of vendors, with addresses, phone numbers, account numbers, and other information. You can add to your list of vendors at any time, but you may want to set up a list of your regular ven-dors when you first set up your books.

Set up categories within accounts. In personal accounting systems, you assign your transactions to income and expense categories. The preset cate-gories in a personal system apply mostly to personal expenses. A better start-ing place for your home business is the categories in Schedule C, the govern-ment's form for reporting profit or loss. Or your accountant may give you a worksheet that has preset categories. You can use subcategories if you want to track more details. In professional accounting systems, you can also set up classes within your various accounts. Sometimes these classes are called accounts. So you have accounts within accounts within accounts. You can also use the classes to track information that's unique to your business—for example, by class of product, if you sell several different kinds of products. Or you can track by local, national, or international jobs if you want to compare the profitability of each of those categories.

Here's the take-home point: You have to do some thinking here. Don't just rely on the preset categories your software gives you. Think about your system of accounts, classes, and categories carefully before you start entering your day-to-day data. Otherwise you'll end up editing a lot of entries—which will make you wonder what's so great about having all this stuff computerized.

Tax law is a profession unto itself—one we profess very little knowledge of. If you want complete legal advice, see an accountant or tax spcialist. If you just want a quick tour of the territory, we can do the honors.

THE BASIC STRATEGY

If you're self-employed, the killer tax is the so-called self-employment tax, which is really your contribution to Social Security. When you work for someone else, that someone else pays half of your Social Security tax. When you work for yourself, you pick up the whole tab, and it's a straight percentage of net income—which is your gross income minus your business expenses.

So the basic strategy is to try to get your net income as low as you legally can. Your legal deductions include:

- Advertising
- Business auto expenses
- Employee wages
- Business travel and entertainment costs
- The cost of supplies
- Office expenses such as postage and shipping, online services, equipment repair and rentals, and even cleaning
- Depreciation of office equipment
- Depreciation of office furniture
- Special telephone lines and long distance charges (you can't deduct the monthly payment for your main home phone)
- Subscriptions and professional dues
- Business gifts
- A percentage of your health insurance
- Some portion of your home expenses (see below)

Look for ways to move things that you normally deduct as personal expenses into your business expense sheet. For example, if you give to charities, you can get more tax mileage if you give through your company in ways that gets your company name in the public eye.

(continued)

STREET SMART

TAXES: THE QUICK (AND NOT TOO PAINFUL) LOOK

This counts as advertising. (It's a good advertising strategy, in fact.) If you deduct a home office space, and you have deductible mortgage payments, deduct a percentage of those as business rather than personal expenses.

ABOUT THAT OFFICE-IN-THE-HOME DEDUCTION

If you work a full-time job and you have an office in your home, you probably can't claim it unless you can prove your company requires it of you.

If you have an office in your home and another office for meeting clients, you'll have trouble deducting your home office.

If you have an office in your home and it happens also to be your dining room and sewing room and hobby room, the IRS will be very fussy about how much time you actually spend using that room for your business.

If you have a dedicated home office that looks like a home office and you do all of your work there and never do anything else there, you can deduct it worry free—provided you can prove it.

All of this gets worked out on Form 8829, which you must file if you claim an office in your home. If you qualify for a home deduction, you can deduct not only a portion of your mortgage and rent payments, but also a portion of mortgage interest and taxes, a portion of your utility bills, your homeowner's insurance, and your general home maintenance costs.

TAX SOFTWARE OR A TAX ACCOUNTANT?

Most of the work in preparing taxes will be trivial if you've set up your Macintosh bookkeeping with taxes in mind. You just print out a report at the end of the year—and then decide whether you want to use a software package like MacInTax to plug the numbers into the right forms, or whether you want to pay a few hundred dollars to a tax accountant to do it for you.

We recommend the latter—particularly if taxes make you nervous. A tax accountant will keep you up-to-date with changes in the tax law and interpret your situation with an expertise you and your software can't bring to the task. Also, you actually stand a higher chance of being audited if you file with forms from a tax software program. The IRS trusts the tax accountants more than you or the software.

TAXES: THE QUICK (AND NOT TOO PAINFUL) LOOK (continued)

STEP 3: CREATE A BUDGET

You're probably thinking limits, right? Somehow, budgeting always conjures a stack of threatening brown envelopes with just enough money to scrape by for the month. This is a mistake. Business budgeting is not about getting by on as little as possible. Business budgeting is about growing your business. Its about setting income goals and tracking them. It's about knowing that you'll have the money you need for your Christmas advertising budget in August—when you have to buy the advertising space.

All the accounting packages include budgeting tools. You set projections for income and expenses by week, month, year, or some other regular financial period. Then you get reports that show how your actuals compare to your projections. In the business accounting packages like MYOB and QuickBooks, you can budget by individual accounts. Remember that accounts are typically things like expense accounts and income accounts in these packages.

The way you set up your accounts will shape the way you create your budgets. For example, if you create global income accounts such as consulting, merchandise, and investments, you budget your monthly income from these sources. If you create income accounts by clients, you budget your monthly income from each client. Expenses work the same way.

A budget isn't a fixed description of your financial world. It's a tool for experimenting in that world. You can play "what if" with budgets. What if you wanted a monthly growth of 1 percent? How much do you have to increase your sales or your hourly fee or your markup rate? Can you get the extra sales you need by increasing your advertising expenses and reducing your packaging expenses?

How often you play this game depends on your business. If it's a business with steady clientele and fixed expenses, once a year is probably enough. If it's a business with changing products, customers, and expenses, you should play the budget game once per quarter. Of course, you should check your budget reports once a month just to make sure you're on track.

STEP 4: GET REPORTS

Once you set up your accounts, you can start to get reports. You want two main reports:

- A **balance sheet** that shows the state of your financial affairs on any given date—usually the last day of the month. It includes a summary of all your assets and all your liabilities. The assets should equal the liabilities plus your equity. Here's a sample balance sheet from MYOB:

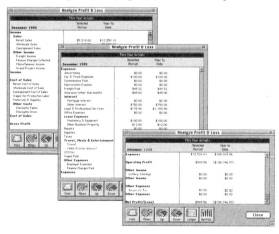

■ An **income statement** that measures the total revenue and expenses over a period of time—such as a month, quarter, or year—to show the net profit or loss for that period. The income statement is sometimes called the profit and loss statement. The revenues include all of the income from services rendered or goods sold. They include your accounts receivable and the value of any goods you may have received in exchange for services or other goods. From this total you deduct the cost of sales—including inventory costs. The expenses include all your operating expenses and taxes. The revenue minus the expenses is your net profit or loss. Here's a sample income statement from MYOB.

Analyze Balance Sheet		
This Year Actuals		
December 1995	Selected Period	% of Total
Liabilities		
Credit Cards		
MasterCard	$3,200.00	1.7%
Visa	$1,000.00	0.5%
American Express	$0.00	0%
Total Credit Cards	$4,200.00	2.3%
Bank Loans	$80,000.00	43.3%
Accounts Payable	$17,359.90	9.4%
Deposits from Customers	$500.00	0.3%
Taxes Payable		
Sales Tax Payable	$2,303.76	1.2%
Withholding Tax Payable	$80,003.10	43.3%
FUTA Payable	$421.09	0.2%
Total Taxes Payable	$82,727.95	44.8%
Total Liabilities	$184,787.85	100%
Equity		
Paid in Capital	$100,000.00	(213.6%)
Owner's Draw	($136,976.07)	292.5%
Retained Earnings	$128,898.00	(275.3%)
Current Year Earnings	($138,746.97)	296.3%
Historical Balancing	$0.00	0%
Total Equity	($46,825.04)	100%

Print Filters Up Down Ledger Asset Liability Equity   Close

With these two reports you can track the overall health of your company. You can also use your accounting software to get lots of other reports:

Accounts receivable reports that show outstanding receivables, including overdue invoices and balances for individual customers.

Accounts payable reports that show your outstanding bills, including tax liability.

Sales reports that show sales by item, by customer, and by salesperson if you have employees.

Purchase reports that show your purchases by item and by vendor, as well as outstanding purchase orders.

Inventory reports that show the status of stock by item and by vendor as well as their value.

Budget reports that show your budget projections and actuals.

Payroll reports that summarize payroll expenses by employee.

Transaction reports that list transactions by account, by customer, by vendor, and by date.

General ledger reports that list all of your transactions for all of your accounts.

You'll need these reports for your day-to-day business—to pay your bills, collect money, prepare your taxes, borrow money, and seek investors. But to grow your company, you need to go further. You need to step into the world of financial analysis. Read on.

Sometimes your customers or clients just don't pay. Sometimes they say it's your fault—you didn't do the job. Sometimes they just avoid you.

To ensure that you get paid for the services or products you sell, follow these guidelines:

■ Always start out with a written contract or purchase order—or both. (A contract may spell out details that the purchase order doesn't. You'll need to refer to those details if your customer claims you didn't deliver.)

■ Get a credit report for your customer.

■ Bill your customers in a timely manner.

■ As soon as an invoice becomes overdue, send a polite reminder. If they still don't pay, send a firmer reminder. Don't threaten, harass, or publicly announce their debt. Don't say you'll sue if you don't intend to. Don't include words like "Overdue Notice" on the envelope. It's against the law.

If two, three, or four letters don't do the job, you have three choices:

Turn the account over to a collection agency.   The agency has no legal authority to force payment, but many people don't like to deal with collection agencies. They'll pay an agency even when they won't pay you. Agencies charge a percentage of the bill—from 30 to 50 percent. But it may be the best you'll get. (We've used Dun and Bradstreet's service with good results.)

Take the customer to small claims court.   The advantage of small claims court is that you don't need an attorney. You can present your case yourself. However, states have different limits for the amount of money you can sue for in small claims court, and most of them are relatively low. You generally have to sue delinquent customers in their own state, rather than yours.

Hire an attorney to sue the customer.   This is expensive. Sometimes it's more expensive than the amount you're trying to collect. Anything above the small claims limit but under $50,000 is generally not worth suing for. This is bad-breaks land. And remember that even if you can win the suit, your customer may not be able to pay—in which case you still have to pay the attorney fees.

If you're in doubt about what you can legally do, consult an attorney. The half hour you pay for may save you a lot of headaches—and even a lot of money.

COLLECTIONS: WHAT TO DO IF YOU CAN'T GET PAID

UPSIZING: Growing Your Profits

To succeed and grow, you need to manage your working capital with skill. Most small businesses fail for lack of working capital. Businesses that grow make expert use of their working capital—to get the most out of every asset. That expertise comes from two main types of financial analysis that you can do with your accounting records and a simple spreadsheet.

Ratio analyses—The liquidity of your business

Liquidity is a measure of the money that's available for paying projected expenses as well as investing in growth—by expanding your advertising budget, paying for a die for a new product, or taking courses to expand your areas of expertise, for example.

You can measure liquidity in several ways. One of best measures is the current ratio—the ratio of assets to liablities. Here's how to set it up:

	Ratio Analyses	
	A	**B**
1		
2		
3	Current Ratio	
4		
5	Total assets	
6	Total Liabilities	
7	Current ratio	B5/B6
8		
9		
10		
11		

Sheet1 / Sheet2 / S

You can check your current ratio at any time by running a balance sheet report in your accounting package and plugging the assets and liabilities into the spreadsheet. You can also track your liquidity over time by recording the current ratio on a monthly basis.

Common wisdom is that you need a 2:1 ratio of assets to liabilities to guarantee enough liquidity to meet your current debts and have a good safety margin. However, this figure varies from industry to industry. You can get more-accurate target ratios from the Small Business Administration, as well as trade associations and industry organizations such as Dun and Bradstreet.

If a lot of your assets are tied up in goods or other vehicles that are hard to convert to cash, you may want to do an acid test ratio. As its name suggests, this ratio measures your ability to meet existing debts if all of your sources of revenue disappeared immediately. For the acid test, you need a ratio of at least 1:1. Here's how you set it up:

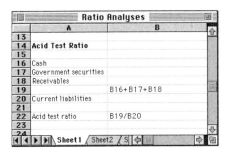

Another measure of liquidity is the **average collection period**. This is the average number of days between the time you make a sale and the time you receive payment. This figure helps you understand, in general, how liquid your accounts receivable are—how quickly you can convert them to cash. You set up this analysis with net sales from your income statement and accounts receivable from your balance sheet:

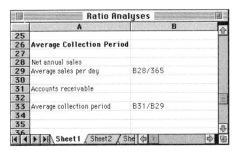

If your accounts are healthy, the average collection period is less than or equal to your standard terms of credit.

Got inventory? Then you also need a measure of how fast your products are moving: the **inventory turnover rate**. Again, you can use the figures from your income statement and balance sheets for the current and previous periods. For example, if you have an annual income statement, you need the current year's end balance sheet as well as the previous year's balance sheet. You set up the analysis like this:

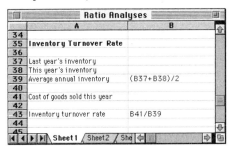

The higher your inventory turnover rate, the faster your goods are moving. When products move fast, you're tying up less capital in your inventory, and your products are clearly salable. A slowdown in the turnover rate signals a mismatch between your products and the market. You can analyze your turnover rate for individual products in your inventory, too, to determine how well each product is selling.

Profitability measures—How much you're making

One of the biggest problems with solo businesses is that it isn't always obvious whether you're really making any money with your business. Your days are spent in your home office, your work becomes your life, and your business expenses seem to be as personal as your grocery expenses. If you make ends meet without too much pain, you think you're doing okay.

You may be. But if you're looking for long-term growth, or even retirement with a measure of comfort, you need to make a profit. So how do you know if you are? Several profitability measures can give you clearer picture.

The first measure is **asset earning power**. It's a measure of your ablity to increase your assets. The higher the earning power, the better. If your asset earning power is very low, you may end up depleting your assets—particularly capital equipment that deteriorates and loses value over time. You calculate asset earning power from the total earnings before taxes and interest as shown on your income statement and the total assets from your balance sheet.

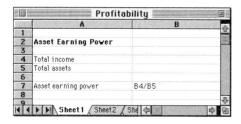

Another measure of profitablity is return on equity. Your equity goes up and down each month as you clear more or less money after you've met your monthly liabilities. If you use it as working capital, it's an investment. The return on equity shows how much you got for this investment. You need a year's worth of balance sheets to establish your average monthly equity and an income statement for the current month to compute your return.

If you want to evaluate your operating costs and pricing policies, measure your **net profit on sales**. Divide the net profit from your income statement by the net sales. The result shows you what you make on each dollar that you receive from sales of products or services.

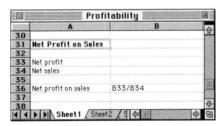

Finally, your **return on investment** (ROI) is one of the best measures of profitability. And one way to measure return on investment is to divide the net profit from your yearly income statement by your total assets from the year-end balance sheet.

There are other ways to measure return on investment. But whichever method you use, you want a high return—certainly higher than you could

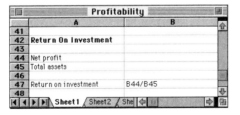

get simply by investing the same amount in a secure fund. (Otherwise, there would be no point in working.) A high return signals strong profitability. A declining return is a sign your company is not operating as efficiently as it could—or that your market is weakening.

As a solo worker, you should pay yourself a salary. You are, in fact, one of the expenses of doing business. You can't measure your profitability until you figure out what you cost yourself to work.

It's easy to fall into a habit of just drawing on the business account whenever you need cash for personal expenses. But for your own personal finances and for the health of your business, it's better to give yourself a fixed monthly salary. If you can't meet your own salary expenses in any given month, it's a strong signal that you may need to look at how you're doing business—either your operating costs or your pricing of products and services. If you have money left over after you pay your salary and bills, that becomes your equity in your company. And your equity is what enables you to grow.

ARE YOU PAYING YOURSELF A SALARY?

POWER PLAY: Building A Business with a Plan

Everybody who gives advice on starting a home business will advise you to start with a business plan. It's good advice. It helps separate the real possibilities from the harebrained schemes. It's also good advice for someone who's been in business for a while. It focuses your thinking on how you want to grow or what might force you to change directions.

Here's a basic strategy for building a business plan.

What you need
- Word processor
- Spreadsheet
- Current balance sheet
- Most recent income statement
- Time: Ongoing

First, create a template

The best place to start your business plan is with a template. You can buy a business plan template, such as JIAN's BizPlan Builder or Palo Alto Software's Business Plan Toolkit. The ClarisWorks Small Business Solutions Pack also comes with a very simple template for a business plan. Or you can create your own, following these steps.

1. Create a title page.

Include your company name, the date, your name and title (or the name of the head of your company), and your address and phone number. You may want to include a notice of confidentiality.

2. Create an executive summary page.

This page will summarize your business plan when you're done. For now, just create the headings:

EXECUTIVE SUMMARY
Objectives
Company Background
Product (or Service) Strategy
Market Analysis
Marketing Plan
Financial Plan

3. Create a page for each of the headings in the executive summary.

Now you have the skeleton of your business plan. You can continue to build it at your own pace—over the next couple of days, weeks, or months.

Second, make notes

Your next step is to start filling in the details in the plan. But don't start by trying to write a bunch of formal paragraphs. Just type notes under each of your headings.

Or print out a copy and scribble notes in the blanks as they occur to you. (Keep the copy on your kitchen counter or take it with you when you go out for your afternoon coffee break at the local coffee shop.)

1. Start with what you know.

You don't have to write your plan from start to finish. Start with the easy parts—your company background, for example, or your product strategy.

2. Ask yourself questions to get you going.

For example, if you're working on the market analysis section, ask yourself questions like: Who wants this product? How much are they willing to spend? How many of these potential customers exist? Who else is selling similar products to these customers? Make a list of key questions like this for each heading in your plan.

(If you're using a commercial business plan template, it will have these questions built in.)

3. Make notes of things you don't know.

You probably don't know everything you need to know to write your plan. Figuring out what you don't know is as important as writing what you do know. Some of the unknowns may concern technical know-how. Some may concern your market. Some may concern finances. Make a list of unknowns. Be as specific as possible.

Begin to research the unknowns. If you don't know where to start, start with an Internet search. Or talk to the reference librarian at your local library. Contact an appropriate professional society for leads. Talk to friends and colleagues. You may need to buy a little consulting time with a few experts, too.

Cut to the $$$

The Finance section of your report is where the rubber meets the road. It's where you get to see if your efforts can put food on your table. A complete financial plan includes your balance statement and income statements for an appropriate period (six months to five years), as well as other ratio and profit analyses.

But even if you don't yet have your books in order to create these reports, you should do two types of financial reports to help you make better decisions in the short run.

If you've been through Chapter 8, "The Marketing Plan," you should already have one of the most important components of your business plan in place.

1. Do a break-even analysis on any new product you're planning to introduce.

A break-even analysis helps you make decisions about whether a product or service is viable at a particular price—and how long it will take before you see a return on it. In its simplest form, its just the answer to the question, How many of these thingamajigs do I have to sell to recover my costs? Your costs, of course, include development time, manufacturing costs, marketing expenses (such as advertising), and distribution expenses.

Here's a simple spreadsheet for a basic break-even analysis. You break even when the bottom line, Net Income After Tax, becomes positive.

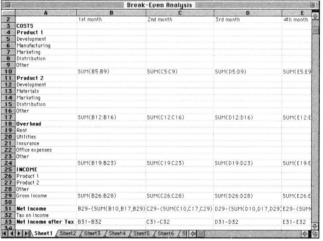

2. Do a six-month cash flow analysis.

A cash flow analysis helps you anticipate cash requirements. It compares all your incoming cash to your outgoing cash and calculates the effect on your cash reserves. For example:

These are simple forms of the analyses. You can check with your accountant or use a standard business planning product if you need more sophisticated analyses. The important thing to remember about these analyses, though, is that they're not oracles of doom. If the numbers aren't working out, don't give up right away. Check your assumptions. You may be able to find the right combination of pricing, manufacturing, and marketing decisions to make your business fly.

Tidy it up

If you're not looking for outside funding or making formal presentations to potential collaborators, you don't really need to clean up your notes. Just keep adding to them. But if you need to present your company formally, you should do a bit of tidying up.

1. Rewrite notes in simple, straightforward text. (Get an editor if you're not good at it.)

2. Get an outside review.

Pay a business planning consultant to review it. You may also want to hire a designer to help you in the good-looks department.

3. Put together a complete presentation package: corporate brochure, advertising materials, sample products or photographs of products, and letters of reference.

Now you're ready to share your plan with the world.

To make sure you get all your business planning details just right, you probably need either a financial consultant or—you guessed it—templates! You can get them from Palo Alto Software or JIAN.

Palo Alto Software's package is called Business Plan Toolkit. It asks all the right questions. It includes a traditional outline template for your business plan, with probing questions for each topic to help you think through all the issues. It also includes some spreadsheets for calculating the key financial figures you need.

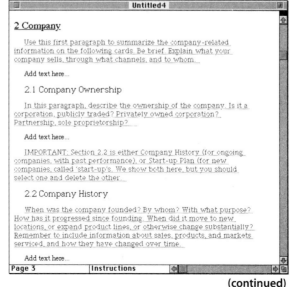

TAMING THE TASK WITH TEMPLATES

(continued)

**TAMING THE
TASK WITH
TEMPLATES**
(continued)

JIAN's product is BizPlan Builder. It uses a more contemporary style and even puts most of the words in your mouth—which is a great help, whether you're an accomplished writer or not. It has a sophisticated set of well-documented spreadsheets to help you with the dollars-and-cents stuff. Both products list for about $150—considerably less than you'll spend on a financial consultant.

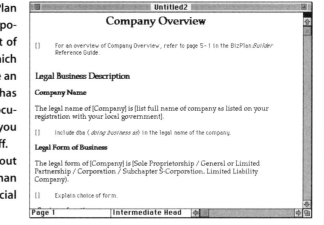

ON THE HORIZON: E-Cash and Beyond

You can pretty much assume that digital banking is the banking of the future. But if you've already set up your online accounts and are writing checks electronically, things are just going to get simpler in this arena. More things will happen automatically, or with a couple of mouse-clicks. Everyone who supplies financial software is looking for ways to cut out any remaining tendrils of tedium. Good news.

The biggest unknown in the future of finances—as in the world of computing, in general—is the Internet. The uncertainty, as of this writing, is about financial transactions on the Internet. The issues here are privacy and security. Privacy is about buying whatever you want without anyone knowing what you're buying. Do you really want your banker to know that you spend all your spare cash on *Loony Tunes* videos?

Security is mainly about protecting customer credit accounts. The various solutions include debit systems—where you buy e-cash from a bank and keep it squirreled away on your computer like pennies in your piggy bank—or some sort of encryption system that ensures no one can hijack your credit card number. The problem with debit systems is that you have to pay for the money before you actually need it, which is not something Americans generally like to do. The problem with encryption is that the government doesn't want anyone designing an encryption system it can't decode. It's a national security risk. And you thought the budget negotiations were tough!

Rest assured, though, that cash transactions will have a big role to play in the Internet's big future. And your biggest worry, aside from making sure that you get your share of those transactions, is how to track them automatically in your online bookkeeping system. And thanks to companies like Intuit and Best!Ware, you probably don't have to worry about that at all.

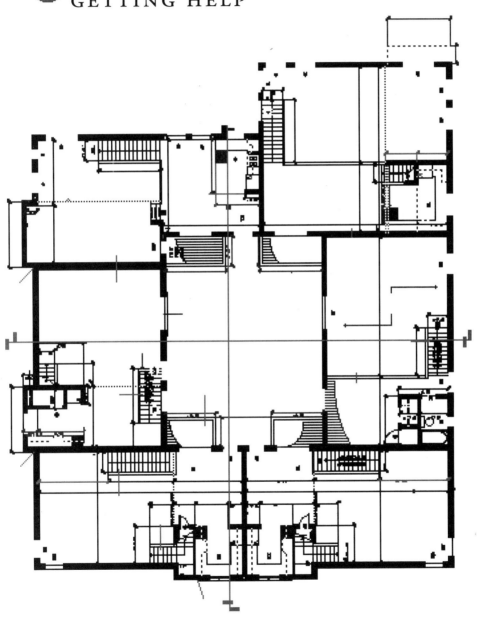

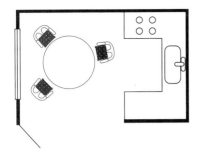

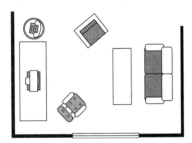

CHAPTER ELEVEN

TROUBLESHOOTING

How to get along with your Macintosh on bad days

Most days, you get along fine with your Macintosh. It does exactly what you want it to. But some days—usually those when you have a killer deadline or a killer headache—it gets sympathy pains and starts acting up. You'd like to call your in-house technical support team, but you can't. You don't have one. This is one of the downsides of working on your own at home.

Your next best bet is to call your Mac guru. Your Mac guru is your old friend from high school who knows everything about Macs, or the gal you met at the computer store who gave you a ton of free advice and her home phone number. This is a person to cherish. Take him or her to dinner on a regular basis. Provide the keys to your cabin in the mountains. Add his or her name to your will. And call when you have a problem.

If you don't have a Mac guru, or if your guru is enjoying the weekend at your mountain retreat, you've got this chapter. It will guide you through the basics, problem by problem.

Problem: Disks don't show up on your desktop

This is the problem to strike terror into the heart of any Macintosh user. Suddenly one day, your hard disk doesn't boot. You get that little floppy-disk icon with a flashing question mark. Or if you have more than one hard disk, the one with all your important work has mysteriously vanished from the desktop. What do you do?

For details about SCSI devices and ID numbers, see "Upsizing" in Chapter 2, "The Tools of Your Trade."

CHECK YOUR CABLES. A missing disk can indicate a range of problems from the simple to the serious. The most obvious thing to check here—and with any apparent hardware problem—is the cables. Check all the cables in the SCSI chain to make sure they're snugly plugged in. If you're setting up an external disk drive for the first time, verify that the SCSI ID number for each SCSI device is unique and doesn't collide with a pre-assigned Macintosh SCSI number.

RESTART AND USE A MOUNTING PROGRAM. First try to restart your computer again and see if it mounts the disk after a second restart. Usually, the Mac OS mounts all attached hard drives on startup. If for some reason it doesn't mount your disk, you can try to mount it manually with a mounting program such as:

- Alliance Power Tools, from APS Technologies, Inc.
- SilverLining, from La Cie Limited
- SCSI Probe, a freeware control panel by Robert Polic
- A formatter or SCSI scan program that (usually) comes with your disk drive

SCSI Probe is the safest tool because it won't reformat your disk if you make a mistake.

(If the missing drive is your startup drive, you may have to start your Mac from a floppy disk or CD-ROM. You can use the Disk Tools disk that comes with your System 7 installation set if your startup drive is down. Then you can try to run a mounting program, but you may have to swap floppy disks if you only have one floppy drive.)

Here's the basic procedure for manual mounting:

1. Run the program from a working disk drive.

The program lists every device it finds attached to the SCSI chain. (If your Macintosh uses one of the newer IDE drives, it won't show up on the SCSI chain.)

2. Select your drive and click the Mount button.

If you're lucky, your hard drive mounts. (If it does, you may still want to do some of the software testing described later because your drive may have a software problem that kept it from mounting in the first place.)

If your drive doesn't appear in the list of SCSI devices, and your cables, SCSI ID numbers, and terminators are all correct, you may have a serious hardware problem.

REINSTALL THE DRIVER PROGRAM. If the mounting program doesn't work, you should try to reinstall the disk driver. This is a low-level program that controls the operation of the disk. The formatting utility that comes with your hard disk usually includes an option for reinstalling the driver. For example, one of the options with Apple's HD SC Setup program is called Update. This updates the disk with a new copy of the driver.

If you can't get anything to show up, you may simply have to take your computer in for repair. But if you have another working drive, you can do some software checking:

RUN A SOFTWARE CHECKING AND DIAGNOSTIC PROGRAM. Your next step is to check for software boot (start up) problems. Run Apple's Disk First Aid or better still, Norton Disk Doctor. These programs list every SCSI device that's attached to your Macintosh. Have them check the drive that isn't booting. Either program can often repair boot block problems and allow your drive to boot. Norton Disk Doctor can often fix problems that Disk First Aid can't fix. If Disk Doctor tells you your drive is so badly damaged that it can't fix it, your only recourse is to use Disk Doctor to copy all the files on the damaged drive somewhere else:

- Your best bet is to copy files to a removable cartridge drive or another hard drive. You might even want to rent a hard drive for a week to make your backup, since copying a large hard drive to floppies is a real chore.
- If you have to copy to floppies, copy all your data files—that is, documents you've created (unless you have current backups). You won't need to copy your applications or your System files to floppies, as you should have the originals as well as your backups. (You *are* keeping backups, aren't you?) Be sure to copy your e-mail archives, preferences folders, calendar data files, and anything else you can't re-create.

Once you've got everything backed up, it's time to reformat your hard drive with the formatting utility that came with your disk drive. Just remember that once you start a format operation, there's no going back. It erases everything that's on your hard disk. You will then need to reinstall your system from the system disks. Once the system is working again, you can copy all your personal files and applications back to your disk and hope this was a one-time fluke.

Problem: Your computer keeps crashing
This is the most typical—not to mention troublesome—problem you'll encounter. Macintosh programs are complex, and they interact with one

another in unusual ways. Sorting out the causes of crashes can be tedious. Here are some basic things to check:

CHECK FOR DISK PROBLEMS. Your disk itself may be corrupted. Use Norton Disk Doctor or Disk First Aid to check for disk errors. These programs find errors and fix them. It's a good idea to run them from time to time as preventive maintenance. You'll not only keep your disks in good repair, but you'll also know how to use them when things start to go crazy.

CHECK FOR EXTENSION CONFLICTS. The most common type of crash is caused by system extension conflicts. Extensions and control panels load when you start the computer. As they load, their icons appear along the bottom of your screen. A simple method to determine whether the problem is due to extension conflicts is simply to turn off all the extensions and then try your application.

- To turn off all your extensions, hold down the Shift key and restart the computer.

Under the "Welcome to Macintosh" message, you'll see a second message: "Extensions Off." Start your application. If things seem to work normally, the problem is most likely caused by an extension conflict. Of course, you still need to figure out which extensions are the problem. The best way to handle extension problems is with a startup manager. Apple provides a simple startup manager, called Extension Manager, with System 7. Now-Startup or Conflict Catcher both have built-in methods for helping you find and resolve startup conflicts.

USE THE SYSTEM MESSAGES TO DIAGNOSE THE PROBLEM. Sometimes your Mac tells you why it's crashing. A dialog box with a bomb icon includes an ID number or error type. Sometimes these codes can help you figure out the problem. For example:

```
Error type 25 (or ID = 25)
Error type 28 (or ID = 28)
Error type -108 (or ID = -108)
```

These are memory errors. The program ran out of memory or had a memory-related problem. Try increasing the memory allocated to the program.

1. Select the application in the Finder and choose Get Info from the File menu.

2. Increase the value in the Preferred Size box by at least 500K (more if you have the RAM for it.)

You may also need to add more memory to your computer or purchase a memory doubler like RAM Doubler.

I f you have a morbid curiosity and want to see what all the system error codes mean, find a little free utility called System Errors Table, written by veteran Mac programmer Bill Steinberg, available through most of the shareware sources.

```
Error type 16 (ID = 16) Floating point error
```

This error occurs when a program expects a floating point processor (FPU) in your Mac but doesn't find one. If your Mac doesn't have an FPU, you may not be able to use the application.

You may encounter this error even if you have an FPU. The Power Mac chip has its FPU built into the chip itself, unlike the older Macs, which used a separate FPU chip. Some older programs can't tell that a newer Mac has an on-chip FPU and generate this error, even though the specs in the back of your Power Macintosh manual assure you that you have a built-in floating point processor. The simple solution to this is to download the shareware extension Software FPU, by John Neil & Associates. It tricks the software into thinking you have the older FPU chip.

```
Error type -34 (ID = -34) Disk full error
```

You've run out of disk space. Even if it seems like you've got a few megabytes left, remember that many programs create large temporary files when you use the program. If these temp files are bigger than the amount of free space you've got left on your disk, you might get this error. Remove some files from your disk.

```
Error type -39 (ID = -39) End of file error
```

The Mac OS couldn't read the file because it couldn't find its end-of-file marker. This generally means that the file you're trying to use is damaged. Replace it with a backup copy or see Chapter 12 for other ways to deal with damaged files.

```
Error type 1 (ID = 1) Bus error
Error type 11 (ID = 11) Miscellaneous hardware exception
error
```

Both of these errors are supposedly hardware errors, but you may see them frequently due to extension conflicts as well as anomalies with the Mac OS. They're harder to debug, but you use the same general strategy as the startup managers do—only you have to do it manually. Start out with a system that's as pared down as you can make it. If everything works, you can slowly start adding applications. In other words, if you get one of these errors when you've got several programs running at the same time, try quitting everything and running only the program that crashed. Then load one of the other programs and continue working in the first program. Continue doing this until you get the crash again. This method may help you find the conflicting programs, but it's by no means foolproof. If you consistently get one of these errors in the same program, read the Read Me file that came with the program or call the manufacturer for a list of known conflicts. The manufacturer may also have an update that fixes the problem.

REPLACE THE APPLICATION AND ITS PREFERENCE FILE. If the same program crashes each time you run it, first try replacing it with a new copy. If it continues to crash, go to the Preferences folder of the System folder and see if your application has a preference file. If so, move it out of the Preferences folder to the desktop, but don't throw it away yet. Run your application again and see if it runs now. Sometimes the preference file gets corrupted and causes a crash. When you remove the preference file, many applications will automatically create a new one. But keep the original pref file until you've resolved the problem—a few applications *don't* create new preference files. If you throw away the only one, you may not be able to run the program at all.

CHECK FOR DUPLICATE SYSTEM FILES. Your Macintosh may also act strangely if you have more than one copy of the System file or System folder. Do this: Use the Find command (in the File menu) to search for the word *system*. If you find more than one copy of the system file on your hard disk, keep the latest version—you can see the date in the Find window—and remove all the older copies.

Sometimes, your Mac system just freezes. The cursor won't move, not even to choose the Restart command. You have to turn the Mac off and then turn it back on—the so-called hard restart. In general, you want to avoid hard restarts for two reasons:

■ A hard restart doesn't save any open files before restarting, but a soft restart (using the Restart command) tries to save them.

■ A hard restart takes considerably longer. When you choose Restart from the Special menu, the Mac OS knows that you're intentionally restarting and assumes that no errors occurred. A hard restart tells the Mac OS that an error has occurred, and it checks the integrity of every hard disk attached to your system before it actually boots up.

Fortunately, there are a couple of tricks you can try to avoid a hard restart. One is a force-quit option:

1. Hold down the ⌘ and Option keys and press the Esc key.
A dialog box asks if you want to quit the current application.
2. Click OK.
The system tries to quit the application and take you into another running application. You can often start working again, but your system may still be in a fragile state.
3. Go to the Finder and choose Restart from the Special menu.
If you don't restart, your computer may crash a few minutes later, and you'll be forced to do a hard restart.

If the force-quit doesn't work, you can try a programmer's trick.

1. Hold down the ⌘ key and press the power-on key on the keyboard (the one that has

WHAT TO DO WHEN YOUR MAC FREEZES

(continued)

a little left-pointing triangle on it). (On older Macs, you have to press the Programmer's Interrupt switch if it's installed.)

If your Mac hasn't crashed beyond hope, this interrupt opens a dialog box with a simple right caret (>) in it.

2. Type SM 0 A9F4 and press Return. (The 0 is a zero.)
Several lines of 4-digit groups appear.
3. Type: G 0 (that's a zero again) and press Return.

Remember to put spaces between the digits as shown. You're really writing a simple, one-command program for the Mac's internal debugger that tells it to return to the Finder. Sometimes this will get you out of a crash even when the force-quit doesn't work. If it does, you should immediately choose the Restart command from the Special menu, as described above.

If all else fails, you'll need to do a hard restart. Either press the power switch on the back of your Macintosh, or hold down the Control and ⌘ keys and press the power key on your keyboard.

WHAT TO DO WHEN YOUR MAC FREEZES (continued)

CHECK FOR DUPLICATE APPLICATIONS. Sometimes you may also have different versions of an application on your hard disk. If you have more than one version of the same program, you may get unexpected results when you open a file. Unless you have a specific reason for using multiple copies, you should remove all but one version of the application.

REPLACE THE SYSTEM FILES. If you continue to get random crashes, you may have a corrupt System file or other system component. The solution here is to reinstall the system from your system installation disks or CD-ROM. Be sure to start up your Mac from a disk other than your normal startup disk—you can't replace the system files on a disk that's running the Mac OS.

Problem: The application can't be found

When you open a document, you may get this message: "The application that created this document can't be found." Every document and application on the Macintosh has a special type and creator code that tells the Mac OS which applications created which documents. Sometimes you may end up with a document for which there is no corresponding application. For example, if someone gives you a MacWrite document and you only have Microsoft Word, double-clicking the MacWrite document is likely to produce that message. You have a couple of options:

■ Try to start a similar application and open the document with the application's Open command.

For example, if you run Microsoft Word first, you can open the MacWrite document with Word's Open command and then save it in Word.

- Use the Macintosh Easy Open control panel to specify applications for a variety of document types.

For example, if you don't have a graphics program, you can tell your Macintosh to open up PICT documents in SimpleText. Easy Open comes with System 7. You have to put it in your Control Panels folder and turn it on.

If you regularly use documents from lots of different sources, you may want to get MacLinkPlus from DataViz. This application is a set of translators that will convert documents from many applications to many others. With it, you can open almost any kind of document, including documents created on DOS or Windows systems.

Problem: You can't empty the trash

You may occasionally get a message informing you that your Trash Can can't be emptied. Try holding down the Option key while you choose Empty Trash from the Special Menu. If that doesn't work, restart your Macintosh and then empty the trash again.

Problem: Your Mac acts like it's trudging through molasses

Sometimes everything on your Mac seems to happen in slow motion. It takes forever to choose a command or save a file, for example. Or everything you do produces massive activity on your hard drive. What's going on?

The Mac occasionally gets confused or has fragmented-memory problems, and everything slows way down. The easiest solution to this problem is simply to restart the computer. Restarting puts everything back to a known and normal state. In fact, restarting is a good general-purpose solution to many problems with the Mac.

Another cause of slow performance may be virtual memory. Virtual memory uses some disk space as a swap area for RAM. Since the mechanical speed of your hard drive is much slower than the electronic speed of RAM, performance takes a big hit with virtual memory. Unless you absolutely need virtual memory to open a big file, you're better off turning it off—you can do this with the Memory control panel. Or you can get RAM Doubler, which uses a much more intelligent approach to extended memory. It's also a lot faster.

Problem: Your printer doesn't work

Here are some simple things to do if you're having problems with printing:

CHECK YOUR CABLES. As with disk drives, the first thing to do if your printer isn't working is to check your cables. (This is true with any hardware device. Loose cables are the most common cause of problems.)

CHECK YOUR PRINTER DRIVERS. You also want to be sure that you have the appropriate printer driver in your Extensions folder. Printer drivers are pieces of software that tell the Mac how to speak to your specific printer. There's a special driver for each printer you install. For example, you might find a file called LaserWriter 8 in your Extensions folder if you're using an Apple LaserWriter. The printer driver should be on a disk that comes with your printer. You might need to reinstall it if you're having trouble printing.

CHECK THE CHOOSER. Be sure your printer is selected in the Chooser. The Chooser is a desk accessory where you select the printer you want to use. If you're on a network, you may choose from several different printers on that network. But even if you only have one printer attached to your computer, you need to choose it in the Chooser.

1. Select Chooser from the Apple menu.
2. Select the printer icon from the list on the left side of the box.
Each printer driver in your Extensions folder appears as an icon in this list.
3. If your printer supports background printing, be sure to click the On button for Background printing.

With background printing you don't have to wait for your document to finish printing before you can start using your Macintosh again.

4. Make sure that AppleTalk is turned on if you're using a laser printer or other AppleTalk printer.
5. Close the Chooser window.

You normally select your Chooser settings only once; the Macintosh remembers them each time you start up. But if you're having printing problems, it's always a good idea to reselect the printer and check your other options in the Chooser.

OPEN THE PAGE SETUP DIALOG BOX. Sometimes you need to open the Page Setup dialog box just to engage the settings, especially if you've just changed the Chooser selection. You don't need to actually change anything in this dialog box (unless you want to change the printing options). You just need to open the dialog box and close it.

RESET THE PARAMETER RAM. The parameter RAM is a special area of memory that holds information about your computer, including values for the modem and printer ports. This memory is kept alive by the battery in your Macintosh, even when the power is off. If the parameter RAM gets messed up, you may have problems printing. You can restore things to normal by resetting it:

- Press ⌘-Option-P-R while you turn on the Macintosh.

You may have to get someone to help you with this procedure if you have only the typical two arms most Homo sapiens enjoy. Resetting the parameter

RAM resets a number of other items—such as the cursor blink rate and the
sound volume—to their default values. If you don't want these defaults, you

**HOW TO SPOT
A HARDWARE
PROBLEM**

It's often hard to know if your Mac problems are caused by hardware or software. In a couple
of cases, though, it's obvious that the culprit is the hardware:

■ If you start up your computer and you see the Sad Mac instead of the usual, smiling
Mac, you know you've got a hardware problem.

■ The startup sound is the other dead giveaway. Instead of the bright, happy *boing*
when you reboot, you hear the "chord of death." This is a four-note arpeggio that signals an
impending trip to the repair shop.

If either of these omens graces your Mac, it's time to call your local Apple dealer.

have to change them manually after you reset the parameter RAM. Also be
sure to set the Memory control panel back to 32 bits if it has changed.

Problem: Your Mac isn't communicating

As soon as you plug your modem into your computer, your Mac is going to
start acting like a sullen teenager with preverbal communication skills.
Resolving these communications problems is a black art better left to techni-
cians with voodoo chants and shrunken heads on long poles. But there are a
few obvious things you can try.

CHECK YOUR CABLES. As always, check your cables first. You also need to
make sure that your modem is connected to the proper port. Modems are
usually connected to the modem or serial port of your Macintosh. In addition, your communications software also specifies where it thinks your
modem is attached. You need to make sure it's plugged into the port your
software thinks it's in.

CHECK YOUR COMMUNICATIONS SOFTWARE. Check any control panels
that come with your communications software or modem to make sure that
all the controls are set properly. (See your user guides for details.) If you're
using MacTCP or ConfigPPP, use the latest version of the software.

RESET THE PARAMETER RAM. As with the printer port, the parameter
RAM holds information about the modem port. If, for some reason, the
parameter RAM gets scrambled, resetting it may solve your communications
problems.

TURN OFF CALL WAITING. If you have call waiting, be sure to turn it off
when you're running communications software over your phone line. Otherwise the click that tells you someone is trying to reach you may disconnect
your online session.

■ To turn off call waiting, press *70 on your telephone before you make
your communications connection.

A better solution is to enter this code in front of the phone number your communications software automatically dials when you set up the software:

■ Type *70, before the number.

Be sure to include the comma—it produces an important pause before the phone number itself is dialed.

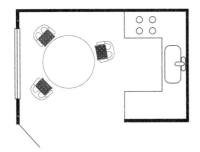

CHAPTER TWELVE

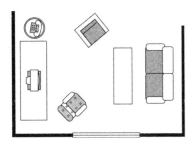

FILE RECOVERY

How to avoid panic and save
hours of work

 One of the most terrifying experiences you can have in your home office is this: you sit down one day to continue work on the document you've been crafting for the last week, only to find that it suddenly won't open. Or even worse, it's gone.

When you work at home, you don't have the kind of technical support center that you might find in a traditional company setting. You're on your own when it comes to dealing with file problems. Well, not quite. You have this chapter. Think of it as *File Recovery 101*—a primer to help you with some of the basic problems. (But keep in mind that you may need to call in a graduate student if your problems are really severe.)

Now, take a deep breath...

Problem: Your file is missing

You sit down in front of your Macintosh, ready to continue work on a document you created yesterday. You were careful to save your work frequently, and when you closed the document, everything seemed normal. However, today, when you look in your work folder, the document isn't there. Yikes.

CHECK ANOTHER FOLDER. The problem may be that when you originally created and saved the document, you didn't save it in your normal work folder. When you select the Save command for a new, untitled document, the Mac OS opens a standard directory dialog box. You name your document and choose where to save it. Often beginners (and even more-experienced users) forget to put the document in the folder they want and simply click Save after naming the document. The document is saved in the folder that was open in the Save dialog box. As far as you're concerned, it could be anywhere on your disk. The solution here is to use the Finder's Find command:

1. Choose Find from the File menu.
2. Type the document name and click Find.
3. If your missing document shows up in the Find command list, drag it to the folder where you want it.

If the Find command doesn't locate the document, your problem may be more serious.

VIEW THE FOLDER CONTENTS BY DATE. You may have selected the document in the Finder and accidentally hit a key while the document name was selected. Now the document has a new name—the key or keys you pressed without noticing. Do this:

1. Open the folder where you expect the document to be.
2. Choose By Date from the View menu.
3. Look at the documents created in the last few days.

If one of them has an odd name (like a few meaningless characters), check it out. It might be the one that's missing.

CHECK FOR DISK PROBLEMS. If your document is truly missing and you're sure you didn't throw it in the trash, you might be seeing the symptoms of a serious disk problem. Follow the procedures for recovering from serious disk crashes described in Chapter 11, "Troubleshooting."

Problem: The document is there but the icon is screwed up

A document usually has the icon that goes with the program you used to create the document. You can immediately identify the type of document by its icon. However, sometimes you may find that your document icon has changed—usually to a generic document icon, which looks like a piece of paper with a corner turned down.

This kind of problem may have several causes, so you can try a few different strategies to deal with it.

OPEN AND SAVE THE DOCUMENT WITH A NEW NAME. You may be having an isolated problem with a document that you can fix by creating another version of the file.

1. Double-click the document to see if its application will open it. If it doesn't, run the application itself and use the application's Open command to try to open the document.

2. If you can open the document using either of these approaches, immediately save it with a new name.

3. If the icon of this new version is correct, check the content and make sure it's all there.

4. Throw the original away.

REBUILD YOUR DESKTOP. If saving a new version doesn't fix your icons, you may need to rebuild your desktop. The Mac OS uses a special desktop file to hold information about files and their icons. Rebuilding the desktop file makes sure that every file has the proper icon associated with it. The only penalty for rebuilding the desktop file (aside from the few minutes it takes) is that you lose any file comments you may have stored in the Get Info box for your files. To rebuild the desktop file:

1. Select Restart from the Special menu of the Finder.

2. When the Macintosh restarts, hold down the ⌘ and Option keys during startup.

A dialog box asks if you want to rebuild the desktop files for each of your hard drives or volumes.

3. Click OK for the volumes you want to rebuild.

RUN DISK DOCTOR. If your icons still aren't right, you may need to run Norton Disk Doctor, which can fix other problems associated with files and icons. See below.

Problem: You threw a document in the trash and now you want it back

The Trash Can on the Macintosh desktop holds documents and files you no longer want. If you throw something away—either by accident or in a fit of foolish housecleaning—you may be able to recover it.

DIG THROUGH THE TRASH CAN. Throwing a document into the trash doesn't really delete it. If you're using System 7 and you throw something away, the Trash Can icon expands—that's how you know it's got stuff in it. Unless you tell the Mac to *empty* the trash, it stays there. So:

1. Double-click the Trash Can icon to open the Trash Can.

2. Drag your document back onto the desktop.

PROTECT AGAINST TRASH CAN ACCIDENTS. If you've emptied the trash (or if you use a utility that automatically empties the trash periodically), you may have a bigger problem. The simplest solution to prevent this potential disaster is to get Guaranteed Undelete, by Utilitron. Guaranteed Undelete is a control panel that keeps track of your trash. If you have it installed, you can use it to recover files even after the trash is emptied.

1. Hold down the ⌘ key and choose Recover Trash from the Special menu.(This command replaces the Empty Trash command.)

When you recover trash, Guaranteed Undelete lists the files and folders you thought you deleted when you emptied the trash.

2. Choose the file you want to recover from the submenu.

A directory dialog box opens. You can use it to save the recovered file on your hard disk.

The program recovers the files and returns them to their original location. Eventually the space used by deleted files will be reallocated by the Macintosh file system, so once you realize you've deleted a file by accident, it's best to recover it as soon as possible.

This is a simple, painless way to recover deleted documents. If you don't have Guaranteed Undelete, Norton UnErase will also recover files that have been deleted, although the process isn't as simple or elegant.

Problem: Your file is damaged

One day when you're least expecting it, you'll try to open a file, and a message will inform you that the file is damaged. This can be a serious problem. But don't panic yet. There are several things to try.

MAKE A COPY OF THE FILE ON ANOTHER DISK. Sometimes a file won't open, but when the Finder makes a copy of the file, it fixes the problem automatically. Be sure to copy to a different disk in case your damaged file is the result of a general problem with your hard disk. When your hard disk has troubles, you don't want to create new files on it until the problems are resolved. (If you have to, however, you can use the Finder's Duplicate command.)

RUN THE APPLICATION AND OPEN THE FILE. If the copy technique doesn't work, try opening the damaged file with the Open command in the application that created it, instead of double-clicking the file from the Finder. Sometimes the application can open the file when the Finder gets confused. If this works, immediately save the file under a new name.

RUN DISK FIRST AID. When a file is damaged, it may be an indication of a serious problem with your entire disk. The best thing to do is run a disk-checking program. Every Macintosh comes with Disk First Aid, which checks the integrity of your hard disks and makes certain kinds of repairs on it. It's on the Disk Tools disk.

1. Double-click Disk First Aid to run it.
2. Click the Drive button to select a disk and then click Open.
3. Choose Repair Automatically from the Options menu.
4. Click the Start button to start checking.

When it's done checking, Disk First Aid gives you a one-line description of the problems found, if any.

If you want a blow-by-blow account of the disk-checking process, press ⌘-S. This undocumented command displays a second window that shows which tests Disk First Aid is doing.

If you're checking the startup disk, Disk First Aid won't be able to repair any problems it finds, but you'll be able to verify any problems. If you want to repair problems on the startup disk, you'll need to start up from a different hard disk, floppy, or CD-ROM that has a System folder on it. Use the Startup Disk control panel to choose a different startup disk.

RUN DISK DOCTOR. In addition to running Disk First Aid, we highly recommend that you run Norton Disk Doctor. Disk Doctor checks the disk much more rigorously and often finds problems that Disk First Aid misses.

1. Double-click Disk Doctor to open it.
2. Select a disk and click Examine to start disk-checking.

When Disk Doctor finds problems, it usually suggests that you fix them.

3. Click the Fix button.
4. Run Disk Doctor again to make sure the problems are really fixed.

For details about Disk Doctor, see its user guide.

USE CANOPENER TO RECOVER A TRULY DAMAGED FILE. If fixing your disk doesn't render your file readable, the file itself may truly be damaged. Your success at recovering this file will be inversely proportional to its complexity. Text files are the simplest to recover. You can almost always recover all of the text in a text file. Word processing files are almost as easy to recover, except you may lose formatting information, such as styles, fonts, size information, and margins. If the file has text *and* graphics, however, you may not get the graphics. Fortunately, a great utility called CanOpener can help in just such a case.

1. Double-click CanOpener to open it.
2. Select the file in the upper left corner of the CanOpener window and click Open.

Can Opener opens the various resources in a file and displays them in a list.

3. Select each resource and save it with a new file name.
4. Recombine these elements in a new document.

(It's a drag, but it's a lot easier than re-creating everything from scratch.)

Even with CanOpener, you may not be able to rescue your file. Files that have structure are the most difficult to recover. Documents like spreadsheets, page layouts, or databases are almost impossible to recover intact if sufficiently damaged. You may be able to recover text or graphics, but you probably won't be able to recover the structure of the file. Your best strategy is defensive: Make frequent backups.

Problem: Your system crashes before you have time to save your file

Okay, you've had a burst of creativity and started writing an epic poem—ideas so delicious and spontaneous that you'd probably never be able to re-create them. You're so caught up in the moment that you forget your normal habit of saving every few minutes. Suddenly, when you're in mid-inspiration, a bread truck down the street clips a utility pole and—*pszzt!*—in the wink of an eye, out goes the power, and you lose your one chance to make it into the dizzying world of the literati.

Is there a way around this problem? It would seem not. If you haven't saved your file, your words exist only in the temporary memory of your machine's RAM. However, never underestimate the creativity of Macintosh programmers.

A couple of products can actually capture individual characters as you type them and save them in a backup file:

- NowSave has a special feature called Key Capture for this purpose.
- Last Resort, by Working Software, does the same thing.

These programs capture everything you type, at the moment you type it, in the order you type it. They capture delete characters, typing corrections, and other unusual junk along with your prose. If you have a power failure, you'll be able to recover most of your text, although you'll probably have to do quite bit of editing to clean up the file. Still, these programs are lifesavers.

But be aware: This kind of software records *everything* you type, including passwords, credit card account numbers, and other potentially sensitive information. It's all available in an unprotected text file for anyone to peruse. So use this kind of software with caution.

Every Macintosh user should have a set of file-recovery tools to call upon when the inevitable happens. Here are our favorites:

DISK FIRST AID, by Apple Computer. It comes with System 7 and can repair some disk problems that may produce unreadable or disappearing files.

NORTON UTILITIES, by Symantec. This package includes Norton Disk Doctor for repairing problem disks, as well as UnErase for recovering files accidentally thrown in the trash. It also has a number of other indispensable utilities to keep your Macintosh running at optimum performance.

NOW UTILITIES, by Now Software. This incredible package has all kinds of useful tools. Of interest here is NowSave, which automatically saves your files after a predetermined amount of time or number of keystrokes. It also includes Key Capture, for saving text even if the file hasn't been saved. You can also use Now Startup Manager for resolving startup document conflicts that may crash your system (see Chapter 11).

CANOPENER, by Abbott Systems. This venerable utility pries open files and extracts their text, graphics, or sound resources. It supports a wide variety of graphics formats.

RESCUE TEXT, also by Abbott Systems. This one searches your disk, block by block, for text you specify. When it finds the text, it displays the block on the screen. You can then choose a clean view of it, select it, and copy it into a new, undamaged file.

GUARANTEED UNDELETE, by Utilitron. This utility provides a simple, easy way to recover files you accidentally throw in the trash.

**THE TOOLS
OF THE
TRADE**

A final word about disaster preparedness

File recovery is a skill you need to learn, like CPR or the Heimlich maneuver. You may not need it very often, but when you do, it'll likely be a matter of (business) life and death. Be sure you have the tools *before* you need them. The first time you have to recover an important document, you'll realize that the money you spent on the recovery tools was well worth it.

RESOURCES

How to find the products and services
mentioned throughout this book

As you set off on your Macintosh home office journey, you're entering resource-rich territory. We've tried to clear a little path through the landscape. That's what this section is—one path to some of the thousands of products and services that are available for Macintosh home offices. We hope it takes you where you want to to go.

Products

The following is an alphabetical listing of the products mentioned in this book and the companies that currently market them.

Acius 4D
Acius, Inc.

ACT!
Symantec Corporation

Adobe Dimensions

Adobe Fetch
Adobe HomePublisher
Adobe Illustrator
Adobe PageMaker
Adobe PageMill
Adobe Persuasion

Adobe Photoshop
Adobe Premiere
Adobe Systems Incorporated

After Dark
Berkeley Systems, Inc.

Apple Quicktime Conferencing Kit
AppleScript
AppleShare
At Ease
Apple Computer, Inc.

BizPlan Builder
JIAN

Business Plan Toolkit
Palo Alto Software, Inc.

Can Opener
Abbott Systems

Canvas
Deneba Software

CE Mail
CE Software

ClarisDraw Pro
Claris Emailer
Claris Organizer
Claris Small Business Solutions Pack
ClarisWorks
Claris Corporation

Color It!
TIMEWORKS

Color One Scanner
Apple Computer, Inc.

CompuServe MacCim
CompuServe Navigator
CompuServe

ConfigPPP
gopher://wuarchive.wustl.edu:70/40/systems/mac/umich.edu/util/comm/

Copy Doubler
Symantec Corporation

CyberFinder
Aladdin Systems

Datebook Pro
Now Software, Inc.

DecisionMaker
Palo Alto Software, Inc.

Design Your Own Home: Interiors
Abracadabra, Ltd.

Disinfectant
John Norstad
ftp://ftp.acns.nwu.edu/pub/disinfectant/

DiskDoubler Pro
Symantec Corporation

DiskFit Pro
Dantz Development

DiskGuard
ASD Software, Inc.

DLS
D. Grant Leeper
Most shareware sources

Encyclomedia II
Apple Computer, Inc.

EZ-135 Removable Cartridge Drive
SyQuest Technology

Farallon Air Dock
Farallon Computing, Inc.

Fileguard
ASD Software, Inc.

FileMaker Pro
Claris Corporation

FolderBolt
Kent Marsh Ltd.

Fractal Design Painter
Fractal Design Corporation

FrameMaker
Frame Technologies, Inc.

Front Office
Pleiades Research Corporation

Geoport Telecom Adapter Kit
Apple Computer, Inc.

Global Village Teleport
Platinum Fax Modem
Global Village Communication, Inc.

Guaranteed Undelete
Utilitron, Inc.

HyperCard
Claris Corporation

infini-D
Specular International

InternetConfig System
Peter Lewis
ftp://amug.org/pub/peterlewis/

Java
Sun Microsystems

Kai's Power Tools 3
KPT Bryce
KPT Convolver
KPT Vector Effects
MetaTools

Last Resort
Working Software, Inc.

Loan Builder
JIAN

MacInTax
MacInTax for Business
Intuit, Inc.

Macromedia Authorware
Macromedia Director
Macromedia Extreme CD
Macromedia Freehand
Macromedia Fontographer
Macromedia SoundEdit 16
Macromedia XRES
Macromedia, Inc.

MacTCP
Apple Computer, Inc.

Marathon
Bungie Software

Market Builder
JIAN

Marketing Plan Pro
Palo Alto Software, Inc.

MegaPhone
Cypress Research Corp.

mTropolis
mFactory, Inc.

Microsoft Bookshelf
Microsoft Encarta
Microsoft Excel
Microsoft FoxBase Pro
Microsoft Internet Explorer
Microsoft Mail
Microsoft Word
Microsoft Works
Microsoft Corp.

Mosaic
NCSA

MYOB
Best!Ware

Netscape Navigator
Netscape Communications Corp.

NewsWatcher
John Norstad
ftp://ftp.acns.nwu.edu/pub/newswatcher/

NightWatch
Kent Marsh Ltd.

Norton Disk Doctor
Norton DiskLock
Norton Utilities
Symantec, Corp.

Now Up-To-Date
Now Utilities
Now Software, Inc.

OmniPage Pro
Caere Corp.

Oracle Media Objects
Oracle Corporation

PhoneDisc PowerFinder
Digital Directory Assistance, Inc.

PhonePro
Cypress Research Corp.

Plan & Track
Mainstay

PowerPoint
Microsoft Corp.

Publicity Builder
JIAN

Publish It!
TIMEWORKS

QuarkXpress
Quark Inc.

QuickBooks
Intuit, Inc.

QuickCam
Connectix Corp.

Quicken
Intuit, Inc.

QuicKeys
CE Software, Inc.

QuickLetter
Working Software, Inc.

QuickTake Digital Camera
Apple Computer, Inc.

QV-10 Digital Camera
Casio, Inc.

RAM Doubler
Connectix Corp.

Ray Dream Studio
Ray Dream, Inc.

Real Audio
Progressive Networks
http:/www.realaudio.com/

Retrospect Remote
Dantz Development

SAM—Symantec
Antivirus for Macintosh
Symantec, Corp.

Scorpio
Abbott Systems

ShockWave
Macromedia, Inc.

SoftWindows
Insignia Solutions

Speed Doubler
Connectix Corp.

StrataVision 3D
Stratus Studio Pro Blitz
Strata, Inc.

Street Atlas USA
DeLorme Mapping

StuffIt Deluxe
StuffIt Expander
Aladdin Systems

Suitcase
Symantec Corporation

Temperament
John Rotenstein
Most shareware sources

TouchBase Pro
Now Software, Inc.

TurboGopher
http://hyperarchive.lcs.mit.edu/Hyper-
Archive/Archive/comm/tcp/

TypeLighter
TypeLighter, Inc.

Virtus WalkThrough Pro
Virtus Corp.

Visioneer PaperPortVX
Visioneer Communications, Inc.

Web Arranger
CE Software

Word Perfect Clip Art
Novell Applications Group

Working Watermarker
Working Software, Inc.

Companies

The following is an alphabetical listing of companies who market the products described in this book, with contact information.

Abbott Systems
62 Mountain Road
Pleasantville, NY 10570
Phone: (800) 552-9157
Alternate: (914) 747-4171
Fax: (914) 747-9115
E-mail: abbottsys@aol.com

Abracadabra, Ltd.
P.O. Box 2440
Eugene, OR 97402

ACI US, Inc.
20883 Stevens Creek Blvd.
Cupertino, CA 95014
Phone: (408) 252-4444
Fax: (408) 252-0831
http://www.acius.com/

Adobe Systems Incorporated
1585 Charleston Road
P. O. Box 7900
Mountain View, CA 94309-7900
Phone: (415) 961-4400

Aladdin Systems
165 Westridge Drive
Watsonville, CA 95076
Phone: (408) 761-6200
Fax: (408) 761-6202
ftp.aladdinsys.com

Apple Computer, Inc.
1 Infinite Loop
Cupertino, CA 95014-2083
Phone: (408) 996-1010
http://www.apple.com/

ASD Software, Inc.
4650 Arrow Highway
Suite E-6
Montclair, CA 91763
Phone: (909) 624-2594
Fax: (909) 624-9574

Berkeley Systems Incorporated
2095 Rose Street
Berkeley, CA 94709-1963
Phone: (510) 540-5535

Best!Ware
300 Roundhill Drive
Rockaway, NJ 07866
Phone: (201) 586-2200
Fax: (201) 586-8885

Bungie Software
PO Box 7877
Chicago, IL 60680-7877
Phone: (312) 563-6200
Fax: (312) 563-0545

Caere Corp
100 Cooper Court
Los Gatos, CA 95030
Phone: (408) 395-7000
Technical Support: (408) 395-8319
Sales: (800) 535-7226
Data: (408) 395-1631
Fax: (408) 395-5120
E-mail: support@caere.com

Casio Inc.
570 Mt. Plesant Avenue
Dover, NJ 07801
Phone: (800) 962-2746
Alternate: (201) 361-5400
Fax: (201) 361-3819
CompuServe: 72662,236

Casady & Greene
22734 Portola Drive
Salinas, CA 93908-1119
Phone: (408) 484-9223

CE Software, Inc.
1801 Industrial Circle
PO Box 65580
W. Des Moines, IA 50265

Phone: (800) 523-7638
Alternate: (515) 221-1801
Sales: (800) 523-7635
Fax: (515) 221-1806
http://www.cesoft.com/
E-mail: CESOFTWARE@aol.com

Claris Corporation
5201 Patrick Henry Drive
Santa Clara, CA 95052
Phone: (800) 325-2747

Connectix Corp.
2600 Campus Dr.
San Mateo, CA 94403
Phone: (800) 950-5880
Alternate: (415) 571-5100
Fax: (415) 571-5195

Dantz Development
4 Orinda Way, Building C
Orinda, CA 94563
Phone: (510) 253-3000
Technical Support: (510) 253-3050
Fax: (510) 253-9099
AppleLink: DANTZ
America Online: DANTZ
CompuServe: 73367,2416

DeLorme Mapping
Lower Main Street
P.O. Box 298
Freeport, ME 04032
Phone: (207) 865-1234

Deneba Software
7400 SW 87th Ave.
Miami, FL 33173
Phone: (305) 596-5644
Fax: (305) 273-9069

Farallon Computing, Inc.
2470 Mariner Square Loop
Alameda, CA 94501
Phone: (510) 814-5000
Fax: (510) 814-5023

Fractal Design Corporation
P.O. Box 2380
Aptos, CA 95001-9973

Phone: (408) 688-5300
Fax: (408) 688-8836

Global Village Communication, Inc.
1144 East Arques Avenue
Sunnyvale, CA 94086
Phone: (408) 523-1000
Fax: (408) 523-2407

Insignia Solutions
1300 Charlston Road,
Mountain View, CA 94043
Phone: (800) 848-7677
Alternate: (415) 335-7100
Fax: (415) 335-7105

Intuit, Inc.
P.O. Box 3014
Menlo Park, CA 94026
Phone: (415) 322-0573

JIAN
1975 West El Camino Real
Suite 301
Mountain View, CA 94049-2218
Phone: (415) 254-5600
Fax: (415) 254-5640

Kent Marsh Ltd.
One Kent Marsh Cir.
3260 Sul Ross
Houston, TX 77098
Phone: (800) 325-3587
Alternate: (713) 522-5625
Fax: (713) 522-8965

Macromedia, Inc.
600 Townsend Street
San Francisco, CA 94103
Phone: (415) 252-2000
Fax: (415) 626-0554

Mainstay
591-A Constitution Avenue
Camarillo, CA 93012
Phone: (805) 484-9400
Fax: (805) 484-9428

MetaTools
6303 Carpinteria Ave.
Carpinteria, CA 93013

Phone: (805) 566-6266
Fax: (805) 566-6367

Microsoft Corp.
16011 NE 36th Way
Box 97017
Redmond, WA 98073-9717
Phone: (800) 426-9400
Alternate: (206) 882-8080
Technical Support: (206) 635-7200
http://www.microsoft.com/

Microspot
12380 Saratoga-Sunnyvale Rd
Suite 6
Saratoga, CA 95070
Phone: (800) 622-7568
Alternate: (408) 253-2000
Fax: (408) 253-2055

mFactory
1440 Chapin Avenue, Suite 200
Burlingame, CA 94010
Phone: (415) 548-0600
Fax: (415) 548-9249
http://www.mfactory.com
E-mail: info@mfactory.com

NCSA
National Center for Supercomputing
Applications
http://www.ncsa.uiuc.edu/SDG/
Software/SDGSoftDir.html

Netscape Communications Corp.
501 East Middlefield Road
Mountain View, CA 94043
http://home.netscape.com/

Northwestern University
NewsWatcher distribution
ftp://ftp.acns.nwu.edu/pub/
newswatcher/

Novell Applications Group
1555 N. Technology Way
Orem, UT 84057
Phone: (800) 451-5151
Alternate: (801) 222-6000
Fax: (801) 228-5377

Now Software, Inc.
921 S.W. Washington Street,
Suite 500
Portland, OR 97205-2823
Phone: (503) 274-2800
Fax: (503) 274-0670
Fax-Back: (503) 274-6370

Oracle Corporation
500 Oracle Parkway
Redwood Shores, CA 94065
Phone: (415) 506-7000
Fax: (414) 506-7200
http://www.oracle.com/

Palo Alto Software, Inc.
144 East 14th Avenue
Eugene, OR 97401
Phone: (541) 683-6162
Fax: (541) 683-6250
http://www.pasware.com
E-mail: help@pasware.com

Pleiades Research Corporation
5904 Monterey Road
Los Angeles, CA 90042
Phone: (800) 73-STARS
Alternate: (213) 257-1710
Fax: (213) 259-1728

Quark Inc.
1800 Grant Street
Denver, CO 80203
Phone: (303) 894-8888
Technical Support: (800) 788-7835
Sales: (303) 894-8899
Fax: (303) 343-2086

Specular International
233 North Pleasant Street
P. O. Box 888
Amherst, MA 01002
Phone: (413) 549-7600

Strata Inc.
Ancestor Square, Suite 2100
2 West Str. George Blvd.
St. George, UT 84770
Phone: (800) 869-6855
Alternate: (801) 628-5218

Sales: (801) 628-9751
Fax: (801) 628-9756

Sun Microsystems, Inc.
2550 Garcia Ave.
Mountain View, CA 94043-1100
Phone: (800) 801-7869
Alternate: (415) 3366299
Fax: (415) 336-0646
http://www.sun.com/

Symantec Corporation
10201 Torre Avenue
Cupertino, CA 95014
Phone: (800) 441-7234
Fax: (408) 253-9600

SyQuest Technology
47071 Bayside Parkway
Fremont, CA 94538
Phone: (510) 226-4000

TIMEWORKS
625 Academy Drive
Northbrook, IL 60062
Phone: (800) 323-7744

Utilitron, Inc.
6079 Madera Dr.
Woodland Hills, CA 91367
Phone: (800) 428-8766
Sales: (818) 883-4646
Fax: (818) 883-4646

Virtus Corp.
118 MacKenan Drive, Suite 250
Cary, NC 27511
Phone: (919) 467-9700
Fax: (919) 460-4530

Visioneer Communications, Inc.
2860 West Bayshore Road
Palo Alto, CA 94303
Phone: (800) 787-7007
Fax: (415) 493-0399

Working Software, Inc.
740 Front Street, Suite 318A
Santa Cruz, CA 95060
Phone: (408) 423-5696
Fax: (408) 423-5699

User Groups and Other Support Groups

Macintosh user groups are a great source of information about your Macintosh hardware and software. They come in all shapes and sizes. You can even create your own. Here are some places to start exploring:

Berkeley Macintosh Users Group is a local users group with a nationwide reach. For information, contact:
BMUG, Inc.
1442A Walnut Street, No. 64
Berkeley, CA 94709-1496
Phone: (510) 349-2684
Fax: (510) 849-9026
http://www.bmug.org/

Boston Computer Society (BCS) is another user's group with national membership, including both Macintosh and PC users. You can get more information at:
BCS
101 First Avenue, Suite 2
Waltham, MA 02154

Phone: (617) 290-5700
Fax: (617) 290-5744
http://www.bcs.org/

User Group Connection is an independent organization that supports user groups all over the world. They can help you find a user group in your area—or start one of your own. Contact them at:

User Group Connection
2840 Research Park Drive, Suite 100
Soquel, CA 95073
Phone: (408) 477-4277
Fax: (408) 477-4290
http://www.ugconnection.org/
E-mail: ugc@ugconnection.com

In addition, Apple Computer lists both user groups and professional Macintosh organizations at its web site: `http://apple.com/documents/user groups.html`

If you need help solving special physical problems, contact the Worldwide Disabilities Solutions Group at Apple Computer.

Books

If you want to plunge into some of the topics covered in this book in more detail, here are a few books we recommend:

Guerilla Financing, by Bruce Jan Blechman and Jay Conrad Levinson. Boston: Houghton Mifflin, 1991.

Guerilla Marketing, by Jay Conrad Levinson. Boston: Houghton Mifflin, 1994.

Guerilla Marketing Online, by Charles Rubin and Jay Conrad Levinson. Boston: Houghton Mifflin, 1995.

The Home Office & Small Business Answer Book, by Janet Attard. New York: Henry Holt, 1993.

Independence Day, Designing Computer Solutions for Individuals with Disability, by Peter Green and Alan J. Brightman. Allen, TX: DLM, 1990.

Sunset Home Offices and Workspaces, by the editors of Sunset Magazine. Menlo Park, CA: Lane, 1986.

The System 7.5 Book, by Craig Danuloff. Chapel Hill, NC: Ventana Press, 1994.

continued

continued

continued

continued

continued

continued

About the Authors

Kathi Vian and Howard Bornstein have shared a home office for more than ten years. Over the years, Kathi and Howard found that the work they each did individually—user interface design and information design, respectively—ultimately merged into a single field. Now they work together in the world of multimedia communication.

Colophon

This book was produced electronically in Foster City, California. Microsoft Word Version 6.0 was used for word processing; design and layout was produced with QuarkXpress 3.32 on a Power Macintosh 8500/120. Line art was created with Adobe Illustrator 6.0. The type face families used are Adobe Garamond and Myriad Multiple Master.

Senior Vice President and Group Publisher   Brenda McLaughlin

Acquisitions Editor   Nancy E. Dunn

Marketing Manager   Melisa Duffy

Managing Editor   Terry Somerson

Development Editor   Kenyon Brown

Editorial Assistants   Suki Gear, Jean Leitner

Copy Editors   Felicity O'Meara, Katharine Dvorak

Production Director   Andrew Walker

Supervisor of Page Layout   Craig Harrison

Project Coordinator   Katy German

Production Staff   Diann Abbott, Laura Carpenter, Stephen Noetzel, Christopher Pimentel

Proofreader   David Wise

Indexer   Liz Cunningham

Illustration   Joan Carol

Book Design   Margery Cantor

Cover Deisgn and Illustration   Eddie Lee, Square Two

Fun, Fast, & Cheap!™

10/31/95

NEW!

The Internet For Macs® For Dummies® Quick Reference
by Charles Seiter

ISBN:1-56884-967-2
$9.99 USA/$12.99 Canada

NEW!

Windows® 95 For Dummies® Quick Reference
by Greg Harvey

ISBN: 1-56884-964-8
$9.99 USA/$12.99 Canada

SUPER STAR

Photoshop 3 For Macs® For Dummies® Quick Reference
by Deke McClelland

ISBN: 1-56884-968-0
$9.99 USA/$12.99 Canada

SUPER STAR

WordPerfect® For DOS For Dummies® Quick Reference
by Greg Harvey

ISBN: 1-56884-009-8
$8.95 USA/$12.95 Canada

Title	Author	ISBN	Price
DATABASE			
Access 2 For Dummies® Quick Reference	by Stuart J. Stuple	ISBN: 1-56884-167-1	$8.95 USA/$11.95 Canada
dBASE 5 For DOS For Dummies® Quick Reference	by Barrie Sosinsky	ISBN: 1-56884-954-0	$9.99 USA/$12.99 Canada
dBASE 5 For Windows® For Dummies® Quick Reference	by Stuart J. Stuple	ISBN: 1-56884-953-2	$9.99 USA/$12.99 Canada
Paradox 5 For Windows® For Dummies® Quick Reference	by Scott Palmer	ISBN: 1-56884-960-5	$9.99 USA/$12.99 Canada
DESKTOP PUBLISHING/ILLUSTRATION/GRAPHICS			
CorelDRAW! 5 For Dummies® Quick Reference	by Raymond E. Werner	ISBN: 1-56884-952-4	$9.99 USA/$12.99 Canada
Harvard Graphics For Windows® For Dummies® Quick Reference	by Raymond E. Werner	ISBN: 1-56884-962-1	$9.99 USA/$12.99 Canada
Photoshop 3 For Macs® For Dummies® Quick Reference	by Deke McClelland	ISBN: 1-56884-968-0	$9.99 USA/$12.99 Canada
FINANCE/PERSONAL FINANCE			
Quicken 4 For Windows® For Dummies® Quick Reference	by Stephen L. Nelson	ISBN: 1-56884-950-8	$9.95 USA/$12.95 Canada
GROUPWARE/INTEGRATED			
Microsoft® Office 4 For Windows® For Dummies® Quick Reference	by Doug Lowe	ISBN: 1-56884-958-3	$9.99 USA/$12.99 Canada
Microsoft® Works 3 For Windows® For Dummies® Quick Reference	by Michael Partington	ISBN: 1-56884-959-1	$9.99 USA/$12.99 Canada
INTERNET/COMMUNICATIONS/NETWORKING			
The Internet For Dummies® Quick Reference	by John R. Levine & Margaret Levine Young	ISBN: 1-56884-168-X	$8.95 USA/$11.95 Canada
MACINTOSH			
Macintosh® System 7.5 For Dummies® Quick Reference	by Stuart J. Stuple	ISBN: 1-56884-956-7	$9.99 USA/$12.99 Canada
OPERATING SYSTEMS:			
DOS			
DOS For Dummies® Quick Reference	by Greg Harvey	ISBN: 1-56884-007-1	$8.95 USA/$11.95 Canada
UNIX			
UNIX® For Dummies® Quick Reference	by John R. Levine & Margaret Levine Young	ISBN: 1-56884-094-2	$8.95 USA/$11.95 Canada
WINDOWS			
Windows® 3.1 For Dummies® Quick Reference, 2nd Edition	by Greg Harvey	ISBN: 1-56884-951-6	$8.95 USA/$11.95 Canada
PCs/HARDWARE			
Memory Management For Dummies® Quick Reference	by Doug Lowe	ISBN: 1-56884-362-3	$9.99 USA/$12.99 Canada
PRESENTATION/AUTOCAD			
AutoCAD For Dummies® Quick Reference	by Ellen Finkelstein	ISBN: 1-56884-198-1	$9.99 USA/$12.95 Canada
SPREADSHEET			
1-2-3 For Dummies® Quick Reference	by John Walkenbach	ISBN: 1-56884-027-6	$8.95 USA/$11.95 Canada
1-2-3 For Windows® 5 For Dummies® Quick Reference	by John Walkenbach	ISBN: 1-56884-957-5	$9.95 USA/$12.95 Canada
Excel For Windows® For Dummies® Quick Reference, 2nd Edition	by John Walkenbach	ISBN: 1-56884-096-9	$8.95 USA/$11.95 Canada
Quattro Pro 6 For Windows® For Dummies® Quick Reference	by Stuart J. Stuple	ISBN: 1-56884-172-8	$9.95 USA/$12.95 Canada
WORD PROCESSING			
Word For Windows® 6 For Dummies® Quick Reference	by George Lynch	ISBN: 1-56884-095-0	$8.95 USA/$11.95 Canada
Word For Windows® For Dummies® Quick Reference	by George Lynch	ISBN: 1-56884-029-2	$8.95 USA/$11.95 Canada
WordPerfect® 6.1 For Windows® For Dummies® Quick Reference, 2nd Edition	by Greg Harvey	ISBN: 1-56884-966-4	$9.99 USA/$12.99/Canada

For scholastic requests & educational orders please call Educational Sales at 1. 800. 434. 2086

FOR MORE INFO OR TO ORDER, PLEASE CALL ▶ 800. 762. 2974

For volume discounts & special orders please call Tony Real, Special Sales, at 415. 655. 3048

Official Hayes Modem Communications Companion
by Caroline M. Halliday

ISBN: 1-56884-072-1
$29.95 USA/$39.95 Canada
Includes software.

1,001 Komputer Answers from Kim Komando
by Kim Komando

ISBN: 1-56884-460-3
$29.99 USA/$39.99 Canada
Includes software.

BESTSELLER!

PC World DOS 6 Handbook, 2nd Edition
by John Socha, Clint Hicks, & Devra Hall

ISBN: 1-878058-79-7
$34.95 USA/$44.95 Canada
Includes software.

PC World Word For Windows® 6 Handbook
by Brent Heslop & David Angell

ISBN: 1-56884-054-3
$34.95 USA/$44.95 Canada
Includes software.

BESTSELLER!

PC World Microsoft® Access 2 Bible, 2nd Edition
by Cary N. Prague & Michael R. Irwin

ISBN: 1-56884-086-1
$39.95 USA/$52.95 Canada
Includes software.

PC World Excel 5 For Windows® Handbook, 2nd Edition
by John Walkenbach & Dave Maguiness

ISBN: 1-56884-056-X
$34.95 USA/$44.95 Canada
Includes software.

PC World WordPerfect® 6 Handbook
by Greg Harvey

ISBN: 1-878058-80-0
$34.95 USA/$44.95 Canada
Includes software.

QuarkXPress For Windows® Designer Handbook
by Barbara Assadi & Galen Gruman

ISBN: 1-878058-45-2
$29.95 USA/$39.95 Canada

NATIONAL BESTSELLER!

Official XTree Companion, 3rd Edition
by Beth Slick

ISBN: 1-878058-57-6
$19.95 USA/$26.95 Canada

NATIONAL BESTSELLER!

PC World DOS 6 Command Reference and Problem Solver
by John Socha & Devra Hall

ISBN: 1-56884-055-1
$24.95 USA/$32.95 Canada

SUPER STAR

Client/Server Strategies™: A Survival Guide for Corporate Reengineers
by David Vaskevitch

ISBN: 1-56884-064-0
$29.95 USA/$39.95 Canada

Macworld® Mac® & Power Mac SECRETS,™ 2nd Edition

by David Pogue & Joseph Schorr

This is the definitive Mac reference for those who want to become power users! Includes three disks with 9MB of software!

WINNERS 1994-95
TECHNICAL PUBLICATIONS AND ART COMPETITIONS OF THE SOCIETY FOR TECHNICAL COMMUNICATION

ISBN: 1-56884-175-2
$39.95 USA/$54.95 Canada

Includes 3 disks chock full of software.

NEWBRIDGE BOOK CLUB SELECTION

Macworld® Mac® FAQs™

by David Pogue

Written by the hottest Macintosh author around, David Pogue, *Macworld Mac FAQs* gives users the ultimate Mac reference. Hundreds of Mac questions and answers side-by-side, right at your fingertips, and organized into six easy-to-reference sections with lots of sidebars and diagrams.

ISBN: 1-56884-480-8
$19.99 USA/$26.99 Canada

Macworld® System 7.5 Bible, 3rd Edition

by Lon Poole

ISBN: 1-56884-098-5
$29.95 USA/$39.95 Canada

NATIONAL BESTSELLER!

Macworld® ClarisWorks 3.0 Companion, 3rd Edition

by Steven A. Schwartz

ISBN: 1-56884-481-6
$24.99 USA/$34.99 Canada

NATIONAL BESTSELLER!

Macworld® Complete Mac® Handbook Plus Interactive CD, 3rd Edition

by Jim Heid

BMUG SPRING 1995 CHOICE PRODUCT

ISBN: 1-56884-192-2
$39.95 USA/$54.95 Canada

Includes an interactive CD-ROM.

NEWBRIDGE BOOK CLUB SELECTION

Macworld® Ultimate Mac® CD-ROM

by Jim Heid

ISBN: 1-56884-477-8
$19.99 USA/$26.99 Canada

CD-ROM includes version 2.0 of QuickTime, and over 65 MB of the best shareware, freeware, fonts, sounds, and more!

Macworld® Networking Bible, 2nd Edition

by Dave Kosiur & Joel M. Snyder

ISBN: 1-56884-194-9
$29.95 USA/$39.95 Canada

Macworld® Photoshop 3 Bible, 2nd Edition

by Deke McClelland

ISBN: 1-56884-158-2
$39.95 USA/$54.95 Canada

Includes stunning CD-ROM with add-ons, digitized photos and more.

WINNERS 1994-95
TECHNICAL PUBLICATIONS AND ART COMPETITIONS OF THE SOCIETY FOR TECHNICAL COMMUNICATION

NEW!

Macworld® Photoshop 2.5 Bible

by Deke McClelland

ISBN: 1-56884-022-5
$29.95 USA/$39.95 Canada

NATIONAL BESTSELLER!

Macworld® FreeHand 4 Bible

by Deke McClelland

ISBN: 1-56884-170-1
$29.95 USA/$39.95 Canada

Macworld® Illustrator 5.0/5.5 Bible

by Ted Alspach

ISBN: 1-56884-097-7
$39.95 USA/$54.95 Canada

Includes CD-ROM with QuickTime tutorials.

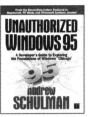

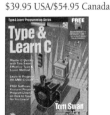

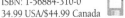

ORDER FORM

IDG BOOKS WORLDWIDE

Order Center: **(800) 762-2974** *(8 a.m.–6 p.m., EST, weekdays)*

Quantity	ISBN	Title	Price	Total

Shipping & Handling Charges

	Description	First book	Each additional book	Total
Domestic	Normal	$4.50	$1.50	$
	Two Day Air	$8.50	$2.50	$
	Overnight	$18.00	$3.00	$
International	Surface	$8.00	$8.00	$
	Airmail	$16.00	$16.00	$
	DHL Air	$17.00	$17.00	$

*For large quantities call for shipping & handling charges.
**Prices are subject to change without notice.

Ship to:

Name _____

Company _____

Address _____

City/State/Zip _____

Daytime Phone _____

Payment: ☐ Check to IDG Books Worldwide (US Funds Only)

    ☐ VISA   ☐ MasterCard   ☐ American Express

Card # _____ Expires _____

Signature _____

Subtotal _____

CA residents add
applicable sales tax _____

IN, MA, and MD
residents add
5% sales tax _____

IL residents add
6.25% sales tax _____

RI residents add
7% sales tax _____

TX residents add
8.25% sales tax _____

Shipping _____

Total _____

Please send this order form to:

IDG Books Worldwide, Inc.
7260 Shadeland Station, Suite 100
Indianapolis, IN 46256

Allow up to 3 weeks for delivery.
Thank you!

IDG BOOKS WORLDWIDE REGISTRATION CARD

RETURN THIS REGISTRATION CARD FOR FREE CATALOG

Title of this book: **Macworld® Home Office Companion**

My overall rating of this book: ❏ Very good [1] ❏ Good [2] ❏ Satisfactory [3] ❏ Fair [4] ❏ Poor [5]

How I first heard about this book:

❏ Found in bookstore; name: [6] _____ ❏ Book review: [7] _____

❏ Advertisement: [8] _____ ❏ Catalog: [9] _____

❏ Word of mouth; heard about book from friend, co-worker, etc.: [10] _____ ❏ Other: [11] _____

What I liked most about this book:

_____

_____

What I would change, add, delete, etc., in future editions of this book:

_____

_____

Other comments:

_____

Number of computer books I purchase in a year: ❏ 1 [12] ❏ 2-5 [13] ❏ 6-10 [14] ❏ More than 10 [15]

I would characterize my computer skills as: ❏ Beginner [16] ❏ Intermediate [17] ❏ Advanced [18] ❏ Professional [19]

I use ❏ DOS [20] ❏ Windows [21] ❏ OS/2 [22] ❏ Unix [23] ❏ Macintosh [24] ❏ Other: [25]_____
(please specify)

I would be interested in new books on the following subjects:
(please check all that apply, and use the spaces provided to identify specific software)

❏ Word processing: [26] _____ ❏ Spreadsheets: [27] _____

❏ Data bases: [28] _____ ❏ Desktop publishing: [29] _____

❏ File Utilities: [30] _____ ❏ Money management: [31] _____

❏ Networking: [32] _____ ❏ Programming languages: [33] _____

❏ Other: [34] _____

I use a PC at (please check all that apply): ❏ home [35] ❏ work [36] ❏ school [37] ❏ other: [38] _____

The disks I prefer to use are ❏ 5.25 [39] ❏ 3.5 [40] ❏ other: [41]_____

I have a CD ROM: ❏ yes [42] ❏ no [43]

I plan to buy or upgrade computer hardware this year: ❏ yes [44] ❏ no [45]

I plan to buy or upgrade computer software this year: ❏ yes [46] ❏ no [47]

Name: _____ Business title: [48] _____ Type of Business: [49] _____

Address (❏ home [50] ❏ work [51]/Company name: _____)

Street/Suite# _____

City [52]/State [53]/Zipcode [54]: _____ Country [55] _____

❏ **I liked this book!** You may quote me by name in future
IDG Books Worldwide promotional materials.

My daytime phone number is _____

IDG BOOKS

THE WORLD OF
COMPUTER
KNOWLEDGE

YES!

Please keep me informed about IDG's World of Computer Knowledge.
Send me the latest IDG Books catalog.